14.99

Oxbow

THE ARCHAEOLOGY OF
MEDIEVAL BRITAIN

Series Editor: Dr Helen Clarke

Medieval Towns

MEDIEVAL TOWNS

—— JOHN SCHOFIELD AND ALAN VINCE ——

LEICESTER UNIVERSITY PRESS
London

Leicester University Press
(a division of Pinter Publishers Ltd.)
25 Floral Street, London WC2E 9DS, United Kingdom

First published in 1994

British Library Cataloguing in Publication Data

A CIP catalogue record for this book is available from the British
Library

ISBN 0 7185 1294 4

Cover photograph: Aerial view of York.
© Royal Commission on the Historical Monuments of England
CROWN COPYRIGHT

Typeset by Mayhew Typesetting, Rhayader, Powys
Printed and bound in Great Britain by SRP Ltd., Exeter

Contents

Foreword

This is the fourth publication in the series *The Archaeology of Medieval Britain*, initiated in 1990. The aim of the books in the series is to present up-to-date surveys of the archaeological evidence for specific aspects of Britain in the Middle Ages. The core period to be covered in depth is from the Norman conquest of 1066 to the Reformation, but there are no hard-and-fast chronological boundaries and examples of sites, artefacts and archaeological discoveries are drawn from before and after the period, where appropriate. The books are not narrowly site- or object-orientated, emphasising rather the social and economic aspects of the subjects in question, and pursuing the most recent thoughts and research in the field. Although primarily devoted to knowledge gained from archaeological excavation and research, they also refer to written, cartographic and pictorial evidence and are of interest to archaeologists and historians alike. Their style of presentation and lavish illustrations also make them attractive to general readers interested in their medieval heritage.

Each topic is covered by experts in that field, whose depth and breadth of knowledge will throw new and exciting light on the Middle Ages. Archaeological excavations and surveys in recent decades are used as the basis for wide-ranging conclusions and synthesis, and also for discussions of the current state of the subject and pointers to future research.

The previous volumes (*Medieval Fortifications* by John R. Kenyon (1990), *Medieval Monasteries* by J. Patrick Greene (1992) and *Medieval Ships and Shipping* by Gillian Hutchinson (1994)) have all fulfilled the aims of a series designed to stimulate new thoughts and ideas. The readers of subsequent volumes will have high expectations, and those will not be disappointed by the current publication. *Medieval Towns* by John Schofield and Alan Vince is an outstanding contribution to the scholarship of this complicated subject. The development, topography, economy and cultural background to medieval urbanism are described in detail and reviewed afresh in the light of the most recent research, both that undertaken by the authors themselves and by their colleagues and contemporaries. This is the first time that the multifarious strands of life in medieval towns have been brought together in such an exciting and enlightening way. The material remains, both standing structures and excavated features, are given detailed treatment, but the authors never lose sight of the fact that the inhabitants of towns were as important as what they created. We see here towns as dynamic and living organisms, not as compilations of statistics.

Both authors of the present work are uniquely qualified to write such a book. John Schofield has been unearthing London's past since 1974, and has also played a major role in shaping the course of urban archaeology elsewhere in Britain and abroad. After a period in London, Alan Vince now works in Lincoln. He also has been influential in moulding current thinking on the value of urban archaeology to our understanding of, in particular, the economics of the Middle Ages. Their complementary interests and experience have here been melded together to produce a book full of new insights into the physical structure of towns and how it reflects their social and economic life. Moreover, the relevance of towns to the overall development of Britain in the Middle Ages is never forgotten and this sets the subject firmly in the context of the life of the times.

Helen Clarke
August 1994

Acknowledgements

This book has been a joint effort, but the division of labour should be admitted. John Schofield wrote Chapters 1–3 and 6–8; Alan Vince wrote Chapters 4 and 5.

We wish to thank the people and institutions which have helped with provision of information and illustrations: Peter Armstrong (Humberside Archaeological Unit), Brian Ayers (Norfolk Archaeological Unit), Malcolm Atkin, James Bond, Bristol Museum and Art Gallery, Paul Bennett (Canterbury Archaeological Trust), M.O.H. Carver, Cheshire County Council, Andy Chopping and Maggie Cox (Museum of London Archaeology Service), Helen Clarke, Steve Clarke (Monmouth Archaeological Society), Robin Daniels, the École d'Architecture de Toulouse, Mike Eddy and M.R. Petchey (Essex County Council), James Greig and Julia Wakefield, Robina McNeil, Jean Mellor, National Monuments Record, National Trust for Ireland, Patrick Ottaway (York Archaeological Trust), Oxford Archaeological Unit, Mark Samuel, Terry Slater, D.R. Vale (City of Lincoln Archaeological Unit); and the editors of *Archeological Journal* and *Medieval Archaeology*.

The figures have been redrawn where necessary by Susan Banks, Alison Hawkins, and Tracy Wellman. Parts of the text have been read by Jane Cowgill, Roberta Gilchrist, Tony Dyson, John Manley, D.M. Palliser, James Rackham and Kate Steane, and their comments have been welcomed. At Leicester University Press we thank Alec McAulay, Jane Evans, Sarah Bury and the series editor, Helen Clarke.

We also thank all who have worked on the archaeology of British towns, particularly in the last twenty years, whether digging on site or patiently cataloguing and drawing finds. This book is a first survey of their achievements, and is dedicated to them.

List of figures

1 Introduction

This book is an archaeological journey through some of the towns of medieval Britain. Its emphasis is on the discoveries by archaeological teams over the last thirty years, nearly always on sites to be developed or already under construction. Like any travel guide, this study must be selective and it will not attempt to be comprehensive in listing these discoveries. Some of our views of towns or their component parts such as castles, churches and houses will be fragmentary and fleeting, not because we are speeding by too fast, but because our knowledge is incomplete. And yet, from the vast haul of information now at our disposal after thirty years of data gathering, we can begin to ask questions of many kinds. What went on in medieval towns? How did the rich and poor live? What nourished them? What did they die of? What was the weather like, the quality of life, the restrictions or special pleasures of living in towns? All these questions, and many others, can be answered at least partially by archaeological study.

As with any good travel guide, we must start with some basic information for the traveller. In this case there are three introductory sections, dealing with the growth of medieval urban archaeology in Britain, the necessity to see medieval British towns in their European context, and a brief chronology of the period 1100–1500 as offered to us by historians and geographers. The subsequent chapters will examine the archaeological contribution to the evolving investigation of medieval towns.

Medieval urban archaeology in Britain

The development of medieval urban archaeology in Britain has gone through three overlapping phases: the first heroic phase of 1946–70; the Winchester experience from 1961 and establishment of the units in the 1970s; and the spreading of the practice of developer-funding from about 1978. A fourth stage was perhaps reached with the publication of the government's procedural note PPG16 in 1990, but the effect of this new thinking on the conduct of archaeology in towns has yet to be felt and is at present unknown.

Since the middle of the nineteenth century, archaeologists in the larger towns of Britain sought to rescue medieval finds on building sites, and sometimes recorded medieval remains in their notebooks. Urban archaeology in Britain really only begins in the bomb-damaged cellars of London, Canterbury and a small number of other towns immediately after the last War, where medieval buildings and monuments had suffered destruction along with those of more recent centuries (Fig 1.1). In Canterbury, Shepherd Frere's objectives were mainly Roman; in the City of London, W.F. Grimes conducted excavations from 1946 to 1962 and besides many spectacular Roman discoveries (such as the Cripplegate fort of the early second century) he also recorded portions of the city wall and towers in the medieval period,

Figure 1.1 Thirteenth-century effigies of knights beneath bomb rubble in the Temple Church, London, 1941 (National Monuments Record)

secular buildings, the Charterhouse and two other religious houses, three parish churches, and an investigation of a Jewish burial ground (Grimes 1968). The work in London was sufficiently innovatory that an essay by Grimes was included in a volume entitled *Recent Archaeological Excavations in Britain* in 1956, along with reports of Star Carr, the mesolithic site in Yorkshire, the Roman treasure at Snettisham, the excavation of the Sutton Hoo ship burial and other famous sites; the chapter represented 'a sustained campaign to make the most of the unique and passing opportunity offered by the clearance of bomb-damaged areas in the oldest part of London, the City' (Bruce-Mitford 1956, xxiii). It was not fully realised at the time that towns would need consistent archaeological coverage for all future major redevelopments.

Urban excavation in the modern sense began seriously at Winchester in 1961; the research unit founded there by Martin Biddle became a prototype for many similar developments in other towns, and was especially influential in its methodology. Winchester was a good choice to reinforce Biddle's argument (e.g. Biddle 1974) that all periods of a town's history were important, not just the Roman which was the chief objective of many excavators at the time. It was also a good choice because throughout its late medieval decline and subsequent quiet centuries the core of the modern city had shrunk, leaving medieval strata intact towards the edges of town and only now threatened with development. Thus the Lower Brook Street site, with its many medieval buildings, lanes and a small church, produced spectacular and clearly important results (Biddle 1967).

By the end of the 1960s many archaeologists were concerned about the destruction of physical evidence for Britain's history in towns. This resulted in the national survey *The Erosion of History* (Heighway 1972), which drew attention to the 'crisis in urban archaeology'. It argued that the most important towns of all historical periods would be lost to archaeology in twenty years, if not before; half of the 906 historic towns remaining in mainland Britain were threatened with some sort of development, 159 of them seriously. The responsibility for this situation could be laid at several doors. Archaeologists were poorly organised and urban archaeology was a new discipline; historians did not often see the importance of other than written records. Government spokesmen continued to assert, against all experience, that existing voluntary procedures and legislation were adequate and effective (for instance, a Commons Written Answer of March 1971). Most of all, there was general ignorance about the value of the strata lying below nearly every modern town centre.

The arguments in *The Erosion of History* emphasising the importance of a town's archaeology are worth presentation here because they formed the agenda of the subject for the next twenty years, and because the document itself was so influential in changing attitudes throughout Britain. The following paragraphs are taken verbatim, slightly condensed.

Archaeology and written records: very few towns possess more than occasional written records earlier than the thirteenth century. Yet the urban life of many of our towns has continued unbroken since the tenth or eleventh century, while the origins of some lie in the Roman or even pre-Roman periods. A town may have been in existence for a thousand years before there is written record of much more than its name. But the physical remains of the past, the tangible results of man's activity, are as important a source of history as written records. This physical evidence is the raw material of archaeology, whose purpose is to study the history of man through the material remains of his past activities against the setting of the natural environment in which he acted.

Archaeology is relevant to all periods of a town's history: archaeological evidence may relate to any and every period of a town's existence, from the moment of its origin. It is therefore often the only source of evidence for the beginning and early centuries of urban life. For these centuries archaeological deposits are the town's only archive. Nor does archaeological evidence lose its importance when documents begin. Until at least the nineteenth century, the evidence of archaeology and of documents is complementary. Each records aspects of the past with which the other does not deal.

Archaeology often has evidence wider than that from written sources: the original written evidence for a town's history is always selective, dealing with those matters which required written records, such as government and records of land-holding. Archaeological evidence, whether buried or above ground, may provide information on activities which have a concrete or physical component. As a result archaeological research is concerned with the environment within which human action takes place.

Archaeology has a place in determining the future form of the town: in the designation of conservation areas and the selection of features to figure prominently in these areas, archaeological considerations are essential. The preservation of a unique identity is often the crucial problem facing a town's planners today. A successful solution to this problem requires a mature comprehension of the factors that led it to take its own particular course. In this comprehension the results of archaeological enquiry are essential.

Urban archaeology is complex: the below-ground archaeological deposits resulting from the growth of a town are by nature very extensive both in area and in depth. The former reflects the absolute size of the town as the most complex of human settlements; the latter is a function of long-continued occupation on one site. Two further factors must be added: the extraordinary complexity of town sites due to frequent disturbance of the ground throughout a town's life, and the difficulty that the entire archaeo-logical area lies below a living community with its own requirements of daily life. It is this last fact which now threatens to destroy without record the deposits of our history.

Archaeological work in towns will always be selective: not every site can be excavated, and a minimum coverage must be what came to be called 'watching briefs', that is observation of the site during contractors' work. Such observations, if properly recorded and continued over years, can produce good results; but they must be accompanied by the proper investigation of selected sites by controlled excavation. The selection of priorities will vary from town to town, but questions of origin and the evolution of the street plan and defences (if any) will always be fundamental.

Though it outlined the threat to all the towns considered, the survey highlighted six representative places, in several of which some archaeological work had already begun. But large portions of towns had already been lost to development: a quarter of Gloucester, a third of Abingdon, and nearly half of Cambridge. These examples were reminders of the vulnerability of the archaeology of towns.

   Archaeological enthusiasm and determination grew in towns where archaeologists (often amateurs and volunteers) already worked, and began to spread to other towns: in Southampton, Oxford (Fig 1.2), Gloucester, Lincoln, Colchester, Leicester, York (Fig 1.3) and Chester (Jones 1984, 17–29). In Scotland an important survey document had appeared in 1972, and this drew attention to a similar threat to the town centres north of the border (Simpson 1972); projects quickly blossomed, at Aberdeen and Edinburgh in 1973, and at Perth in 1974. The City of London itself was late in this process, and provision of a proper archaeological unit there at the end of 1973 was due to a combination of patient negotiation by the Guildhall Museum and the impending development by the Corporation of the site of the late medieval and Tudor Baynard's Castle on the waterfront. This site, excavated in 1972, was crucial in the development of archaeology in the capital, for it was clearly important; it was a powerful example of the potential damage being inflicted on our heritage, and was used by the increasingly vocal and expert pressure

Figure 1.2 Oxford Castle, 1970s: a section through the outer bailey of the castle. Saxon occupation layers which preceded the castle are paradoxically at the top of the section (Oxford Archaeological Unit)

groups such as RESCUE (founded 1971); and, incidentally, the wealth of finds from the site (not so much from the Tudor castle, but from the fourteenth-century watergate beneath it which was filled with objects of all kinds) made archaeologists throughout the country sit up. The waterfront of London, and by implication waterfronts in other historic towns, was to become a major archaeological priority in the next two decades.

During the 1970s and early 1980s archaeologists widened the debate and scope of their activities from being purely reactive to formulating strategic plans. Several county-wide surveys of threats to towns were produced: for example, for Berkshire (Astill 1978), Dorset (Penn 1980), Essex (Eddy and Petchey 1983), Oxfordshire (K. Rodwell 1975), Somerset (Aston and Leech 1977), Surrey (O'Connell 1977) and Sussex (Aldsworth and Freke 1976). There were also policy statements for individual towns (e.g. for Boston (Harden 1978), Gloucester (Heighway 1974), Lichfield (Gould 1976) and Newcastle (Harbottle and Clack 1976)). As an example of this kind of survey, we can cite the case of Taunton in Somerset (Aston and Leech 1977, 136–9).

Taunton's urban origins go back to the eighth century; a Saxon royal estate grew into a religious and administrative centre. By the end of the tenth century, it had a mint and probably defences. At the time of Domesday Book it had 64 burgesses, a market and mint, and three mills; it was the third largest town in Somerset after Bath and Ilchester. In the twelfth century the

Figure 1.3 Excavations in York, 1970s: medieval structures being investigated at the Bedern site (York Archaeological Trust)

bishop of Winchester converted the bishop's hall into a castle, and the Saxon minster was later replaced by an Augustinian priory.

Though some excavations had recently taken place, the centre of town was, in 1977, of 'enormous archaeological potential'.

> No excavation has ever been carried out on the large Augustinian priory site; even its exact site is unknown. Little is known of the archaeology of the castle, particularly of the outer bailey area, even though the documentary evidence is good. Little is known about the town's defences and nothing about the precise dating and arrangement of the recorded town gates. The sites of various chapels, hospitals and features mentioned in documents are uncertain and details of structures and activities represented on individual tenements are usually totally unknown. (Aston and Leech 1977, 137)

Large areas of medieval Taunton had been redeveloped since the 1930s, mostly since 1945. Redevelopment had not been preceded by adequate archaeological investigation and many more areas, although not destroyed archaeologically, had been effectively buried under permanent car parks. The town was in grave danger of trashing its own heritage permanently. In the years since 1977, archaeological work has fortunately taken place in Taunton: notably investigations of the castle, defences, and the site of the Saxon minster of St Peter and St Paul, later the medieval priory (Leach 1984); but questions still remain, especially concerning the town's Saxon origins.

The development of town and city centres in the 1970s provided the necessity, as well as the opportunity, for urban archaeology to learn its business very quickly; and the results were encouraging. Investigations of medieval strata and buildings were plentiful. In 1981 a summary of work in 146 English towns reported excavations of bridges (at Beverley, Bristol, Exeter, Pleshey), castles (in 37 towns), cathedrals (Canterbury, Durham, Exeter, Peterborough, Wells, York), cemeteries (14), churches (14), defences (26), land reclamation and waterfront structures (Bristol, London, Plymouth, Poole, Weymouth, Yarmouth), religious houses (Benedictines, friars, Knights of St John and Templars), streets (18), suburbs (Bristol, Exeter, London, Winchester, York), and domestic and industrial buildings of all kinds, both buried and still standing (Schofield and Palliser 1981).

Urban archaeology also blossomed in other countries of Europe during the 1960s, 1970s and 1980s: for instance in Dutch towns (Van Regteren Altena 1970; Sarfatij 1973; for Amsterdam, Baart 1977), in France (Baudry 1982), Germany and Switzerland (Flüeller and Flüeller 1993), Sweden (Ersgård et al. 1992) and other European countries (Barley 1977). Irish public interest in a large Viking and medieval site at Wood Quay, Dublin, changed the direction of Irish archaeology for ever (Bradley 1984; Barry 1987, 2). Notable advances in technique were being produced in Lübeck; principally the application of dendrochronology to buildings in towns, the interpretation of standing buildings from detailed archaeological drawings, and a strategy based on the twin purposes of first informing the public about their archaeological and architectural heritage through excavations, exhibitions and publications, and secondly a city-wide study of fundamental historical problems not yet answered.

But this work, impressive in extent and determination both in mainland Europe and Britain, was often desperate and frustratingly insufficient. As the archaeologist for Bordeaux wrote in 1982,

> the results [in Bordeaux] are nevertheless far from being satisfactory; too-rapid excavations, destruction of the remains, accumulation of masses of material which are difficult to study, synthetic publications always pushed back because of the interruptions caused by new rescue excavations. (Baudry 1982, 372)

This was the story in too many European towns, even those (unlike Bordeaux) which had a permanent archaeological unit.

In the larger British centres, at least, the available money was not matching the growing need as the pace of redevelopment quickened. During the post-war rebuilding of British towns, developers often allowed access to sites and sometimes made a contribution towards archaeological investigation on their sites; sometimes the sympathetic and educated attitude of a developer aided the provision of archaeological coverage in the town, for everyone's future benefit, as in 1974 at Perth (Jones 1984, 47–9). But during the late 1970s it became clear that the existing combination of government (then Department of the Environment) funds and occasional sponsorship was not enough to provide an efficient service on all sites where archaeology was certain to be encountered.

Nor did the existing legislation adequately cover town sites. In England, part II of the *Ancient Monuments and Archaeological Areas Act 1979* (an act of the kind recommended in the original *Erosion of History*) provided for a statutory period of four and a half months for archaeological investigation on sites in areas designated under the *Act*; but only five historic town centres were ever so designated (Canterbury, Chester, Exeter, Hereford, York), and there is no prospect of additions in the future. Archaeologists in York have found that the *Act* was helpful for persuading, or coercing, statutory authorities such as the gas and water services to allow for archaeological scrutiny of emergency works in the town centre, though they occasionally continued to claim exemption. On ordinary sites, access was made easier. The *Act*, however, said nothing about funding the archaeological work, and in that sense made the discovery of archaeological strata a problem.

In London in 1978, the Museum of London's archaeologists began suggesting to *every* developer that he should assume the responsibility of dealing with the archaeology on his site in an appropriate way. Since that time over 350 site investigations in the City have been sponsored by developers (Fig 1.4), and the custom spread, first to larger towns in Britain and abroad (including the USA, where international companies were ready to contribute funds, having previously developed a site in London).

At the present time, therefore, urban archaeologists are equipped with a fairly well-developed methodology, the product of the last twenty or thirty years of common experience. The town or regional archaeological unit deals with the town as one archaeological entity. Most often, sites are brought to the attention of the unit through planning applications. If a building site is archaeologically significant, the unit will negotiate with developers or their agents to try to eliminate or reduce the threat to the archaeological remains,

Figure 1.4 Excavations of 1982 at Billingsgate, City of London: a large area of medieval buildings is uncovered within a box of steel shuttering inserted by archaeologists (Museum of London Archaeology Service)

or to secure the time and resources required for excavation and the associated immediate tasks.

Accurate site evaluations are crucial to justify the archaeological involvement and the developer's expense. The unit holds or has access to records and finds of previous excavations in the town, and from this archive has developed a keen sense of how much archaeology survives beneath a particular development. Nevertheless, site evaluation techniques can involve joint exploratory test pits where structural engineers and archaeologists derive different data from the same groundworks. Other techniques being developed include ground radar scanning and power auguring.

Site investigation techniques (usually forms of excavation) aim to reduce the amount of time required on site as far as possible; much of the specialist recording and analysis (for instance of ancient timbers, decorated stonework from former churches or sampling for environmental archaeology) takes place off site. The finds are removed to the local museum, to which they have usually been donated by the developer. Upon completion of the excavation the site is handed back to the client, the archaeological responsibilities having been discharged.

But sponsoring excavation need not be merely a necessary duty for the developer; it can bring good publicity and the satisfaction of knowing that he has in fact paid for knowledge to be produced, and of that he has every reason to be proud. The educational benefits are enormous (Fig 1.5). Archaeology and property development can co-exist, with a proper recognition of each other's needs.

Figure 1.5 Billingsgate, City of London, later in 1982: while excavation of well-preserved medieval buildings takes place, a viewing gallery is under construction (Museum of London Archaeology Service)

In rare cases, archaeological remains may merit preservation. Some of these sites are already Scheduled as Ancient Monuments by the Secretary of State for the Environment; others deserve to be. Scheduled Monument Consent is required before Ancient Monuments can be touched in any way. The structures which might merit preservation of some kind are usually of stone or brick, especially those of the Roman period (walls, gates, or public buildings). The normal constituents of archaeological strata however are clay, timber and gravels, which are fragile and unlikely to survive in the open air without extensive conservation. Medieval monuments likely to be preserved after excavation in town centres are town walls and gates, and other structures of stone such as parts of religious houses or former churches.

For the developer faced with preservation requirements there are a number of options: incorporate the structure into the building (some examples of which figure in this book); leave the structure out of doors, to form a garden for city workers (as in London with stretches of the city wall and three bombed church sites); or seal the ruin carefully and build over it. Often it is possible, and beneficial both to the developer and to archaeology, to bridge over the archaeological deposits – to avoid deep basements for instance, or to pile only around the perimeter of a new building.

The rescue and research exploration of British towns is not only a matter for professionals; in many places amateur societies provide an essential service of support to professional colleagues, and occasionally take welcome

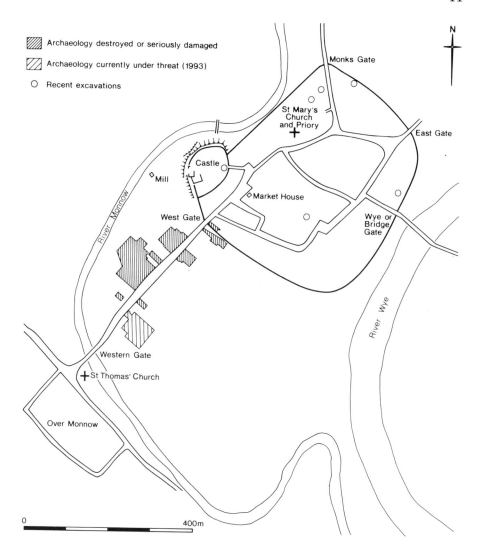

Figure 1.6 Monmouth: excavations of recent years and future prospects (Soulsby 1983 and Monmouth Archaeological Society)

initiatives. One of the most successful in recent years has been the Monmouth Archaeological Society. At least ten sites in the main street of Monmouth have been developed, with largescale destruction of up to 2m of archaeological strata (Fig 1.6). Confronted at first with unsympathetic developers, the Society used media pressure and public demonstrations to protest at illegal demolition of a listed building and the threat to archaeology beneath. The Society acquired shares in the supermarket company which was developing one of the main sites, and asked questions at shareholders' meetings. As a result the company not only funded excavations, but devised an environmental policy which includes the recycling of old buildings. Meanwhile the archaeological work of the Society in the town has elucidated its Roman and Norman stages of growth, locating defences and industrial sites (*Current Archaeology* 115 (1989), 254–7; *Rescue News* 53 (Sept 1991), 3; *Medieval Archaeology* annual summaries).

What do archaeologists seek to study in towns? Let us start with the formation of the layers of evidence itself. Layers in towns tend to be distinctive, even colourful, by comparison with those on rural sites. Although gradual and natural accumulations do occur, the majority of urban *contexts* (the word generally used for both individual deposits and traces of past digging actions such as ditches and pits) are the stratigraphic traces of events of short duration, such as construction or demolition programmes. Urban deposits also have a high proportion of crisply definable forms such as brick and stone or waterlogged contexts containing timbers. Thus, it can be suggested, urban layers are in the main more easily defined.

Urban deposits are found in great variety and often in complex sequences, and they survive to varying degrees throughout the length and breadth of the town. We first need to identify the types of evidence available (organic deposits, pockets of strata preserved by terracing, surviving medieval structures) and then use them to evaluate the town as an archaeological resource (often with the use of specially prepared maps of the deposits). The variety of survival in the evidence will affect the strategy of our excavations and the likely results. Deposits of bulky proportions, for instance, were left in Roman and Victorian times, with periods of lesser detritus between. A likely conclusion will be that not all periods are available for examination everywhere. The first factor in archaeological excavation strategy must be the nature of the site.

Urban finds are of several kinds: ceramics (largely pottery), animal bones, human bones, buildings and loose building material, non-ceramic artefacts (in leather, wood, and metals), biological and botanical evidence. Buildings and streets are types of artefact, to be analysed in the same general ways as pottery or smallfinds. The town's archaeology is the result of a bundle of influences – climatic regimes, physical factors in the environment such as the influence of geology or gradual pollution, or biological factors (e.g. dietary differences between people). The archaeologist seeks to identify economic and social groupings (including industrial, military or religious groups) in the town by purely archaeological means. Once these groups have been described and delineated, the archaeologist can move to consider the relationships between groups, both within the town – how did these military, industrial, commercial, social and religious functions fit together in the comparatively confined space of the town? – and over time, by comparing how groups rose and fell, infiltrated each other or disappeared from view. The keywords in urban archaeology are *groups, spaces* and *change*.

Origins of medieval towns in Europe

The development of urbanisation in medieval Britain must be seen in a wider, European context (Barley 1977; Clarke and Simms 1985). Herrmann

Figure 1.7 Herrmann's Inner, Middle and Outer Zones of urbanisation in western Europe (1991)

(1991) has recently provided a useful overview. He divides Dark-Age Europe into three zones (Fig 1.7), based on the boundaries of the former Roman empire. The Inner Zone comprised for our purposes southern France and Italy, centred on the Mediterranean. North of this was a Middle Zone, whose axes were the Rhine and the Danube (flowing north-west and south-east respectively), up to the geographical boundary of Roman power and of Roman urbanisation. Beyond this, to the north and east, lay the Outer Zone, where Roman settlements did not exist. Roman Britain (that is, apart from most of Scotland and Ireland) lay in the Middle Zone, and its development

14   *Medieval towns*

should be compared with that of the Low Countries, southern Germany, Switzerland and Austria.

How did town life start again in this zone? Archaeological work in many European towns, especially since the last war, has produced much evidence demonstrating different solutions and regional variety, but some common themes are evident. The old Roman sites developed in four ways. First, there was often continuity of site without necessarily continuity of town functions such as civic order and a continuous market. In Vienna, for instance, there was certainly occupation of some kind (*Fortleben*, 'after-life') in the ruins, until after 1030 when a new town became evident within the outline of the Roman fortress (Ebner 1991; Fig 1.8).

Secondly, there was continuity of fortifications or defences; Roman walls were renewed, in the main with more primitive techniques of construction. These rebuildings presumably indicate groups of people sheltering in the towns and using them at least periodically. An example of this is Regensburg in Bavaria, where parts of the Roman defences, including their towers, served as centres of religious and political power from which the suburbs were organised and governed.

Thirdly, many ancient towns show that settlement in them continued, but in phases which do not seem connected to each other. In Cologne, for instance, there were farms within the Roman walls. In the eighth century, new buildings and the establishment of a Frankish aristocratic centre followed, with a religious reorganisation of the area.

Fourthly, a few places demonstrate continuity of town institutions (and principally the Christian church), crafts and industries. Paris was chosen by Clovis as his capital in 507, and in the following two centuries many churches were built on both banks of the Seine. The town developed into three separate districts: from north to south, the former centre of the Roman city, a restricted enclave of religious and royal power (the Ile de la Cite) and a new urban settlement on the right bank of the river (Velay 1991). Another example of this kind is Huy on the Meuse in Belgium, which by 1000 had become a favoured trading-partner of London. Originally a small Roman town, at a crossing-point of an important river, Huy maintained its regional importance in the Merovingian period, minting coins in the seventh century and exacting tolls from wayfarers in the eighth century. Recent excavations have suggested that a craft-working settlement occupied a suburb alongside a princely residence (Verhaeghe 1991).

The first three of these levels of development do not demonstrate urban continuity, but merely sporadic reuse of the site by separate groups at different times. The Dark Ages is a term applicable to the archaeology of this period in Britain, the Rhineland and around the Danube. From the seventh century, however, and largely through French centres, international trade began to percolate to Britain and other parts of the Middle Zone; even beyond, to Scandinavia (Hodges 1982). Major land routes, such as that to Kiev in the east, were used by merchants, and along them grew many of the larger eastern European towns of today.

In the Outer Zone, where there were no Roman towns to reuse, new types of urban settlement were created; and further new towns were added to trade and communications networks within the former Roman provinces

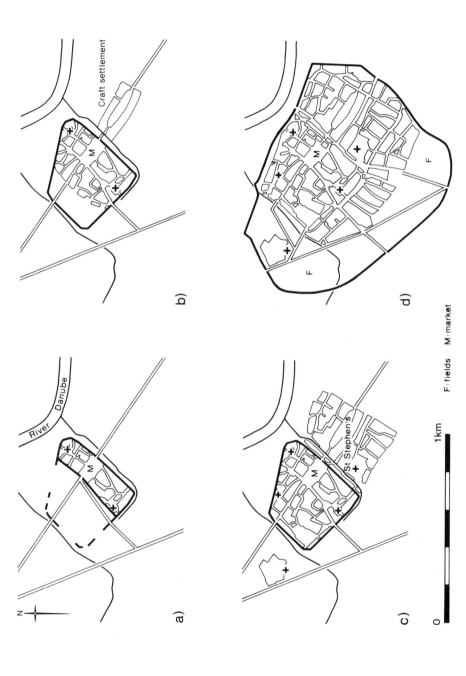

Figure 1.8 Stages in the growth of Vienna: (a) fifth to eighth century; (b) eighth and ninth century; (c) eleventh century; (d) at the end of the twelfth century (Ebner 1991, based on the work of R. Pohanka)

such as lowland Britain. These new settlements were of three general forms. First, independent villages might come together into a regional centre which, while defended by a princely stronghold, specialised in crafts and industry: examples of this are towns on the Danube such as Bratislava (Habovstiak 1991) or Novgorod (Dejevsky 1977). In a similar way, it is clear that centres such as Ribe and Haithabu (Hedeby), on or near the Baltic, were closely related to their rural surroundings, spreading artefacts from abroad into the villages and presumably receiving provisions and exports in return.

Secondly, there were new towns with two clear elements: a lord's castle or fortified stronghold, and a mercantile settlement often called a suburb. This type of town became common in the tenth and eleventh centuries, when the dual character of many towns is evident in all parts of the Middle Zone, and beyond in Denmark, Norway and Sweden. There was a surge of foundations in the twelfth and thirteenth centuries, but not always on bare territory. Recent archaeological work has shown that in some cases, such as the important town of Lübeck on the north coast of Germany, the documented foundation of 1143 was based on an existing Slavic stronghold and mercantile quarter (Fig 1.9; Fehring 1991). Excavation has also shown that the double town of Cölln-Berlin, mentioned in documents in 1237 and 1244, was preceded by settlements of probably commercial character (Seyer 1991).

A third type of new urban settlement was the coastal trading place. These were important distribution points for foreign products and luxuries, and for that reason were assiduously controlled by local kings and princes. Some of these ports grew up at a distance from the royal centre, or flourished on the borders between kingdoms. In the eighth century London, for instance, was the port of land-locked Mercia. These places took on a great importance in international trade from the seventh century, and spread through the Outer Zone of northern (Baltic) Europe in the ninth century: for instance Reric and Ralswiek on the north coast of Germany, Wolin (Poland) and Birka (Sweden). London's port was resited within the old Roman walls. The most graphic illustration of the growth and vigour of these towns is their waterfront installations, which have now been excavated in many cases (Milne and Hobley 1981). The topography of the ports was varied, but they were based on access to the sea (or a major river), and this appears to have influenced the street layout of many. A major street would run along the crest of the river bank or sea shore, and from it lanes or alleys would descend to the quays. Though the major landing-places were natural markets, this function was shared with landward markets on these parallel streets, at one remove from the ships.

These three types of town formation, characteristic of Herrmann's Outer Zone (that is, beyond the Rhine and Danube) but also common in the Middle Zone, form the background to our enquiry about medieval towns in Britain.

An outline of period in Britain, 1100–1500

The medieval period in the British Isles is conventionally divided into three consecutive phases: (i) the development of towns and the countryside in a

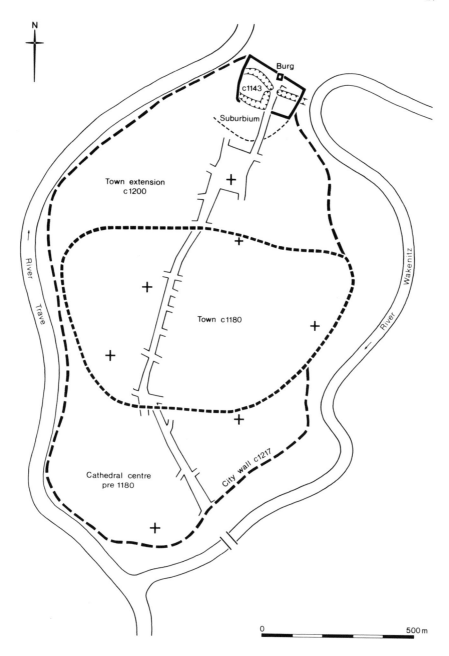

Figure 1.9 Lübeck: general conclusions about development of the town from recent excavations. Prior to the archaeological work, it was widely held that the town was built at one instant in the mid-twelfth century (Fehring 1991 and other sources)

period of growth, 1100–1300; (ii) the crises of the early and mid-fourteenth century, including the Black Death; (iii) a long period of mixed fortunes from about 1350 to 1500, which comprised both decline for some towns and the rise of others, including in England the increasing dominance of London over a widening hinterland.

The period 1100–1300 was one of rapid population growth, in towns and in the countryside. In 1340 England's population may have been 5–6 million. Such a figure had not been reached since the third century and would not be reached again until the eighteenth century.

The powerful pressure of an expanding population in the early Middle Ages found its most immediate expression in a widespread movement of colonization. This filling-out of the web of the established settlement pattern, of which eastern Norfolk provides an extreme example, was going on all over England and Wales. As the farmed area expanded, so existing settlements got larger, although sometimes secondary settlements were also brought into being in the form of isolated farms, farm clusters, and hamlets. This process of internal colonization and the natural increase of population gradually changed the face of the countryside as wood, heath, and fen were reclaimed and converted into productive farmland. The process pushed out into estuarine marshes, and to abandoned lands in the north of England; the new monastic orders proved active.

In the eleventh century there were already many towns in Britain, though the majority were in England, where Domesday Book records 112 places called boroughs in 1086. They were based on royal residences, or trading settlements, or the defended places of Saxons or Danes in the ninth and tenth centuries (Hill 1981, maps 226–34; Hinton 1990, 82–105). Some major centres such as London, Lincoln and York had longer histories, being Roman foundations of the first century AD.

The dominant foci during the eleventh and twelfth centuries for European trade were the fairs of northern Italy, Flanders and Champagne. These fairs did not usually produce towns, but the repeated and prolonged residence of merchants at fairs brought wealth to nearby towns, and occasionally fairs would weld together loosely formed places into a town (Verlinden 1963).

In the towns this period of comparative wealth and growth is illustrated by the range of civic and religious buildings which were constructed (Platt 1978, 1–29; Hinton 1990, 106–32). The great majority of urban defences in England and Wales, for instance, were built, or at least begun, before 1300. The Normans moved the seats of bishops to towns, which meant many new cathedrals. In the thirteenth century the friars arrived in Britain seeking populous locations, and hospitals were founded in and around many towns.

Weekly markets in the smaller towns are mentioned in the twelfth but especially in the thirteenth centuries; sometimes the grant of the market itself is recorded. The fair, on the other hand, was a kind of glorified market, usually held once a year and lasting for at least three days and sometimes for as long as six weeks. As the market was the centre for exchange within the neighbourhood, so the fair was the centre for foreign wares, brought from outside the locality.

Between 1200 and 1500 about 2800 grants of market were made by the Crown, over half of them in the period 1200–75. Village markets and seasonal local fairs were augmented by weekly or bi-weekly markets held in centres of production – both existing towns and new towns. This was happening all over Europe, for instance in south-west France (the interface between the English and French kingdoms) and along the Baltic coast. Towns were valuable pieces of property, for the lord gained revenue from the court, tolls on merchandise, and from the demands of the market which benefited his own rural manors in the surrounding countryside (Platt 1978, 30–90).

In this early phase the merchants of many small British towns participated in overseas trade and London's dominance was a thing of the future. Ships still came to the river-ports of York, Lincoln, Norwich, Gloucester and Chester. Wine from the English lands in Gascony (south-west France) came to Boston in Lincolnshire; wool exports through the town rivalled those of the capital. Along the eastern and southern coasts, small and medium-sized towns fed their regions with imports, and shipped out the local produce. This led to country landowners and religious houses acquiring properties in the ports, where they could trade with the surplus of their own manors and farms, and have access to the market in imported luxuries.

London, however, had been the largest and wealthiest town in England from the tenth century, and by the twelfth century was also the primary distribution centre for inland trade. Its size and wealth began to dominate south-east England. At the time of the Norman Conquest, Winchester was the centre of the Old English kingdom, but during the twelfth century Winchester's connections with the Norman kings slackened and after the loss of Normandy in 1204 the centre of the kingdom moved away from the south coast to the superior attractions of London. In 1340, London's population may have been between 80,000 and 100,000. In this respect it would bear comparison with other large cities of Europe, such as Milan, Venice, Naples, Florence and Palermo (all over 50,000 in the thirteenth century); Ghent (56,000 by about 1350); Cologne (40,000) and Bruges (35,000 in about 1340). Four towns in the Iberian peninsula were in the same league: Barcelona, Cordoba, Seville and Granada (Hohenberg and Lees 1985, 11). By this time, London's pull on people and resources was affecting the whole country: only 9 per cent of immigrants came from within a radius of 10 miles or less; a large proportion (39 per cent) came from within 11–40 miles; 25 per cent from 41–80 miles; and a notable 27 per cent from over 80 miles away (Keene 1989).

In Wales, the Norman kings inherited from their Anglo-Saxon pre-decessors a claim to overlordship. Border raids by the Welsh in the 1060s prompted serious consideration of the Welsh question. By 1135, under successive Anglo-Norman kings, a boundary zone of castles and nascent towns had been established along the Marches from Cardiff to Chester. Towns flourished particularly in south Wales during the eleventh and twelfth centuries: places like Monmouth, Cardiff, Abergavenny, Brecon (where the first civil town was laid out in the castle bailey, a pattern found elsewhere in the Welsh zone), Carmarthen and Pembroke. This southern group was complemented by a second wave of fortress towns added in the north and west by Edward I's campaigns in the 1270s (Davies 1991; Soulsby 1983). The importance of towns in the economic life of medieval Wales was out of proportion to their small size, because the society was underdeveloped in urban terms, and localised. Towns were here, in pure form, the lubricators of trade and cash in every direction.

In Scotland, by the eleventh century, there were also political and economic systems which could organise and support substantial centres of population, but urban history is obscure before the widespread introduction of the 'burgh' and its privileges by King David I (1124–53) and his successors. Some towns, like Edinburgh and Stirling, grew next to citadels; while others, such as Lanark, Selkirk and Dunfermline, are on unprotected sites (Lynch et al. 1988). It is important (especially for English readers) to remember that Scotland was a different kingdom. The bulk of her overseas trade was with Flanders and Artois; by the 1290s Scottish merchants had their own district in Bruges. Some of the more prominent early Scottish burgesses seem to have come from Flanders; much of the Scottish country-side was given over to sheep farming to feed the Flemish demand for wool. Spanish iron was imported at Ayr, and Spanish merchants may have bought fish at west-coast ports (Stevenson 1988).

In England, towards the end of the thirteenth century, there are signs of economic strain and social tensions, at least in the larger towns (Bolton 1980, 146–8, 156–9). The most important single industry was cloth, but in the thirteenth century, in the face of the highly urbanised Flemish industry, England became an exporter of raw materials, that is, wool. This placed England in the position of being a colony of Flanders. Flemings and Italians organised the trade, and English merchants resorted to repressive policies at home: more rigid enforcement of rules about trading (shown in the sudden increase of written records), seeking out cheaper labour in the countryside, and the development of monopolies.

Ecological, demographic, socio-economic and political factors all con-tributed to a period of crises in the fourteenth century. By 1300 the imbalance between population and resources had become such that the economy was ill-equipped to cope with extreme events, yet the next half century delivered a succession of them: bad harvests, tax demands accompanying a declaration of war on France, and bubonic plague.

During the second half of the thirteenth century reserves of colonizable land were gradually exhausted. Part of the reason for this mounting imbalance between population and resources was the rate of population growth itself. Some localities coped with the problem of population pressure by diversifying their economy, and this gave them resilience. It has been suggested that natural ecological limits were exceeded and environmental degradation set in. Certainly some localities experienced difficulties in the first half of the fourteenth century. Yet even in these hard-pressed places it is far from clear whether the ecological breakdown was cause or effect. For some historians, it is the nature of a feudal society based on land tenure which ultimately hindered medieval economic growth and eventually precipitated the crisis which the economy experienced in the fourteenth century (R.M.S. Campbell 1990).

The Black Death of 1348 was the *coup de grâce* to a country already weakened by political problems and natural disasters. England was at war with Scotland and from 1337 with France, which resulted in heavy taxes to pay for the king's campaigns. Crop failures and cattle disease caused widespread famines in 1315–25; a 50 per cent drop in production brought a 400 per cent increase in grain prices. Land prices in the middle of the City of London show that there was a decline in the fourteenth century (which lasted virtually to the middle of the sixteenth century), and it was under way well before the Black Death, which seems to have had no special impact of its own (Keene 1985a; 1989).

The population's failure to recover from the plague inaugurated a century and a half of demographic stagnation and malaise. The fifteenth century has been called the 'golden age of bacteria'. Migration redistributed population from the countryside to the town (and hence from areas of lower to higher mortality), and redistributed the population locally and regionally. In England the net effect of these moves was to boost the proportion of the total population resident in eastern, south-eastern and especially south-western England at the expense of the Midlands and the North. In Wales, also, towns experienced a lengthy period of decline characterised by reductions in populations and the disappearance of some small communities (Soulsby 1983, 24–7).

Yet this late medieval period, from about 1350 to 1500, has produced great cathedrals, scores of beautiful parish churches, and many of the sturdy medieval buildings which have survived six hundred years in market towns. Rural housing improved, and there was a certain amount of conspicuous show in public and domestic building (for reviews of the archaeological evidence, see Platt 1978, 138–204; Hinton 1990, 191–213).

In wider Europe, the structure of medieval trade now gave dominance to towns. By the fourteenth century the fairs of Champagne, such as those of Troyes and Provins, were in decline, being replaced in importance by industrial and commercial towns such as Frankfurt (Verlinden 1963).

During the late fourteenth and fifteenth centuries cloth replaced wool as England's main export. By 1500 the bulk of the country's overseas trade was in English hands; so was the transformation of raw materials into finished products. However, the merchants had now also captured foreign markets (Bolton 1980, 193–5).

But many towns, some sooner than others, went into decline. At York around 1400, the textile industry was flourishing and the town's merchants engaged in overseas trade through the nearby port of Hull. Within 30 years, the textile industry had migrated to the countryside and wool exports had slumped. Hull could not compensate by more exports of cloth, for it faced Hanse opposition in the Baltic and London's interests in Flanders. Lincoln was declining more rapidly, initially from the effect of the plague and then from problems with its vital waterways, the Fosdyke to the Trent and the Witham to Boston. At Nottingham in 1376 houses were falling into decay; Bedford and Warwick similarly stagnated. The problem of how to identify decline in the archaeological record is one of those considered at the end of this study (pp. 212–14).

Other towns, however, succeeded. Gloucester and Coventry switched attention from wool to cloth production. Salisbury and Norwich did likewise, and whole regions came to specialise in cloth: notably the south-west (Totnes, Castle Combe), East Anglia (Lavenham, Hadleigh) and the

West Riding of Yorkshire (Halifax and Wakefield). Ports also fared better, as demonstrated by the fortunes of Bristol and London; but not so much the southern and eastern ports such as Southampton, within the increasing range of London's pull. Even Bristol would succumb to the capital's dominance after 1500 (Platt 1976, 108–14; Bolton 1980, 246–55).

In the capital, whereas the earlier period had been one of urban industrial production and the growth of guild or craft power, this later period is one of decline in urban industry and the subsequent waning of the power of the guilds. At the same time London rose as the principal distributor of luxury goods (as shown in the Paston letters of the fifteenth century). Trends in this direction had started by 1300, when the pewter and brass industries were based primarily in the capital. All manufacturing trades were also stimulated by the increasing crystallisation of the royal and government offices nearby at Westminster. In Scotland, Edinburgh probably had a similar strangling effect, controlling key sectors of overseas trade and contributing to the decline of many Scottish towns until 1500 or later (Lynch et al. 1988, 6). In general, trading zones within Britain (that is, the distribution of products) were larger in 1500 than in 1300.

We have thus sketched out three introductory topics: the rise and nature of medieval urban archaeology in Britain, the medieval town as a European phenomenon, and an outline of the period. The rest of this book looks at selected themes in the archaeology of the medieval town. First, two chapters form a more detailed introduction to study of the medieval townscape: the main features in the town plan, and the domestic setting of many activities within the urban space. Then follow three chapters exploring functions against this background: crafts and industry, trade and commerce, and the role of the church (both parish churches and religious houses). To some extent military functions will be dealt with in Chapter 2 on the town plan, in brief consideration of castles and defences, but we have regretfully omitted detailed study of them, and leave that to others. Chapter 7 deals with the ecological study of medieval life in towns, its processes and their consequences. The final chapter both lists unfinished business and looks ahead to the next set of questions.

2 Topographical factors in the growth of towns

During the late eleventh, twelfth and thirteenth centuries urban expansion took place, to varying degrees, in all parts of Britain. In the existing, Anglo-Saxon towns this took the form of filling-out the unsettled areas within the town and spreading beyond boundaries such as defences (sometimes of Roman origin) into new suburbs. Away from the established centres, expansion took two clear forms: the foundation of new towns, and the spread of market rights and fairs which might be a catalyst to the transformation of a loosely formed place into a town. Kings, lords and bishops promoted villages to boroughs, often by adding new areas of settlement.

As far as general patterns can be seen in England and Wales, royal foundations were common before 1100, but seigneurial foundations – that is, those founded by a secular or religious lord – were more conspicuous in the late twelfth and early thirteenth century. Medieval towns in Scotland can be divided into two groups (Carver 1987): first, 'long-lived central places' of twelfth-century foundation, which flourish as towns today, such as Jedburgh, Stirling, Dumfries and Perth; their origins are often attributed to King David I (1124–53), but they were also part of the wider urbanisation movement throughout Europe during the century (Lynch et al. 1988), and fitted into the largely rural pattern of medieval Scotland (Ewan 1990, 1). A further group of towns are generally added or stimulated later, and are now smaller settlements, villages or even deserted: towns of the eleventh/twelfth centuries (Crail, Fife), thirteenth century (Fyvie and Newburgh, Grampian), fourteenth century (Tarbert, Argyle) and fifteenth century (Carnwath and Douglas, Lanarkshire).

In this chapter, we are essentially concerned with natural and man-made boundaries (rivers, defences), definable zones inside and outside the town (trade quarters, suburbs) and major constructions or spaces in the urban landscape which were usually the focus of specific activity (castles, market-places, public buildings, bridges). As we review the evidence, we should keep in mind that we are seeking *patterns* of location or relationship – if the castle is *here*, the later market will probably be *there* – and evidence of how the principal monuments of the town affected each other by the functions they expressed. The existence of walls might cramp the limit of settlement, or the town might expand around its defences, fanning out from the gates. The expanding influence of a nodal point for public resort such as the gate of a large monastery would affect the character of its surroundings, and in particular other prominent buildings such as parish churches in its immediate vicinity. We can attempt to gauge how much architectural and artistic energy went into the construction and embellishment of public buildings and structures such as town gates or quays. Some patterns, for instance the division of towns into quarters which reflected trade specialisations, are now difficult to identify from archaeology alone; this particular question is dealt with below (Chapter 4, pp. 117–22).

Geology and contours

The siting of a town in relation to its underlying geology will affect the survival of deposits to be read by the archaeologist. A soft, high site such as Shrewsbury, it is suggested, seems to get generally lower over time, due to constant foundation-digging (Carver 1978). Stream-valleys, where they either run through the town or next to it, are extremely useful reservoirs of strata, often comprised of domestic and trade rubbish from the town itself in waterlogged and therefore well-preserved condition.

In the medieval period, many towns were moulded to contours of hills which affected the design and development of the place. Some, like Durham or Lincoln, still display the crags or steep slopes on which they were built; others, like the City of London, far less so. At Edinburgh (Fig 2.1), the old town still clings to its narrow ridge of rock, with the High Street forming the spine for properties to either side; settlement spread below it on the south into the Cowgate valley, since the main approach roads to the citadel were from the south and east. Expansion here from the thirteenth century was such that the hastily erected Flodden Wall of 1513 was half-way up the gradual slope beyond the Cowgate valley, and yet it cut through existing suburbs.

Thus the physical topography of a town is a worthwhile subject of archaeological research; the skeleton of the town is often natural features, such as hills and streams (e.g. for minor streams in Norwich: Ayers 1992), or includes a man-made reaction to the elements, such as sea embankments. One of the first duties of an archaeological survey of a town must be to chart the contours of the underlying natural soil (and therefore the varying depth of archaeological strata), as has been undertaken for only a small number of British towns (London, Shrewsbury, Worcester and York) and abroad at Trondheim, Norway (Lunde 1985, 125–7), and in several German and especially French towns (a series of reports by the Centre National d'Archéologie Urbaine which, at the time of writing, deals with the towns of Angers, Arles, Bayeux, Besançon, Castres, Douai, Grenoble, Metz, Saint-Amand-Montrond and Strasbourg). Such a chart is then refined by each excavation.

Coasts, rivers and roads

Towns multiplied on coasts, on rivers, and along major roads. The ports in particular were stimulated by an export trade in corn, minerals and wool from their hinterlands, but also by the use of the sea as a highway which linked one part of Britain to another. Nearly half all medieval new towns in England were ports, on the coast or at estuaries; the majority of these were on the south coast, acting as shipping and landing points to and from the continent. In Wales, 24 towns occupied coastal sites. The majority were

English foundations, whose garrisons could be landed and supplied by ship. Several also had profitable fishing industries during the medieval period, and the economic life of the town centred as much on the public quay as on the castle.

The majority of medieval Welsh towns were sited on rivers, which brought many advantages. Rivers were major routeways, and towns such as Monmouth gained importance, both strategic and economic, from being at a river-junction (Fig 2.1; Soulsby 1983). Rivers also provided lines of natural defence, sometimes making a full circuit of walls unnecessary (as at Llanidloes). They supplied power for the town mills (as at Chipping Campden or Winchester (Biddle and Keene 1976, 282–5) and water for both home and trade consumption. Some towns, such as Cork in Ireland (Fig 2.2), were surrounded by channels and there was probably more traffic on water than on routes by land.

Rivers also had to be crossed, or made accessible by bringing roads to them for the loading and unloading of goods and persons. Bridges were often instrumental in the siting of new towns, and in the development of old towns. In some cases land routes were diverted to new boroughs with new bridges, as at New Sleaford (Lincs) or Boroughbridge (N Yorks); the names Stockbridge (Hants), Uxbridge (Middx) and just plain Brigg (Lincs) emphasise the main reason for the place. The detailed scrutiny of medieval bridges, aided by surviving building and repair accounts in municipal records, can say much about the town's understanding of its position in the hinterland, and which routes it saw as important in furthering its economic prospects (see for example Bristol and Exeter, Schofield and Palliser 1981, 10, 37; for general discussion, Steane 1985, 109–15). The bottleneck or limiting effect of a bridge could define different archaeological cultures: in fourteenth-century Bedford, for instance, glazed pottery from Lyveden in Northamptonshire was widespread north of the river, while the comparable ware south of the river came from Oxfordshire; this despite the existence of the stone bridge since the late twelfth century – or, the excavator suggests, perhaps because of the tolls levied upon it (Baker et al. 1979, 294). Alternatively, the effect of building a bridge at one town could be damaging to another: the construction of a bridge over the upper Thames at Abingdon in the fifteenth century was a cause of decay to nearby Wallingford, also on the river, but now placed at a severe disadvantage.

A main road running through a town was probably as important a cause of growth as any other. The Roman road system contributed to the rebirth of London after each of its periods of destruction or decline; then, as now, it was a difficult place to avoid. In England and in Wales, many medieval towns grew up on or near parts of the Roman road system. Most of the 24 medieval towns of Essex, for instance, developed on the radial roads north and east of London. Chelmsford was founded *de novo* in 1199 by the Bishop of London, who also extended the existing settlement at Braintree; both were on routeway junctions. St Osyth's priory founded Brentwood on one side of the road between London and Colchester and Ipswich in 1176 (Eddy and Petchey 1983, 27) and Epping was founded by the canons of Waltham Abbey in similar fashion in the mid-twelfth century (ibid., 50). Both these settlements were markets and yet occupation was for a long time

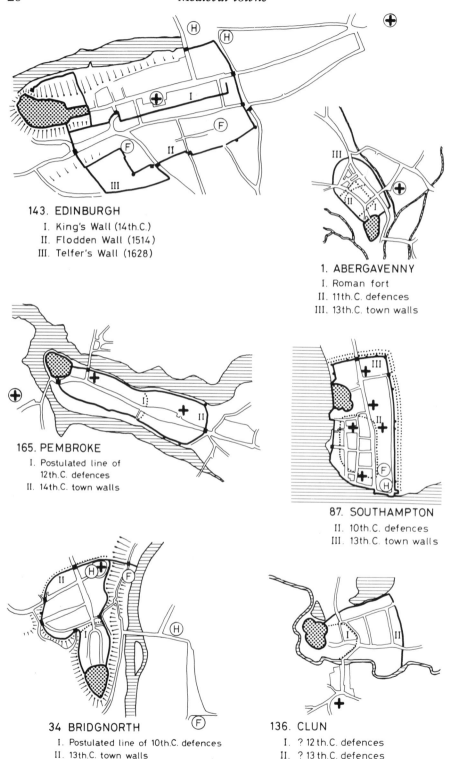

143. EDINBURGH
I. King's Wall (14th.C.)
II. Flodden Wall (1514)
III. Telfer's Wall (1628)

1. ABERGAVENNY
I. Roman fort
II. 11th.C. defences
III. 13th.C. town walls

165. PEMBROKE
I. Postulated line of
   12th.C. defences
II. 14th.C. town walls

87. SOUTHAMPTON
II. 10th.C. defences
III. 13th.C. town walls

34 BRIDGNORTH
I. Postulated line of 10th.C. defences
II. 13th.C. town walls

136. CLUN
I. ? 12th.C. defences
II. ? 13th.C. defences

Figure 2.1 Maps of selected medieval towns: those which enlarged their area of settlement and enclosed it with defences (Bond 1987)

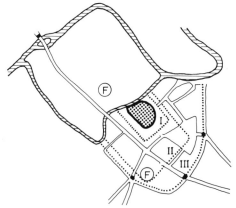

25. DONCASTER

   I. Late Roman fort, partly reutilised
     as outer bailey of castle
   II. Postulated line of burh defences
   III. Medieval town ditch

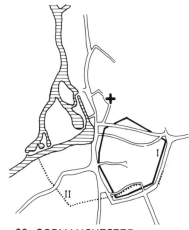

26. GODMANCHESTER

   I. Roman defences
   II. 9th–11th.C. defences

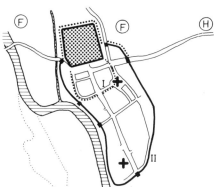

132. CARDIFF

   I. Postulated line of 12th.C. defences
   II. 14th.C. town walls

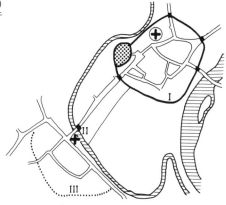

160. MONMOUTH

   I. 13th.C. town walls
   II. Monnow Gate
   III. Clawdd Du (Over Monnow)

N

 Castle
 Monastery or Cathedral
 Church
 Friary
 Hospital
——— Town walls
·········· Bank / ditch defences

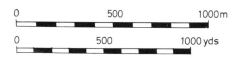

0   500   1000m

0   500   1000 yds

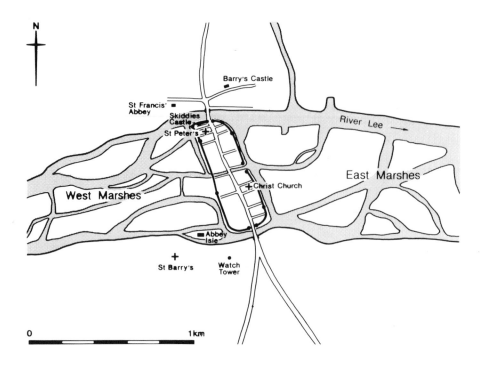

Figure 2.2   Cork in 1545, showing its remarkable position on several islands, surrounded by water (National Trust for Ireland)

confined to one side of the street only (ibid., 4, 23). A combination of studies of kings' itineraries round their castles and manors and maps such as that of Matthew Paris (*c.* 1250) and the Gough map (*c.* 1340) can produce a map of medieval roads, at least in England (Hindle 1982; Steane 1985, 104–9). The importance of the road itself to a settlement can be seen in the number of inns which accrued to make the village or town a stopping-place along the route.

Factors in growth: planned towns and planned parts of towns

An enthusiasm for studying medieval towns over the last 20 years has given rise to an impression (i) that they arrived as a new form of settlement in the twelfth and especially thirteenth centuries, and (ii) that they were usually fully formed and of a single period of planning. On the contrary, we now know that the tradition of planned towns can be traced back to Mercia and Wessex in the eighth and ninth centuries; and secondly, towns and villages usually contain a number of planned elements of different periods.

Medieval towns can be divided into two groups: those planned largely at a single instant (and often also called 'planted' towns) and those of organic growth, which are usually towns with long histories. The distinction was firmly made by Beresford in his study (1967, repr. 1988) of medieval new towns, which identified 251 English and Welsh towns created between 1066 and 1368. Though this approach was criticised by urban historians (e.g. Reynolds 1977, 54–5) as leading to over-simplification, new towns remain a significant feature of the period.

From the modern street-plan of towns, or from maps showing their former state, we can identify certain layouts which were shared by new towns and by planned extensions to existing (pre-medieval) settlements. Three main variants have been identified. First, in a small number of towns there is clear evidence of planning. A chequerboard pattern formed by at least four streets and nine squares is found rarely (Salisbury (Rogers 1969); Winchelsea (Fig 2.3; Beresford 1988, 14–28)) and must always have been exceptional. Ludlow, which now comprises a grid of streets, probably grew in a series of stages (Platt 1976, 38–44). A second grid-plan produced a ladder-like effect with two main streets in parallel (e.g. New Shoreham, Melcombe Regis). Thirdly, particularly in the years up to 1200, an urban castle might dominate the town plan to the extent of making it circular or D-shaped, following the castle's outer defences (Barnstaple, Pleshey).

A second group of apparently planned elements were more irregular, and concern the emphasis placed upon the market, especially as defensive considerations declined during the thirteenth century. Markets might be in the main street, causing its edges to bulge into a cigar-shape, or the meeting of two or three ways might produce a triangular space. These two market-forms are very common in towns, and one might ask what, if any, deliberate policy of planning they represent, apart from the initial decision to start the market.

Ideas of what may be termed medieval town-planning are most evident in the new towns associated with Edward I. In the north at Berwick, and in Wales at Flint, Conwy and Caernarvon, he hoped both to keep the peace by establishing garrison towns but also to encourage it by promoting ports and markets; incidentally ensuring effective markets to feed the garrisons. New towns in Gascony, then held by the English Crown, are called *bastides*; the name is related to *bâtir*, to build, and the streets, public buildings and market-places of the new towns bring into clearer focus the factors at work in the design of towns. Edward I gathered together experts in the field of town-planning, as it then existed as a subject; the new towns of the years around 1300 in Wales and Gascony are the most 'planned' of all the English foundations.

Flint (1277; Fig 2.4a) was the first of Edward's bastides in Wales, and work began simultaneously on the castle and the town. Here the land allowed regular blocks to be laid out, with space for the market inside the walls; as at Caernarvon, the castle could be defended separately and would not have to suffer the fate of the town if attacked. The town's defences, though on a large scale, were however of earth, and this despite being sited on a sandstone outcrop. It is possible that the design owed something to Edward's recent visits to Gascon towns, or the Mediterranean bastide of Aigues Mortes which he would have seen in 1270 when departing on a crusade (Beresford 1988, 39–40, 550).

Caernarvon (1283; Fig 2.4b) was to be a fortified town on the edge of the hostile kingdom of Gwynedd; in 1284, a year after work started on it, the

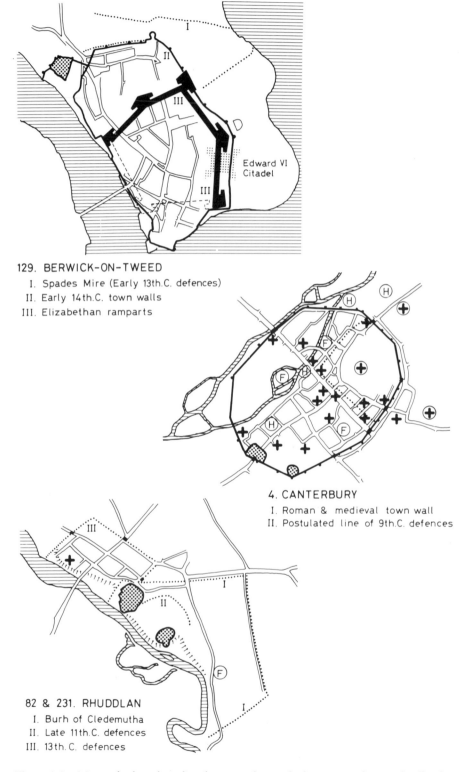

129. BERWICK-ON-TWEED
   I. Spades Mire (Early 13th.C. defences)
   II. Early 14th.C. town walls
   III. Elizabethan ramparts

Edward VI
Citadel

4. CANTERBURY
   I. Roman & medieval town wall
   II. Postulated line of 9th.C. defences

82 & 231. RHUDDLAN
   I. Burh of Cledemutha
   II. Late 11th.C. defences
   III. 13th.C. defences

Figure 2.3 Maps of selected medieval towns: those which contracted, or radically changed the area of settlement in the medieval period, as shown by their defences (Bond 1987)

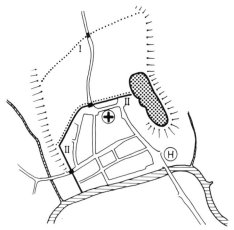

127. ARUNDEL

   I. Outer defences (? Early 13th.C.)
  II. Town wall (1294-5)

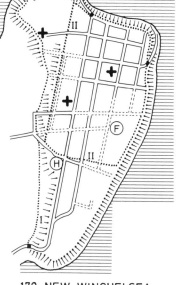

179. NEW WINCHELSEA

   I. Late 13th / early 14th.C.
     defences
  II. Defences of 1414-15

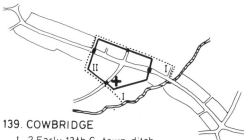

139. COWBRIDGE

   I. ? Early 13th.C. town ditch
  II. 13th.C. town wall

N

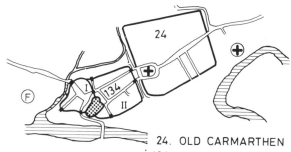

24. OLD CARMARTHEN
134. NEW CARMARTHEN

   I. Town wall (1233)
  II. Town wall (1415)

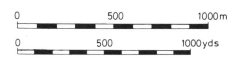

   Castle
   Monastery or Cathedral
   Church
   Friary
   Hospital
   Town walls
   Bank / ditch defences

| 0 | 500 | 1000m |
| 0 | 500 | 1000yds |

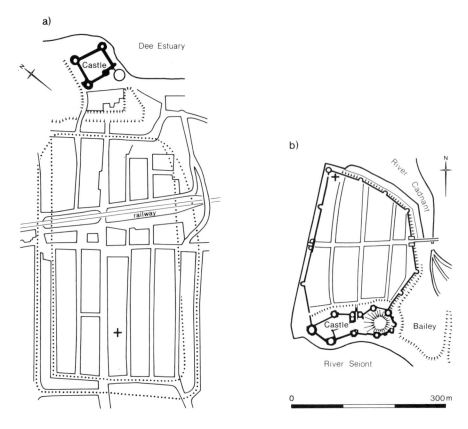

Figure 2.4 Plans of (a) Flint, (b) Caernarvon, showing main topographical elements

town became the administrative and judicial capital of the Principality of North Wales. There was a Welsh settlement on the site, but no concessions were made to it in the new rectangular grid of streets. Outside the remarkable castle, the small town was enclosed with stone walls, complete with towers at regular intervals and two opposed gates which marked the ends of the High Street (RCHMW 1960, 115–58). Other streets at right angles divided the intramural area into eight blocks; the market-place lay outside the walls to the east, on the site of the previous Norman castle, next to which a large mill-pool was crossed by a stone bridge of seven arches (Soulsby 1983, 89–91; Beresford 1988, 42–5). Sadly we cannot say if the principles of order and uniformity evident in the design of streets extended to house-design, since no medieval houses survive in the town; though accounts show that unused stone from the castle was sold off cheaply to the burgesses for building. Indeed, interest in the plan of Caernarvon should not obscure ultimately more significant aspects. The town's importance was political and its commercial life was never vigorous; there is no evidence of developed industry, and craftsmen were engaged mainly in supplying essential needs in food, clothing and housing for the garrison. To an extent this is true of all the Welsh planted towns.

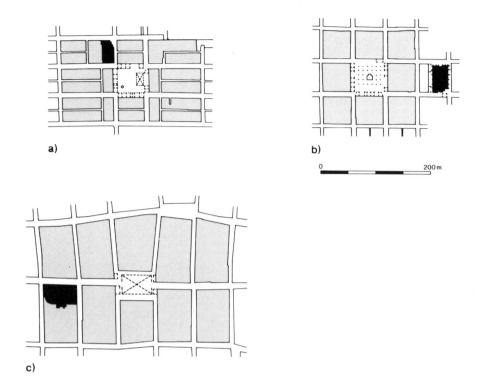

Figure 2.5   Three distinctive plans of bastide towns: (a) Monpazier (Landes); (b) Mirande (Gers); (c) Gimont (Gers) (Lauret et al. 1988). In each case the church is shown in black

The bastide towns of Gascony furnish interesting parallels, and it may be that their relatively unchanged forms (in comparison to many of their British equivalents) hold lessons for students of British towns. Recent work by French scholars (Lauret et al. 1988) has emphasised the great variety of plan among the bastide towns, but three groups sharing similar characteristics are noteworthy. They are all roughly contemporary in the period 1260–1320. The first group, called the Aquitaine type, comprises 27 towns in the northern, largely English part of the region; Monpazier is the best example (Figs 2.5a and 2.6). Four large streets divide the urban space like the framework of a noughts-and-crosses board. Between them are smaller streets, and the middle blocks have transverse alleys so that the central market-place is surrounded by thin blocks of housing. The church is most often immediately off the square, at one of the corners.

A second Gascon type comprises 15 towns largely founded by the French king or his nobles, to the south of the first group; Mirande is the model (Figs 2.5b and 2.6). Here streets are of the same width throughout, and the blocks are square, giving a chequerboard appearance; at least eight blocks are formed around the square. The church is normally in a block to one side and outside the basic rectangle of inner blocks.

A third group of six towns, founded by French lords towards the south of

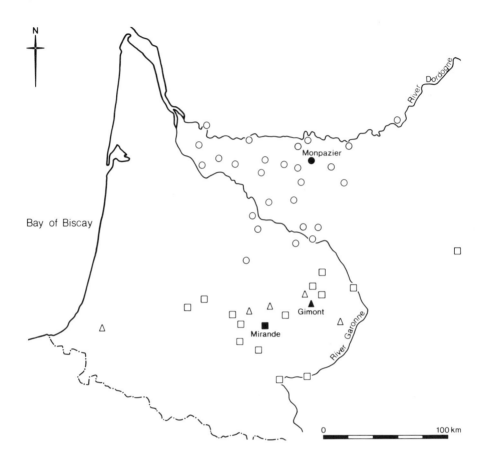

Figure 2.6 The distribution of the three types of plan in bastide towns in Gascony: circles, the Aquitaine model (like Monpazier); squares, the Gascon model (like Mirande); triangles, the Gimontois model (like Gimont) (Lauret et al. 1988)

the region, are named after their type-site, Gimont (Figs 2.5c and 2.6). The Gimontois type has two or three parallel major streets crossed by smaller transverse streets so that the blocks have a rectangular shape, and the square, sometimes narrow, is placed across the axis of the main street. The church is on this axis but a block away from the square.

These are only 48 towns out of nearly 800 in the study; and quite a few bastides, like their conterparts in England and Wales, were additions to existing settlements, so that deduction from the plan alone can be hazardous. They are also different from the majority of British towns in that very few contained a castle which would distort the topography. But these three varieties show different approaches to town-planning which may reflect local or political preferences. Though some of these towns were in English territory at the time of their foundation, their squares and the arcades around the squares were features not repeated in England.

In sum, though types of plan can be collected and analysed (e.g. Butler

1975; for geographers' approaches, Dickinson 1961, Carter 1981), a more profitable approach is to accept that many town plans were composed of a series of units of different periods. The clearest examples are those towns of great age, such as Abergavenny, Doncaster, Godmanchester (all shown in Fig 2.1 on pp. 26–7), and Hereford, but the apparent homogeneity of planted towns should also be regarded with caution. New towns might be laid out systematically at first, but soon spilled over and developed their own idiosyncracies. In addition, as demonstrated in many 'planned' cases, the units of new settlement were based on field boundaries and ridges, as in the twelfth century at Stratford and Lichfield (Fig 2.7 from Slater 1980; Bassett 1982a on Lichfield). Little is known of what precedes the town of Salisbury on its site, but the alignment of some streets may have been influenced by previous drainage ditches (Rogers 1969, 2) or, more significantly, the intention to run water-channels along the middle of the streets (RCHM 1993, 3–4). The completed plan there is not particularly regular; only three of the streets are parallel.

The larger Scottish towns of the twelfth century show a variety of plans, including single-street designs (Elgin, Forres, Montrose), three streets converging on an important church (St Andrews), two streets at right-angles to a river or the coast (Perth, Arbroath), and triangular market-places (Haddington, Dundee, Dumfries). Their apparently homogenous designs by the post-medieval period were however often the result, again, of cumulative phases of settlement from the twelfth to the fifteenth centuries and later, as suggested at Perth by analysis of street-blocks, plan units and plot widths (Spearman 1988; Fig 2.8; for archaeological work in Perth, Bogdan and Wordsworth 1978, Holdsworth 1987). The emphasis of wider European studies (Barley 1977; Clarke and Simms 1985; Brachmann and Herrmann 1991) has also been to emphasise the cumulative character of town plans, often with many stages from a Dark Age or Carolingian fortified centre, through markets, extensions and suburbs, to the fully expanded city of Renaissance times.

A number of shrunken medieval towns throughout Britain still need basic fieldwork to outline their extent and component parts. At New Radnor (Powys), for instance, the town in 1335 was evidently prosperous, but is now only a village; several sections of the original grid of streets are beneath fields, some marked by hedge-lines (Beresford and St Joseph 1979, 245–6). The shrunken port of Torksey on the River Trent is now only a small group of buildings, but was formerly of much more substantial extent, with embellishments such as three parish churches and two monasteries.

Defences

Two clear influences on the shape, extent and rate of growth of towns were their defences and their castles. Another book in this series (Kenyon 1990) is devoted to them; but brief reviews are in order to explore both the kinds of evidence they have to offer and the interleaving of their functions with others in the confined space of the town.

Defences signified the town limits, and the size or the intended size of the

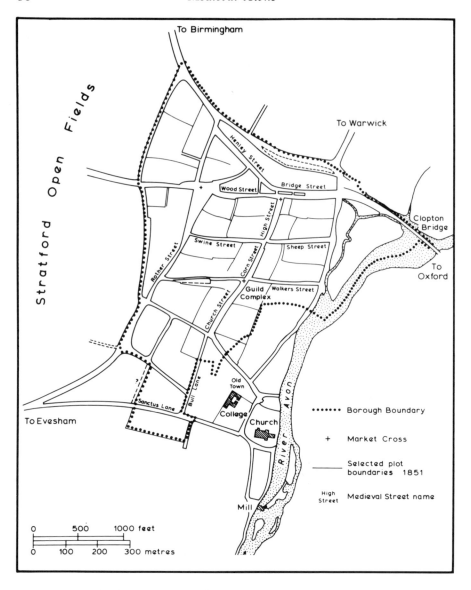

To Birmingham

To Warwick

Stratford Open Fields

Henley Street

Wood Street

Bridge Street

Clopton Bridge

To Oxford

High Street

Swine Street

Sheep Street

Rother Street

Corn Street

Guild Complex

Walkers Street

Church Street

River Avon

Old Town

Sanctus Lane

Bull Lane

College

Church

To Evesham

Mill

•••••• Borough Boundary

    +   Market Cross

———— Selected plot
        boundaries 1851

High
Street   Medieval Street name

0   500   1000 feet
0   100   200   300 metres

Figure 2.7 Stratford-upon-Avon: the burgages in the central area around Sheep Street and High Street are demonstrably based on open-field strips of the earlier village (Slater 1980)

settlement. Extensions to circuits might therefore be caused by growth of population or expansion of building beyond original boundaries, as at Abergavenny, Bridgnorth and Southampton in the thirteenth century, or Cardiff and Pembroke in the fourteenth century (Fig 2.1). Only Bristol (Figs 2.9 and 2.10), Lincoln, Norwich and York developed extensions in several directions which resemble the concentric rings of defences seen in continental cities, though there may be more examples to be identified. We need to know

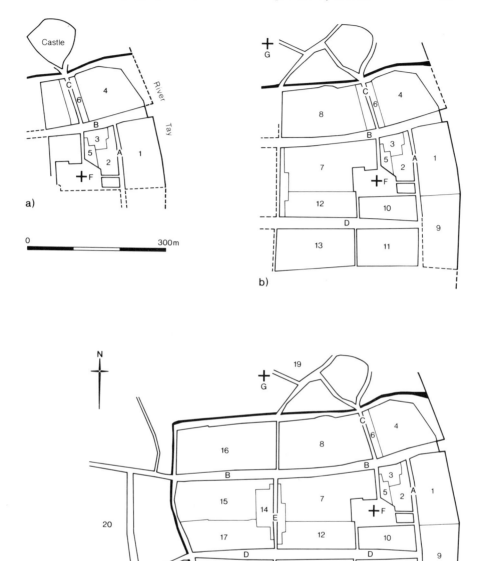

Figure 2.8 Perth in (a) the mid-twelfth century; (b) the thirteenth century; (c) the fifteenth and sixteenth centuries (Spearman 1988). This example of plan analysis shows twenty numbered plan units in proposed chronological order. Main streets and buildings: A Watergate; B High Street; C Skinnergate; D South Street; E Meal Vennel; F St John's church; G Dominican friary; H Franciscan friary; I Carthusian monastery

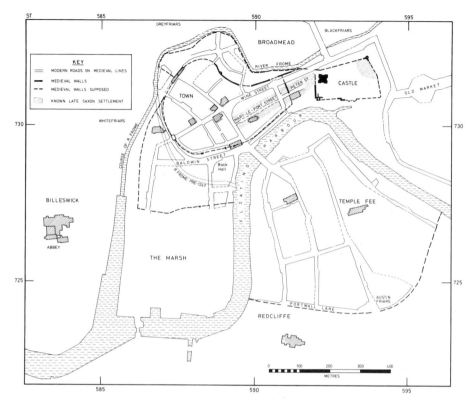

Figure 2.9 Bristol: plan showing the castle and main areas of medieval growth (City of Bristol Museum and Art Gallery)

more about towns where defences were built but the expected new housing did not follow, or where, as in Hereford and Nottingham, the enclosed spaces lapsed into cultivation or dereliction. Rebuilding the defences to define a smaller area than before, which presumably reflects urban decay or retrenchment, is rare but there are examples at New Winchelsea, where the defences in 1414–15 reduced the area of the town, and at Berwick-on-Tweed, where the Elizabethan circuit covered only two-thirds of the area of the fourteenth-century town (Fig 2.3 on pp. 30–1). Alternatively, city walls might be built, or lines of defence strengthened, by joining together existing lines of the walls of stone houses and blocking up openings such as doors and windows, as is documented at Southampton in the fourteenth century, and in Edinburgh in both the fifteenth (the King's Wall, 1425–50) and the sixteenth centuries (Flodden Wall, 1513; Schofield 1975–6; Fig 2.1 on pp. 26–7).

Bond (1987, with extensive bibliography) has distinguished seven major types of urban defences in the medieval period. Roman defensive circuits were reused by medieval towns on the same sites, for instance at Canterbury, Lincoln, London and York. The walls were of masonry, and the surviving Roman gates formidable structures, so that it was usual for the majority of a town's medieval gates to occupy the same sites as their Roman predecessors.

Figure 2.10 Bristol: excavation of a length of the Portwall by Temple Meads, showing the wall leaning outwards (City of Bristol Museum and Art Gallery)

Any new gates, such as London's Moorgate of 1415, therefore signify new
interests: in this case, reclamation of the marsh outside the walls to provide
an open space for the citizens.

At other towns, a defensive circuit originally of Anglo-Saxon date was
partly or wholly reused by the medieval town, as at Barnstaple, Bridgnorth
(Fig 2.1), Oxford, or Totnes; this was usually of earth, though some, for
instance at Hereford, Cricklade and Wallingford, had been reinforced with
masonry before the Conquest. Elsewhere, Saxon circuits were superseded by
expansion in the medieval town, as at Hereford, Norwich, Stamford and
Worcester, and thus evidence of ramparts or ditches might lie unsuspected
beneath ordinary medieval house-sites or backyards. In a further, numerically
larger group of towns, the new Anglo-Saxon circuit of defences was by
contrast of no post-Conquest importance (e.g. at Bedford, Maldon,
Northampton, Rhuddlan (Fig 2.3), Southampton (Fig 2.1), Warwick and
Worcester). This presumably relates to a change of emphasis within the town
after the Norman Conquest; the abandonment of older defensive concerns
must mean new settlement (within the town or outside it, in another place)
and changes in economic direction.

New medieval circuits or extensions were substantially of masonry in the
larger towns such as Berwick (Fig 2.3), Bristol (Fig 2.10), Edinburgh (Fig
2.1), London (Blackfriars), Newcastle, Norwich, Oxford (where towards the
end of the thirteenth century the north-eastern side of the town was given a
stretch of double walling, resembling a concentric fortification (Durham et al.
1983)), Shrewsbury, Southampton, Stirling and Worcester. Here one might
look for contemporary defensive developments such as interval towers,
crenellations or gunports, which appear in the later fourteenth century at the
more important south-coast towns such as Southampton (*c.* 1360), Dover
and Canterbury; on the Continent the development of artillery rendered
medieval city walls useless during the following century. Smaller towns could
also have walls mainly or wholly of masonry, such as at Arundel, Clun and
Monmouth in the thirteenth century, or New Carmarthen twice, in 1233 and
on a different scale in 1415 (Figs 2.1 and 2.3).

Gates of masonry were an essential part of these defences, and a good
number survive, though some of the circuit walls have been lost. In a further
group of towns the gates were of masonry but the defences of earth and
timber, giving both strength and prestige to the entry points into the town.
This was the case, for instance, at Aberdeen, Cardiff (twelfth century, before
the later stone walls), Coventry, Pontefract and Tewkesbury. At Banbury
there were four gates, but no walls (Harvey 1969, 4); Glasgow also had
gates across its streets, but no defences (Kellett 1969, 4).

Bond identifies three further types of urban defences which would make
good research projects. The first are new medieval defences for towns which
were subsequently deserted or destroyed; many are in Wales. The walled
borough of Old Denbigh declined at the expense of its suburbs because it
was virtually inaccessible; the division between the borough and the market
outside was mentioned in 1334 (Soulsby 1983, 123). Towns at Dolforwyn
(Powys) and Dryslwyn (Carmarthen) were suppressed or destroyed by the
English and Owen Glendower respectively; Glendower's forces also
destroyed the town at Old Kidwelly (Dyfed), an important port with

connections with Ireland, Gascony and Aquitaine (ibid., 152–4). A second small group of towns intended to erect defences, but they were probably never built or never completed, as at Holt (Clwyd), one of the largest Welsh boroughs in the early fourteenth century, or Woodstock (Oxon). This need not have been a result of lack of cash; at prosperous Salisbury, only two gates and very little of the defensive circuit were ever built. Thirdly, certain villages gained defences – were they unsuccessfully trying to be towns, or are we underestimating their medieval importance? Bond mentions in this context Bourne (Lincs), Pirton (Herts) and Pontesbury (Salop).

Defences performed many primary and secondary functions besides defence of the town and exclusion of the outsider. Walling of towns along the south coast of England, or later on the east coast of Scotland, were part of a regional programme of defence against a neighbour (in the latter case, England). Gates were used as accommodation for civic officers, as chapels, lock-ups and meeting-rooms. The defensive system included fishponds at Stafford and York, and a lake at Edinburgh; at Hereford water from the town ditch drove mills.

Defences – that is, the ditch, wall and bank behind – have several archaeological virtues. The ditches are often waterlogged, producing a different range of rubbish from that thrown in the waterfront zone along the town's river. The line of the defences often crosses earlier occupation, which is therefore sealed and preserved. Scrutiny and stone-by-stone recording (often by photogrammetry) of masonry gates and walls interlocks with documentary evidence in identifying structures, techniques, and extensions to the town.

Work in Canterbury (Frere et al. 1982) provides an example. Several excavations and observations of 1947–77 show that the medieval defences of Canterbury followed the line of their Roman predecessors, reusing three or more of the Roman gates. Twenty-four medieval towers, of at least two periods of construction, have been identified. An interesting sequence of archaeological deposits comes from an excavation of 1977 in Church Lane, on the defences by the North Gate. Most of the recorded periods of occupation are shown in one of the drawn sections (cross-sections through a number of deposits), which illustrates the pressure on space near major obstacles to expansion like a stone city wall (Fig 2.11). This section was only of the wall and the layers behind it; any ditches in front had been removed by later activity.

Probably in the late third century, Roman occupation (layer 88) had been interrupted by the building of the first city wall (81, 82) and its bank or rampart (80, 77, 76, 75, 74). In the late Saxon or early Norman period an intramural street was laid along the back of the rampart, shown by the layers of pebbled street-metallings, resurfaced at least three times (66, 64, 62, 60; roadside gulley, 67). Five human burials were found in the small excavation; two of the graves can be seen in the section, with a general level of graveyard soil (54, 55, 53; later street, 52). These appear to form part of the graveyard of the church of St Mary-upon-Northgate which was built on top of the adjacent gate at this time; crenellations on the city wall, probably of early Norman date, were embedded and fossilised in its north (exterior) side. The cemetery and streets were sealed by construction debris of the

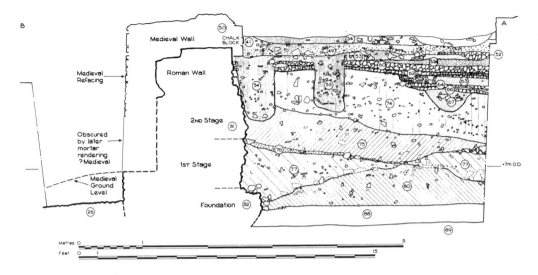

Figure 2.11   Canterbury: section of strata at Church Lane (Frere et al. 1982)

rebuilding of the city wall in the 1380s–90s (49); the original Roman wall was replaced with one in chalk with a knapped flint face (50). Medieval buildings immediately behind the wall also survive, in altered form, across the street.

Much archaeological work has taken place on medieval town defences in England and Wales, and a little in Scotland, but most of this work has been piecemeal and hurried, often ahead of bulldozing for ring roads and other modern necessities such as pedestrian subways. In avoiding historic centres which have clear amenity value, modern planners have destroyed large sections of medieval defences and the immediate suburbs. This may be inevitable, but it is certainly to be regretted. Towns were acquiring or refurbishing their walls late into the Middle Ages; the impetus rose from the insecurity of invasion or baronial warfare. But in the sixteenth and seventeenth centuries few defences were put to the test (except in the English Civil War), and town walls thereafter became an unwanted luxury. Churches have continued in use, and castles have proved difficult to eradicate; but defences were quickly overtaken by new pressures on space, and have largely disappeared. As a class of monument, they have become an endangered species.

Castles

A distinction should first be made between castle-boroughs, where a castle was the point of attraction for a new town, and truly 'urban castles', where castles were inserted into existing settlements (Drage 1987).

The Norman kings and their tenants built new castles which were often powerful stimulants to urban growth. Besides offering security, any aristocratic residence would generate a market, and it is therefore not surprising that 80 per cent of all new towns in Wales and 75 per cent of new towns in

England before 1150 grew up or were established next to a castle; the association of castle and burgh is even more marked in Scotland, where 31 of the 33 burghs founded by the king before 1286 were beside castles. At some places, such as Pleshey and Devizes, the design of the town in its defences suggests that both were founded at the same time; occasionally castles moved site, perhaps to encourage settlement in a better situation (as at Knighton (Powys) and Newport (Dyfed) (Soulsby 1983, 155, 200). But in other cases the castle-borough failed, and several deserted sites in Wales and the adjacent border area show the form of these boroughs in their early stages. At Richard's Castle (Hereford/Worcs), for instance, the large bailey of the castle contains a church, market-place, and traces of burgage plots; the prominent defensive bank which surrounds the town was, however, not a primary feature, but added in the thirteenth century, perhaps when the settlement, like many others, was aspiring to be a town (Curnow and Thompson 1969, 108).

A similar case is Saffron Walden (Essex), where the town has survived, but a period of building prompted by the lord of the castle failed to bring the hoped-for rewards (Bassett 1982b). In about 1144 the Mandevilles rebuilt the castle and enclosed a new town with two roughly concentric earthwork defences (Fig 2.12). A market-place and tenements were laid out within the outer circuit. In the early thirteenth century this nucleus was enlarged by the foundation of the new market-place, within a grid of streets. But the enlarged town was never a success, and Walden remained a shrunken town, though quite large by Essex standards and certainly rich in the fifteenth and sixteenth centuries. In yet further examples, the economic future of the town lay away from the castle: at Salisbury and Thirsk protection was abandoned in the interest of better communications and economic prospects, and the town moved to a new site. Though castle-and-town foundations continued to be the norm in the frontier zone of Wales, England's relatively peaceful life after the civil war of 1136–54 meant that only kings founded new towns with the full defensive armoury of a castle.

In castle-boroughs the castle is usually on the edge of the town, often with its back to an adjacent river. Castles placed in existing towns were similarly on the edge of the settlement, often tied in to the Roman or Saxon defences (as at Lincoln and London). At Stamford, the castle was placed outside the pre-Conquest borough, on a relatively high piece of ground next to the river and controlling the land routes which met at the place; here, between castle and town, the market-place grew up (Mahany et al. 1982, 1–12). Elsewhere, the intrusion was more deliberate, involving the destruction of previous housing and streets, as in Exeter and Warwick; at both Cambridge and Norwich (Ayers 1985) a church and a cemetery were swept aside.

The insertion of a castle into a Saxon town, and its gradual assimilation into the urban topography, is illustrated by work in and around the area of the castle at Oxford in 1965–73 (Hassall 1976). Here were two features of note: Saxon occupation including a timber cellar and pits pre-dating the Norman castle-mound built in 1071, and a catalogue of notable medieval finds, particularly of organic materials (i.e. shoes, clothing fragments and wooden objects), in the castle ditch. As early as the twelfth century, however,

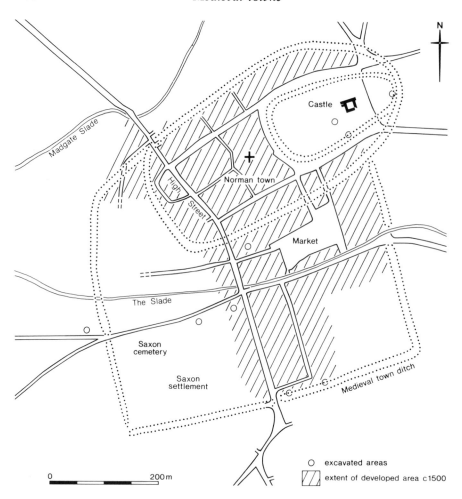

Figure 2.12 Saffron Walden: plan of the medieval town, with main excavations of the 1970s (Bassett 1982)

in a kind of urban reaction, properties along the street behind the barbican were already encroaching on the barbican ditch with their rubbish pits.

Even clearer pictures of the process of imposition of the castle could come from smaller places where later activity has not been great. Ongar (Essex), for instance, was an important centre, as a local moot (meeting-place) and market (Fig 2.13); Ongar Great Park, west of the town, is the earliest recorded park in England, mentioned in 1015 (Eddy and Petchey 1983, 39). What has been tentatively interpreted as a Saxon enclosure, later overlain by the castle, was sectioned in 1982 (Priddy 1983, 165). A castle was imposed on this settlement, with the High Street running through its outer bailey, perhaps in the late eleventh or early twelfth century. At Pleshey (also Essex) the High Street also crosses the outer bailey of the castle (Eddy and Petchey 1983, 75), and a cross-route helps to form the market-place in the bailey at Richard's Castle. There is, therefore, often a strong relationship between a

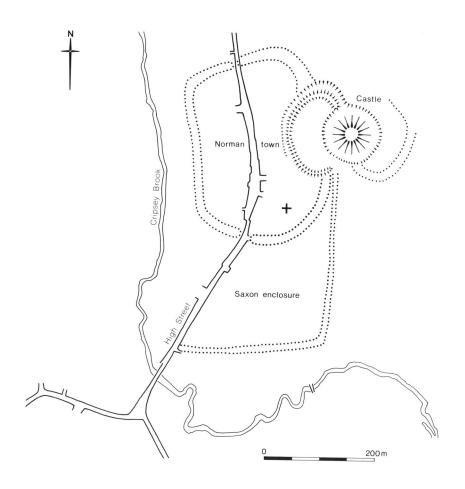

Figure 2.13   Chipping Ongar, Essex (Eddy and Petchey 1983)

major road, the castle bailey, and the subsequent capture of trade by the castle owner.

Castles were used as residences for the king or the local lord and for administrative purposes; usually as the sheriff's court and jail. When Lydford needed a court room and jail in the 1190s, the resulting building, which survives, was erected on a spur of an earlier ringwork, and became, at least in name, Lydford Castle (Saunders 1980). Recent work suggests that the Norman Fleet Prison in London resembled a castle and was wholly surrounded by a moat formed by two channels of the Fleet river. The evidence for castle buildings and the life in and around them – halls, kitchens, lodgings, chapels and other structures – is studied in detail by Kenyon (1990, 97–162) in the companion work in this series.

With so many castle keeps having been cleared in pre-archaeological days, information on the residential aspects of castle history is now likelier to survive in the bailey or castle ditch, as at Pleshey (Williams 1977). Here excavations of 1959–63 in the bailey produced evidence of a twelfth-century rampart and defensive tower, overlain by two successive rectangular buildings, the second in stone and clearly the castle chapel, constructed around 1300. During the following decades, the chapel was embellished with painted window glass, a decorated tiled floor and architectural details in stone. Walls in one chapel were painted, and used glazed wall tiles.

The disuse of the site in the post-medieval period has kept the archaeo-logical strata in good condition, and it is clear that the chapel is only one of many buildings in the bailey; but it tells us much about the chronology and lifestyle of the noble household, in this case the de Bohuns, earls of Hereford and Essex, and later Thomas of Woodstock, seventh son of Edward III. The finds in and around the chapel included locally made floor tiles bearing several contemporary royal and noble coats-of-arms; correlation with those from two other prestigious sites indicates a working lifespan of 40–60 years for the tilery. The metal objects had a military flavour: spurs, knives and buckles. Significantly, perhaps, the original earthen defences do not seem to have been replaced; the place was a courtly residence, not a fortified stronghold. The pottery included imported wares from Spain and the Netherlands.

In studying a medieval town, it is advisable to elucidate and then compare the building-dates of the castle and the town defences; were they constructed and repaired at the same time, or at different times, and does this reflect their relative signficance to the town? During the twelfth century some town defences and castle refurbishments went hand in hand, but from about 1300 many English urban castles declined as military structures, and towns' concern for safety concentrated on their own defences. In Scotland, on the other hand, towns did not, in general, gain substantial defences until the fifteenth century, and they continued to rely on castles for their defence.

Castles in towns can produce several useful kinds of information. First, the castle often makes a major contribution to the topographical history of the place; it is a dominant feature in the landscape, and we can study its creation, rise and fall within the fortunes of the town at large. Secondly, it is the residence of a local lord, and thus a centre of local business of all kinds and a place where luxuries would have been in comparative abundance. Thirdly, the castle may contain information about the town which is in as good or often better condition than elsewhere in the town, because the castle site has remained comparatively untouched and not affected by basements (for a review of the light which castle sites throw on building techniques, military and household life, costume, pastimes and diet, see Kenyon 1990, 163–80).

Streets, markets and public buildings

The castle was only one type of royal and religious building which formed a nucleus of public life and traffic in the medieval town. The network of streets and lanes went through and around other complexes which, by their size and often quality of construction, formed dominant features in the topography of their neighbourhoods. In some towns the meeting of main roads, and the market, was to be found at the gate of the monastery or cathedral church which took over the castle's role as epicentre of the place; and this would have an effect on the neighbourhood round the new centre. The Saxon town of Bury St Edmunds had been enlarged in response to the cult of St Edmund before the Conquest. Post-Conquest examples include Battle and Dunstable. Reading lay at the junction of two important routes, connecting it with Oxford, London and Winchester. The founding of an abbey in 1125, with a market-place developing at its gate, pulled the centre of gravity of the town eastwards. Its attraction to medieval pilgrims (including royal visitors) also ensured that St Laurence's church, next to the abbey, became wealthy (Slade 1969, 5).

New boroughs were often planted on the edges of existing parishes, and sometimes the church for the new place was dependent upon the mother-church. This often created difficulties (for example, the distance over which it was necessary to conduct funerals) and resentment. But where, as in the majority, there was a parish church or chapel, market life was also inextricably mixed with daily religious observance. Markets were held in or near churchyards, as at Llanelli or Haverfordwest; in many other places, churches lay in the middle of broad market streets (Morris 1989, 212–13; and discussed further below in this chapter, pp. 51, 56). Generally, planted towns only had one church, which contrasted with the many churches of pre-Conquest towns, but occasionally, pressure of population resulted in further churches. When King's Lynn was extended northwards, for instance, it acquired a second market-place and a second church (see below, pp. 59–61). The topographical impact of religious precincts and parish churches is considered further in Chapter 6.

Some French towns are clear examples of multiple centres which only later became one place, usually when a wall surrounded all the component settlements. *Bourgs* (separate urban districts) based on churches appeared in the first half of the tenth century, such as at Poitiers and Angers. Sometimes these centres grew to vie with the original town in urban alure and vivacity, as at Tours. Some great churches on the edges of towns, such as the basilica of St Sernin at Toulouse, became rich and famous through being the goal of pilgrims. By the eleventh century Reims had two centres a kilometre apart, the citadel and an ecclesiastical quarter which contained a cathedral, an abbey and at least four churches. Another stimulant was a market, often growing outside an ancient town, as can still be seen at Chartres and Bordeaux (Le Goff 1980, 83–101). At Inverness, excavation of Castle Street has suggested that it originated as a deliberately planned expansion of the existing market during the fourteenth century (Ewan 1990, 10).

The layout and condition of the streets, markets and public buildings presumably reflected contemporary motives. How can we calculate their degree of success? The public life of the medieval community revolved around its central institutions, and these may have been given special prominence, grandeur or increased accessibility to enhance their appearance and function. A parallel here can be made with Islamic cities, where public architecture – chiefly the congregational mosque, the central public bath, and the central market-place – were foci of great artistic and constructive energy.

The major institutional buildings or areas may be located near each other for practical and other purposes; the streets to them from the main city gates may be of a wider, more stately character (a good example of these themes explored by archaeological work is Qsar es-Seghir, Morocco (Redman 1986)).

A market emphasis might find archaeological expression in civic structures such as market buildings, toll-houses, the public weighing-beam, a town well or conduits, public quays and attention to city gates; but it is otherwise not easy to use archaeology to study markets. A characteristic of a market is an open space, used periodically, and therefore devoid of the features or deposits which might leave archaeological traces, except areas of gravel metalling (as from a possible market area inside the north gate of Winchester; Biddle and Keene 1976, 286).

The local ruler controlled the revenue of trade by establishing a market within a town, often on only one site. A central space, often near the main church, would be made available for stalls, which over time became permanent structures and buildings which in some cases survive today (as at Salisbury). By the late thirteenth century covered, specialised markets and civic warehouses for food, grain or cloth were to be found, mostly in principal towns; examples in the large cities of Bruges, London and Paris were considerable pieces of architecture. Recent work has reconstructed the mid-fifteenth-century Leadenhall market in London (Samuel 1989), a model exercise in reconstruction from excavated and documentary evidence. It also shows how the public functions of market and school were in this case intertwined. Leadenhall has been reconstructed from a fragment of wall surviving, to general surprise, within City office-buildings of the nineteenth century; a series of truncated chalk foundations; and 177 loose moulded stones. These represented parts of arches, doors, two- and three-light windows and two spiral staircases. The complex comprised a large market space surrounded by arcades, with warehouses above; a chapel; and a grammar school, endowed by the rich mercer Simon Eyre (Fig 2.14). The layout was established by comparison of the archaeological evidence for foundations with that from maps and plans; the reconstruction above ground (Fig 2.15) by combination of the moulding details on the stones and engravings and sketches of the building before its demolition in stages in the eighteenth and nineteenth centuries.

A concern with the careful ordering of public space in medieval towns may have extended from market buildings to squares and even street widths. Many covered halls, often containing the official town measures for grain, survive in the Gascon towns, and the fabric of some may date back to the fourteenth century. The central square (*la place publique*) was in many ways the symbolic centre of town life: here was the market hall, the public well, and sometimes a belfry which regularised and therefore helped organise the working day. It is therefore no surprise that the square is also the setting for modern civic monuments such as war memorials. The streets of the bastides were usually carefully graded as to their widths: at Monpazier, the longitudinal streets, which connected the central square to the gates, are 8m wide, the transverse streets 6m wide, and the connecting alleys about 2m wide. Such grading of streets might be apparent in British towns.

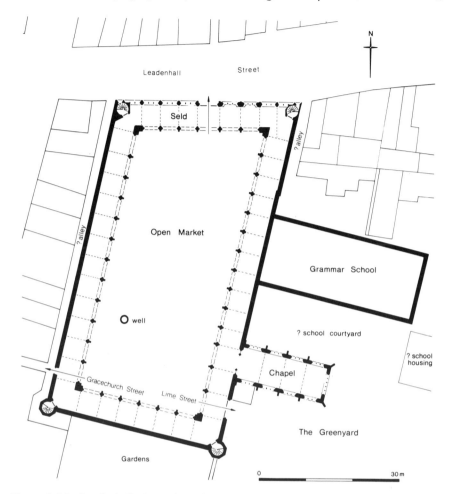

Figure 2.14 Leadenhall, City of London: plan of the market of 1440, which included a chapel and a school (Samuel 1989)

As markets grew, so they specialised. First, it was possible to split the market so that different kinds of produce would be on sale on specific days: livestock, fish and so on. This is not likely to be recognised in the archaeological record. A second development was regional, in that some medieval towns specialised in a commodity which became a regional speciality (Everitt 1976). The third type of specialisation was within the settlement. Those selling certain produce would congregate in certain areas of the market: this may be the origin of street-names such as Milk Street and Bread Street in London. These may not reflect the activity of the streets themselves as much as that of the sections of the main market of Cheapside where the streets branched off.

There were few, if any, open medieval market-places inside the City of London; the main streets were used instead. A similar arrangement can be found at Lincoln, where a single street formed the town's main market. This

Figure 2.15 Leadenhall, City of London: axonometric of north range (Samuel 1989).
The parallels for such civic buildings are only found in larger European cities such as
Cologne and Florence

started at the Stonebow, a ceremonial gate opening on to the river Witham to the south, and finished at the gate into the Bail, the bailey of Lincoln Castle, which lay to the north. Looking back down the hill, one saw first the fish market, also known as the High Market, then the Poultry, and then the corn market. The skin market was off the main road in Hungate and the Drapery or cloth market was in a road parallel with the Strait. The lower part of the main street was occupied by the butchers in the late Middle Ages, and a further market was on Ermine Street in the suburb of Newport, around a market cross. At harvest time this was the appointed place to hire reapers and servants (Hill 1948, 170). Many of the Lincoln markets had originally been held in churchyards adjoining the streets, into which they were officially moved in 1223 (ibid., 154).

There is some evidence that older towns, like London and Lincoln, had their markets in the streets because they developed their main street frontages at a time when large open spaces were not required; in the tenth and eleventh centuries there were no great congregations of people requiring such spaces (or, if they were, they were provided by extramural markets, as in Hereford and London). From the twelfth century, however, virtually all new towns had a market-place as a centre of activity.

The study of tenure of markets can be revealing. A town might, for example, have more than one market grant, reflecting the presence of more than one powerful landowner in the settlement; as at Shrewsbury, where the abbey tried to develop its own borough as a discrete area of the town. Once markets were established in a region, they might be held on different days in different places, so that a greater density of markets could be supported. Any resulting dominance of one market centre over another, or all others, would have a consequence on revenues and thus the rise and decline of markets is an index of the power of local lords.

The influence of the church in controlling and developing urban activity should not be underestimated, as is illustrated by recent work on several Scottish towns. Glasgow was an ecclesiastical burgh granted to bishop Jocelin between 1175 and 1178; it was already noted for housing St Kentigern's tomb, a cult centre which attracted pilgrims. The bishop granted an annual fair and a weekly market. Before 1240 the church authorities were in debt to Florentine merchants, perhaps from a transaction at their fair; excavated evidence so far is, however, largely of local material. The cathedral was in construction for a century from the 1130s, and the Dominican friars were building their own church in the town by 1246; a bridge over the Clyde is mentioned in 1286. Several crafts have been identified from excavations, and the town was a flourishing trade centre, fastidiously regulated by successive bishops (Shead 1988).

The lord took the tolls from markets; but what were people paying the tolls on? Current opinion favours the idea that the proliferation of markets in the twelfth and especially in the thirteenth centuries was for the disposal of rural surplus; and although the buoyant economy of the time prompted demand for manufactured goods and services by the local population, there was little stimulus for industry in the small towns (Astill 1985). Besides the new boroughs, villages also had their markets, and in some counties, such as Leicestershire and Nottinghamshire, there were more markets in villages than in towns (Hilton 1982). There were also many communities on the borderline between villages and towns, so the distinction cannot be forced. Some markets reflect specialised influences: the spread of markets along the Essex coast indicates a rapid growth of coastal trade in thirteenth-century Essex (Britnell 1981), though in time a good roadside location was better than a coastal one. Only in larger market centres could money be spent on luxuries such as wine, spices, armour and quality textiles. These centres were provincial capitals, big fairs, and ports (see Chapter 5 on Trade below).

In Britain, civic authorities do not seem to have been much concerned with the co-ordination of planning of streets or areas, but there was considerable thought given to the provision of amenities and to certain aspects of building design. Besides providing a market-place, sometimes with covered stalls, the town or its lord was concerned to supply clean water, essential both for consumption and for industries such as textile-production, running water drove corn- or fulling-mills. Major European towns organised a public water supply during the thirteenth century, often following the lead set by religious houses such as the friaries (as in London itself). At Gdańsk, Antwerp and many other places, canals were built to bring water into the town for drinking and industrial uses. In Italy, Siena had tunnels and springs in the hillside, but lost out to its rival Florence because the latter could use the Arno for easy transport and in its textile industry.

There seems to be little interest in archaeological research into the water-supply of British medieval towns, though the siting, appearance and efficacy of wells, fountains and washing-places (both for domestic laundry and industrial purposes, e.g. in the cloth industry) were of great significance. A great number of public wells have disappeared, but formerly they provided points of public congregation at street corners or in public spaces. Here, the presence of people, coming for water, may have influenced the volume of traffic into nearby shops and therefore affected their value as properties. One would suppose that a special correlation might be demonstrated between better buildings and the location of public wells and conduits. Similarly, certain industries which constantly required water, such as brewing or dyeing, often congregated around access-points to water, and this sometimes caused friction with domestic consumers.

Suburbs

The previous sections have dealt with intended boundaries to the settlement such as defences, major nuclei and the streets which articulated that organised space. There are two further boundaries to the settlement which were hardly ever static, since they reflected a constantly changing pattern of growth or decline as the settlement waxed and waned. These litmus-papers of the town's growth are suburbs and the waterfront.

Keene (1975) has drawn attention to the way growth or decline in the suburbs may be a reflection of the town's fortunes, and of its position in the hierarchy of neighbouring towns. The form of suburbs was usually dictated by existing approach roads and by the location of markets immediately outside the town gates, as illustrated most vividly by the space called St Giles outside the north gate of Oxford. Nearby is Broad Street, another market which was able to expand over the outer edge of the city ditch. This also happened in Stamford and Worcester.

During the eleventh and twelfth centuries many of the older towns such as Canterbury, Winchester and York expanded their suburbs to reach their largest extent for several centuries. Prominent churches or bridges would be rebuilt as signs of prosperity. At Exeter, for instance, a suburb on Exe Island would have been promoted by the building of St Edmund's church and the contiguous Exe Bridge around 1200. Suburban expansion can be identified by areas of town called Newland, as at Banbury and Gloucester. After 1300, few, if any, towns expanded further, and many contracted in size. By the time of the earliest maps around 1600, great parts of their suburbs had reverted to fields.

Dangerous or obnoxious trades were often banned to the extramural areas. Blacksmiths, potters, tanners and fullers were found here, either banned because of their smoke or noise, or taking advantage of the relatively open space (the bell-founders could dig for brickearth, the dyers stretch their cloths on frames called tenters (potters in Chichester: Schofield and Palliser 1981, 24; tenters in Bristol: ibid., 11). When the hospitals and friaries came, they limited rather than encouraged further growth.

Most suburbs were relatively poor, but some early developments were conspicuously wealthy, for instance in the western suburb of Winchester (where in the thirteenth century smaller properties were being amalgamated into larger units, as shown by substantial boundary ditches: Schofield and Palliser 1981, 106) or outside the north gate at Gloucester. The guild hall of St Mary at Lincoln survives as a reminder of the social independence of the men in the suburb of Wigford (Stocker 1991). In a few cases the town centre moved to what had previously been a suburb: at Hereford and Northampton, for instance, the extramural market became the commercial centre of the town, as already mentioned in the case of Kidwelly, and the later expansion of Leicester was around the East Gate.

One type of building often found on the periphery of towns or in the surrounding villages was the mill. In 1303 there were 28 mills near the City of London, owned mostly by wholesalers in the grain trade or fishmongers. Most of the early examples would be watermills, but windmills are known in other European countries from the early thirteenth century, and were common in southern England by 1300. Though many mills of both types were used for the grinding of corn, some were also used for fulling of cloth, a practice which spread from Normandy in the twelfth century (Cipolla 1981, 171–4). Here again is an item on the agenda for medieval urban archaeologists, since excavations of mills near towns have not occurred in any number.

Suburbs have several archaeological merits: their boundaries, being the boundaries of the whole settlement, indicate general prosperity or decline of the town; and suburbs often offer clean-slate sites, where the occupation will be easier to understand because it is on virgin soil. This occupation is often of an industrial character. Main suburban streets, with their narrow properties, look like main streets inside the town, but they lie in a rural setting and usually without defences. This concentration of housing identifies the major axis routes to the town, and if the date of this settlement can be established by archaeological and other means, the date of development of that route (a trading route out to the hinterland in a particular direction) can be explored. Two excavations of medieval suburban sites in recent years demonstrate these qualities: that of the Hamel, Oxford (Palmer 1980) and Alms Lane, Norwich, which is treated in detail in Chapter 3 below. Alms Lane, in particular, shows a good suburban sequence. In the tenth century it lay north of and outside the Saxon town, and until about 1275 was used as a refuse dump for the crafts of the town, as shown by the artefacts. Wetland plants and bones of frogs and toads indicate the environment. From the late thirteenth century, as shown by archaeological and documentary evidence, the site was owned and used by workers in leather, skinning, bone-working, and especially iron-working. About 1375, however, the land was levelled and became the site of housing from the expanding city, and suburban industries were pushed out (Ayers 1985).

The waterfront

Besides spreading out along approach roads, the town often spread in a rather different manner into the adjacent river or sea. A waterfront zone often developed as a narrow strip of reclaimed land along the river bank or shore, modifying it to suit the needs both of landing and exporting goods, and, in time, for housing, warehouses and other buildings – even churches. Thus many towns actually increased their area – in the City of London, perhaps by as much as 15 per cent – over the medieval period by pushing out into the water.

Waterfront archaeology has been one of the most significant developments of the last two decades within European urban archaeology. In this section we deal with the overall topographical significance of the reclamation process; the other main products of excavations on waterfront sites are the vast array of dated artefacts in the rubbish used to fill in behind the revetments (see below, Chapter 4) and the revetment structures themselves (Fig 7.3, p. 186 below). Here, three points concerning overall topographical development in the waterfront area can be made: (i) the chronology of reclaiming the land tells us about significant centres of human activity within the town, (ii) there was a range of motives for the reclamation, and (iii) the evidence from waterfront sites for changes in river and sea levels. The most intensive study of waterfront reclamation has taken place in London, as a result of the complete change in land-use of the present waterfront within the City over the last twenty years, and the main results from this continuing campaign of excavations can be used as a model to compare with results in other places.

All the present land south of Thames Street, which runs for a mile from the Tower of London in the east to Blackfriars in the west, is a reclamation zone; it began in the Roman period and came to an end largely in the fifteenth century, though pieces of reclamation have been added up to 1962. The third-century Roman quays extended along much of the city's shoreline, but were in decay and eroded by the rising river throughout much of the

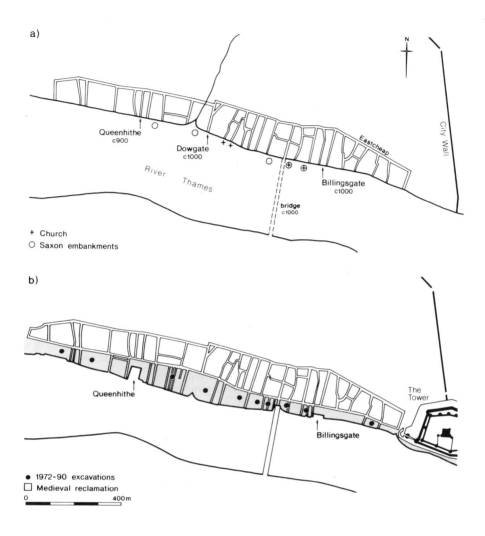

Figure 2.16 London: main Saxon reclamation points and churches on the waterfront, and the area of medieval reclamation which followed, showing waterfront excavations of 1972–90 (Milne and Hobley 1981, revised)

Saxon period. The creation of new land south of Thames Street probably radiated out from three centres: the two Saxon landing-points for merchandise at *Etheredshythe* (later Queenhithe), first documented in 899, and Billingsgate, recorded *c*. 1000; and the pre-Conquest foreign settlement at Dowgate, later the Steelyard (Fig 2.16). By the twelfth century churches were established south of Thames Street at Dowgate (All Hallows the Great and the Less), the bridge (St Magnus) and at Botolph Wharf, just above Billingsgate and perhaps originally part of the landing area (St Botolph). These remained the only churches south of the street, indicating that by the time of formation of parishes in the twelfth century these points represented substantial areas of reclamation, occupation and activity. Thus we can suggest that a combination of public landing area + church + early reclamation = important place in the network of communications and business within the town (Steedman et al. 1992). Again, a church is centre stage, and it is difficult to be sure which came first – church or place of landing and its associated market. Certainly it can be suggested for London and other cities such as Ghent (Belgium) and Lübeck (Germany) that economic stimulus in the tenth and eleventh centuries came by boat, not overland, and development of medieval street patterns may have begun by the waterside, only later stimulating what became major landward market streets in the medieval town. Meanwhile reclamation continued; by about 1500 in London a large linear area south of Thames Street had been reclaimed, in many individual stages, from the river.

Such reclaimed areas, though usually without churches, can be identified at British ports such as King's Lynn (Clarke 1973; 1981; and below, pp. 59– 61), Newcastle (O'Brien 1991), Norwich (Ayers and Murphy 1983; Ayers 1991) and Hull (Ayers 1981), and in many continental ports (for general reviews and detailed reports of many excavations in Britain and Europe, see Milne and Hobley 1981; Herteig 1985; Milne 1987; Good et al. 1991; for Scottish towns, see also Ewan 1990, 6–7). One significant pointer, as illustrated in London, is often the existence of a sinuous street on the original (geological) river-bank, now more or less parallel to the present river-front but some distance behind it; the intervening space is man-made reclamation.

It is also clear that reclamation proceeded at different rates at different times during the medieval period, and there must have been a range of motives behind different pieces of reclamation. In London, the greatest distances between successive revetments is in the period 1100–1250; thereafter, though revetments decayed quickly and were often replaced, it was on the same alignments or only a few feet further, and thus the rate of reclamation was now more gradual. In addition, river walls in stone, found from the twelfth century at larger ports such as Dublin (Wallace 1981) and London, became more common in the latter from about 1300. Not requiring constant repair, these walls tended to put an end to the reclamation process itself. Though the main public landing-places at Queenhithe and Billingsgate have not been excavated, documentary and cartographic evidence suggests that they comprised a public open space (known as a *Romeland*) adjacent to the river. This did not expand very much, but the largely private properties to either side continued to reclaim land, so that by 1300 the landing-places were inlets or indentations in the riverfront.

The process of reclamation has been studied over a large area at the Trig Lane site, now beneath the new City of London Boys' School and south of an urban motorway, the construction of which in the early 1970s sealed waterfront deposits of the twelfth and early thirteenth centuries at the heads of properties stretching south of the medieval Thames Street (Milne and Milne 1982). South of the new road, the area excavated in 1974–6 revealed revetments and river walls dating between the end of the thirteenth to the middle of the fifteenth centuries on several properties (Figs 2.17 and 2.18). When dated by a combination of stratigraphy, dendrochronology and coins, the site demonstrated how individual private properties extended riverwards

Figure 2.17 London: Trig Lane, the excavations of 1974 in progress, looking north-west (Museum of London Archaeology Service)

at different times, and using differing standards of construction; when, finally, a stone wall formed a unified frontage for several properties in the mid-fifteenth century, documentary evidence confirms that the Armourers' Company had bought up all the relevant land.

The remarkable survival of archaeological strata, and especially finds in a waterfront zone, gives the area a general importance for greater understanding of a town's history in a number of significant ways. First, the wealth of finds, especially of organic materials such as wood, leather and bone, is often accurately dated by a combination of dendrochronology and coins. The finds often include trade waste (unfinished products) or industrial scrap. The waterfront revetments constitute dated groups of medieval finds representative of life in the wider city, since backfilling the revetments acted as private and civic rubbish-tips. Secondly, in many ports, the strip of land along the river has often been raised several times against the rising river, and this action buried many medieval buildings whose fairly complete plans may be recovered by excavation. At other ports, previous buildings are buried by attempts to reach the water as the port silted up. In certain towns such as London (Dyson 1989) and Hull (Horrox 1978), the buildings and the finds in and around them may be further illuminated by documentary study of their owners and occupiers, including people of different social standing and of different trades. Thirdly, overall, it is reasonable to suggest that the rate of reclamation in cubic metres is indicative of activity and growth in the city at large; so that as our information increases from a programme of excavations, we may be able to relate the volume of reclamation (measured by archaeological contexts) with periods of growth in

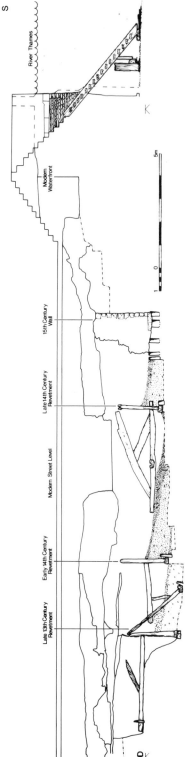

Figure 2.18 London, Trig Lane: simplified section showing stages of reclamation in the fourteenth and fifteenth centuries (Milne and Milne 1982)

the city itself. These general correlations show how the waterfront zone is an index or comprehensive sample of the archaeology of the whole medieval city.

Analysing a town: King's Lynn

Some of the boundaries to the urban settlement, such as gates and defences, were meant to delimit, and had a constraining influence; other boundaries, such as the extent of surburban growth or expansion of the town into the adjacent river as reclamation, were a result of forces pushing against the previous constraints and flowing round them. We can chart the growth of a town by comparing the intended limits by its planners and the actual limits reached as a result of economic development, population growth and other historical circumstances. A final illustration of how archaeology helps to identify the main phases of a town's topographical history is provided by archaeological and documentary work over the last three decades in King's Lynn (Parker 1971; Clarke and Carter 1977, 411–49).

At the request of a group of traders, the bishop of Norwich founded a church and priory on the bank of the river Ouse, within his manor of Gaywood, at the end of the eleventh century (Fig 2.19). The site, near the river's estuary into the Wash, was already surrounded by valuable salt workings, and stood at an important road crossing of the river; it could thus exploit a large agricultural hinterland. Perhaps a small settlement already lay in what was later South Lynn, south of the Millfleet; the new town lay between the Millfleet and the Purfleet, two streams draining the marshy ground into the Ouse.

The first two centuries of Lynn's history have so far little to show archaeologically. Pottery of c. 1050–1250 includes coarse, thick-walled bowls and jugs from Grimston (Norf) glazed jugs from Stamford and a very few continental imports, for example from Andenne in the Low Countries. In the mid-twelfth century, the town was extended again to the north, to encompass an east–west route which crossed the river. This Newland was well settled by the time of a property survey of c. 1267–83. The main street was Damgate (Norfolk Street), which originally ran to the ferry; part of this route still exists as a right of way through a branch of Woolworth's, who have built across the line. The river bank seems to have been marked by King Street (in the Newland) and Queen Street (in the historic core), both of which, like Thames Street in London, now run some distance from the river; two stone houses of c. 1200 have been recorded (one during shameful demolition) on the inland side of these streets. Wharves are documented on the riverwards side of the new area, by its church of St Nicholas, shortly after 1243.

The main relevant excavation has taken place in the northern, Newland part of the town. A site on the north side of Damgate revealed four phases of wattle fences, some probably forming the walls of buildings (Clarke and Carter 1977, 23–30). Pottery suggested an early thirteenth-century start to occupation here; as the site lay in the backs of medieval tenements, the features included ovens, rubbish pits and a cobbled path. If settlement of the

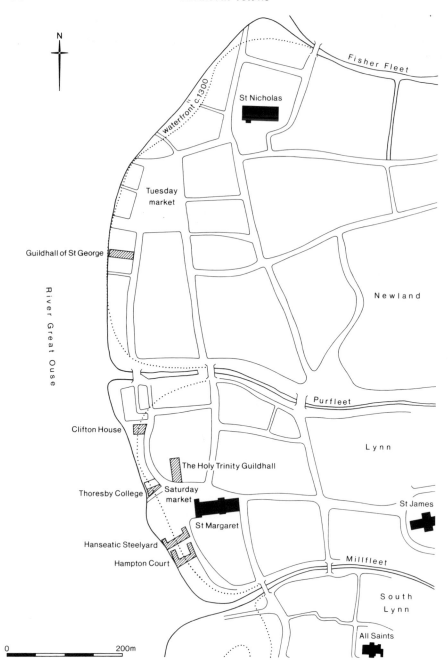

Figure 2.19 King's Lynn: extent of medieval waterfront, relevant buildings and excavations (Clarke 1981)

Newland was vigorous after its foundation, the evidence would lie elsewhere, up by the street frontages. The third phase of fences, of the fourteenth century, included more foreign pottery and some from a wider range of sources in England.

The excavated and surviving evidence from the town changes in character *c.* 1250. Domestic buildings revealed by excavation now had stone foundations, though largely for timber frames; pottery sources included Yorkshire, Nottingham, the East Midlands and the London area, with a wider range of French, Dutch and German imports. A timber wharf excavated in the courtyard of Thoresby College shows the approximate line of the waterfront in the older part of town in 1300, and by 1500 notable medieval buildings, several of which survive, lay in the reclaimed zone, between the river-bank street and the river. These include semi-public buildings such as the Gildhall of St George (its undercroft used as a ware-house), the Hanseatic Steelyard complex, and merchants' houses in King Street and Queen Street (Clifton House and Hampton Court). A number of pre-1500 houses have also been recorded away from the waterfront; they were (and the survivors still are) scattered through all three parts of the town, showing that its late medieval prosperity (having survived 500 years, they must have been among the better examples) was not confined to one locality. Excavation has also located a brick wharf on the Purfleet, demonstrating how the watercourse was embanked and constricted in the fifteenth century as a nearby merchant's establishment sought to create a wharf on one of the contributory creeks to the Ouse (Clarke and Carter 1977, 31–43). Although a town would increase its area by expansion into a major river or the sea, the effect of waterfront reclamation on smaller streams tended to narrow and eventually erase them from the landscape.

Conclusions

In each town, one of the main objects of study should be the outline of each new topographical element; and then what happened to it. From this we may be able both to deduce the intention behind its formation and to judge how successful it was.

How can topographical elements be identified by archaeological means? Some elements have a distinctive character, such as castles, churches and markets. Others, such as the suburbs and waterfront, are perceptible zones where occupation derived from the need for access to roads or rivers, and where the pattern of properties and buildings is often relatively crisp and clear because in either case they were being laid out afresh. A third kind of spatial element can be identified by breaks in the grid of streets, or grids of different proportions in different parts of the town. This is particularly important when studying the successive expansions and areas of growth of the historic town. The town plans of British towns are not crisply differ-entiated in this regard, due to centuries of change in even the more recent plantations; but we can see better examples, and evaluate the technique of analysis, in post-medieval cities, such as in America (for example, New York in the eighteenth century: Rothschild 1990).

From a knowledge of the development of the town and its parts over time, we can hope to move further. Every new element prompted a change in emphasis within the town, and we can therefore ponder the ways in which geographical shifts might reveal organisational shifts in the society which comprised the town itself. This is one of several themes to be explored in the following chapters on housing, crafts and industries, commerce, and churches and other religious institutions.

3 *Houses, properties and streets*

The questions

To understand how the main kinds of secular buildings such as houses, shops and inns functioned in the medieval town, several questions can be posed. We would like to know the framework of streets and property boundaries which constrained the spread of buildings and governed their disposition and size; what the earliest buildings of stone and timber looked like; and, over time, whether they formed a range of types or preferred arrangements on the plot. Although the main discussion will be of domestic accommodation, we can briefly examine other types of building which shared domestic characteristics, and which were adapted from houses, or the form of which grew out of domestic origins: taverns, inns and almshouses for example. The appearance of these buildings can be illustrated by evidence of their construction technique, materials, decoration and internal or external fittings. And finally, we can ask what contribution archaeological study can make to an understanding of three kinds of environment in the medieval town: the built environment (its bulk, shapes, construction), the social environment (how rooms were used; how economic and social factors resulted in differences in the evidence), and the perceived environment (how medieval townspeople regarded their homes, notions of privacy, and mental arrangement of spaces around them).

The number of excavations of medieval house-sites which have now been published, in either final or interim form, allow us to compare the quality of information between a large city such as the City of London and smaller towns. In London, continual and intense digging into the ground at all periods means that, apart from along the waterfront, archaeological evidence of structures from which plots might be reconstructed is scattered and sparse; it is largely confined to the distribution of deep foundations such as sunken timber cellars, the foundations of stone buildings and the lower parts of cesspits and wells. In smaller towns, by contrast, the strata often survive in longer sequences, but not necessarily in more volume. Occasionally, in towns away from the present industrial or commercial centres, also, standing buildings of the period are available for examination. A third source is reconstruction from documentary evidence; for direct comparison this depends on density of information over a long period, and sufficient information of the right type (e.g. measured dimensions) which occur rarely and fortuitously from the twelfth and thirteenth centuries. This evidence tends to occur in the larger towns and cities.

The varied types and strands of evidence can be approached from several points of view. In this chapter we consider the house as a domestic unit, and what functions besides domestic went on in it; particularly rooms such as undercrofts which were built for a trading or storage purpose. In Chapter 5, custom-built shops, market halls and guild halls are considered as buildings concerned with trade and commerce. As will be seen, these two functions, domestic and trade, often overlapped in medieval buildings.

Formation of properties and early buildings

A first matter to explore is the manner in which properties and buildings formed along streets once the latter had been laid out, whether in the eleventh, thirteenth or fifteenth centuries; secondly, how prominent buildings formed first encroachments and then points of permanence in the development of streets; and, thirdly, whether distinctive buildings might congregate in particular areas of towns.

Several of the arguments in this chapter are illustrated by three recently excavated sites around Cheapside in London: one in Milk Street on the north side, and two sites in Bow Lane to the south, at Watling Court and Well Court (Schofield et al. 1990). From the mid-eleventh century, pit alignments at Milk Street, at right angles to the street, seem to indicate property boundaries; the pits left an undug strip between their lines, perhaps indicating a property boundary (Fig 3.1). The formation of properties can be seen in more subtle ways through the disposition of rubbish pits, and in particular, cesspits (i.e. latrines). At Watling Court, properties were undoubtedly physically separate entities from as early as the late ninth or tenth centuries, on the evidence of (i) pits spaced at regular intervals which presumably lay behind surface-laid buildings fronting on to the streets (and which, in the city centre, have otherwise been destroyed by modern base-ments), and (ii) the use of many of these pits as cesspits; here we presume that in general spatially separated cesspits (i.e. one every five metres or so) indicate separate tenements.

The appearance of the properties along Bow Lane in *c*. 1050 can be visualised as a street range of timber buildings, without cellars but otherwise of unknown character, with a substantial range behind and at right angles, of which the timber-lined cellar survives to be recorded (Fig 3.2). This would imply a certain density of occupation and a similarity of construction between properties. It would also imply the emergence of the right-angled medieval house plan by the mid-eleventh century: a range parallel with the street, through which a gateway or passage led to a small yard or alley along the side of a major, usually sunken-cellared building set at right angles to the line of the street (as Building 3 at Watling Court). A similar degree of rectilinearity and organisation of properties, including gradual definition of access to the internal spaces, is found at this period in Northampton, Lincoln and Durham. At Northampton, the St Peter's Street site demonstrated a reorganisation of street and buildings into a rectilinear arrangement, replacing the former loose configuration, in the late eleventh century (Williams 1979, 143); at Flaxengate, Lincoln, this period saw a denser level of occupation and the appearance of an L-shaped range of buildings bordering the street and running back from it (Perring 1981, Fig 34). At Durham the late eleventh century saw the establishment of fences towards the rear of late Saxon properties, presumably parcelling out a backland which was previously common and the site of large middens (Carver 1979, 71).

Figure 3.1 Milk Street, City of London: rows of tenth-century and later pits indicate where a medieval property boundary may have lain. The late Saxon and medieval street is at the top of the picture (Museum of London Archaeology Service)

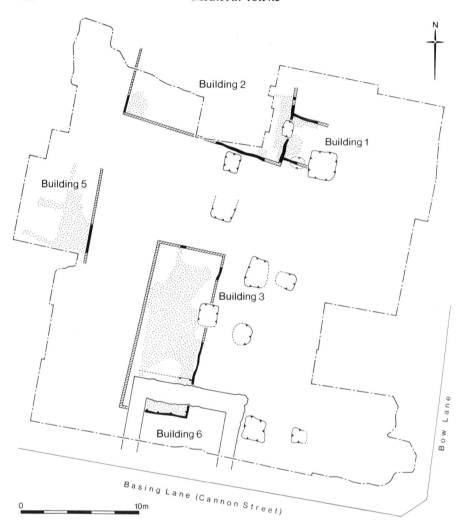

Figure 3.2 Watling Court, City of London: plan of the site in the eleventh century, with a twelfth-century stone building added (Museum of London Archaeology Service)

The shape and size of individual buildings clearly contributed to the outline and definition of properties, particularly along street frontages; by 1200, in London, the frontages of streets such as Bow Lane and Milk Street were defined. In some cases the street frontage was already indented or even slightly curved, taking account of encroachments or obstacles formed by prominent buildings. Some of these encroachments were buildings of stone, commonly with their gables against the street. The erection of a stone building by the street, often in the twelfth or thirteenth centuries (as for example also at Lincoln and Bury St Edmunds), would thereafter tend to anchor that part of the frontage for generations.

The grouping and positions of buildings also show how the plot was

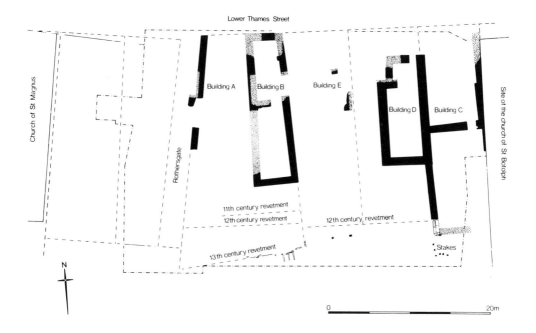

Figure 3.3 New Fresh Wharf, City of London: stone buildings of the twelfth and early thirteenth century on the waterfront, immediately downstream of London Bridge (Steedman et al. 1992)

arranged, especially in relation to the street, and where the main building, and therefore the social centre of the property, lay. At Watling Court, a prominent stone building of the twelfth century (Building 6) coincided with the substantial timber-cellared building of the eleventh century (Building 4); a large building lay in the same place over a period perhaps of two centuries, and the destruction of the former was probably followed closely by the construction of the latter (Fig 3.2). This indicates a continuity both of location of the main building within the property, and perhaps underlines that this corner property was substantial among its neighbours in both periods.

In London and Winchester, stone buildings near the street could occasionally be found by 1100; there are a number of twelfth-century examples, for instance at Well Court in the City of London, also in Bow Lane, or on narrow waterfront properties immediately downstream of the medieval bridge site at New Fresh Wharf (Fig 3.3; Steedman et al. 1992). Some stone buildings might be visible from the street, but placed back slightly within their surroundings of timber buildings; for instance, along the side of a plot and behind a street-range, as at Brook Street, Winchester (Keene 1985b, 156, 169). Documentary work on Canterbury houses has shown that they often occupied properties which, although not large, were nevertheless commodious. One house (Burgate) is first mentioned *c.* 1180 and several others *c.* 1200 or in the early thirteenth century. Properties were all shapes and sizes, though generally rectangular; for example, 52 × 90 ft, 70 × 70 ft, 60 × 106 ft, 65 × 80 ft and 42 × 74 ft. One house occupied an entire plot 40ft square and another house had a frontage apparently of 60ft to a major street, forming the front end of a property 153 ft long (Urry 1967). In general, the stone building with gable to the street must be seen as the successor to the cellared timber building of the eleventh century, with the innovation that the ground floor of the stone structure now communicated directly with the street.

The cesspit probably continued to be sited near boundaries throughout the medieval period in London. The regularity of complaint by one London neighbour against another about leaking cesspits in the surviving rolls of Assize of Nuisance in the period 1301–1437 (Chew and Kellaway 1973) demonstrates that many cesspits were dug close to property boundaries. When a privy was used by more than one tenement, as is recorded in London from at least *c.* 1160, the privy would presumably be sited on the tenement boundary. Secondly, in London, stone-lined privies were generally located deep within the properties (i.e. towards the back); where relationships to recorded or vanished buildings could be suggested, the privies lay behind the buildings fronting on to the streets. In other medieval towns privies were similarly at the rear of buildings with gable to the street, either inside or immediately outside the building, as in thirteenth- or fourteenth-century Stamford or Southampton (RCHM 1977, lii; Platt and Coleman-Smith 1975, 235). Excavations at Worcester have found cesspits across small yards behind buildings on twelfth- to fourteenth-century tenements (Carver 1980, 167). Surveys of London houses in 1607–12 show privies across small yards behind houses, in the same block as the separate kitchen, an arrangement which may date from at least the fourteenth century (Schofield 1987, 16, Fig 3). Together, these configurations suggest that (i) stone privies of the thirteenth and fourteenth centuries were commonly towards the edges of properties, often deep within them; (ii) stone privies often replaced timber predecessors in the same locations (as is demonstrated on several London sites); and (iii) timber-lined cesspits of tenth-century and later date are found near boundaries which are documented by 1300. It therefore seems likely that tenth-century pits can be used to infer boundaries in their own century (Schofield et al. 1990, 153–9).

A wider question concerns the overall distribution of early medieval stone buildings in medieval towns, especially those on or near street frontages. In London, one relative concentration of such structures was the area north of Cheapside, from Milk Street to Old Jewry, the district in which Jews lived in the twelfth and thirteenth centuries. Stone buildings of the twelfth century have also been recorded in the waterfront zone, both south of Thames Street at Dowgate and in the stretch between the bridge and Billingsgate, and on the lanes leading to the river at Pudding Lane and Miles Lane. These main concentrations of twelfth-century stone houses, the central commercial area (or areas, in a large place like London) and the waterfront area, are also favoured by stone houses in other towns. In Colchester, the known fragments of early medieval stone buildings are found within two blocks of the High Street, in an area possibly occupied by Jewish houses (Crummy 1981; Stephenson 1984–5). In Canterbury, the 27 known stone houses are almost all to be found in the centre of the town (i.e. the High Street and streets north and south of it (Urry 1967, Maps 2/5 and 2/6). There is a similar concentration in Lincoln, where parts of eight buildings survive, seven of which are round the cathedral in the upper town. In Norwich, the excavation of a notable late twelfth-century stone building on the waterfront at St Martin at Palace Plain, probably a warehouse for the adjacent cathedral, has occasioned a survey of early secular stone buildings in that city (Ayers 1988, 172–4). Only two are physically extant, but records, principally of the fourteenth century, speak of at least sixteen probable examples. Early medieval Norwich was a port with continental connections; and an apparent concentration of stone structures on King Street, bordering the Wensum on the southern approach to the town, is notable and invites comparison both with London (New Fresh Wharf) and stone houses on the expanding waterfront in King's Lynn (Clarke 1981, 132–3 and Figs 120–1).

While stone houses were no doubt symbols of wealth and the residences of substantial citizens, their survival in some towns should not obscure the need to study the development of timber buildings, which were originally the majority, along street frontages throughout the medieval period. From about 1300, standing buildings begin to show us what street frontages in medieval towns looked like, but we await a body of evidence to work with for earlier centuries. In the absence of many buildings of the period above ground, archaeological work can make a significant contribution by study of timber parts of buildings reused in waterside constructions, preserved by the waterlogged conditions adjacent to streams and rivers, whether still apparent or with their courses now buried underground. A recent summary of work on timber-building techniques from waterfront revetments of 900–1400 in the City of London, for instance, provides many missing links between Saxon and medieval building traditions in timber, and suggests that timber-framed buildings were not introduced into London in a fully formed state, but evolved by stages in the twelfth and thirteenth centuries, and continued to develop thereafter (Milne 1992). Examples of timbers and their joints from the eleventh to the fourteenth centuries, properly recorded, can allow reconstruction of styles of timber-framing which would have been seen on the capital's streets in those centuries.

House typology

The eleventh and twelfth centuries therefore saw the gradual solidification of property boundaries, both along the street and at the back, usually by the erection of buildings, among which stone buildings, which naturally lasted longer, made the greatest contribution. By 1300, archaeological evidence is growing for a range of house-forms and arrangements of buildings on the plot.

Any typology of medieval urban house-plans must build on the work of W.A. Pantin, who based his analysis on 40 medieval houses from seventeen English towns (Pantin 1962–3). He was concerned with the hall as the central feature of the tenement and the problems of adaptation on restricted urban sites, and he therefore deliberately omitted both the smallest houses, in

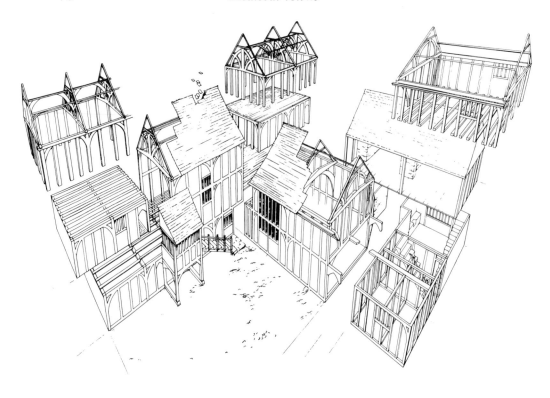

Figure 3.4 Parts of an ecclesiastical town-house at Coffee Yard, York; now refurbished as a historical research and information centre (York Archaeological Trust)

which development was only vertical, and the largest ('such as Arundel House in the Strand, or the Bishop's Palace or the Old Deanery at Salisbury') where space allowed full introduction of the rural manor-house plan. The archaeological typology must now be wider, dealing with these extremities of the continuum, and Pantin's types fit within the middle range.

Many houses in major towns such as London, York and Edinburgh were town houses of a distant lord, whether lay or religious. There were two purposes for such a house: the provision of accommodation for those engaged in the everyday affairs of the house or the see, such as the selling of produce or the buying of goods, especially luxuries; and as the residence of the institution's head when in town. These urban depots of religious institutions from out of the town, whether based in another town or in the countryside, are found in many of the larger centres, such as York, where a hospice of Nostell Priory with fourteenth- and fifteenth-century buildings has been restored by York Archaeological Trust (Fig 3.4); or Edinburgh, where fifteenth-century ecclesiastical town houses have produced excavated evidence of luxurious living such as an unusual amount of imported German pottery (Schofield 1975–6). The wider effects of these religious houses in towns, for instance on patterns of medieval trade, is picked up again below (Chapter 5). A similar class of residence were those associated with major churches (Barley 1986, 58–67): houses of prebendaries (canons of cathedrals who were granted portions of the cathedral revenues as their stipend) as at Stonegate in York, and halls which may have functioned as ecclesiastical guest-houses, as at Beverley (Armstrong et al. 1991).

Coming to London, for many religious and secular lords, also meant attendance on the king at Westminster, though the function of providing an urban base in the largest city had a longer history. Until the second decade of the thirteenth century, when the organs of government and the meetings of parliament began to become permanent fixtures at Westminster, the documented town houses of the religious are to be found in the City or in Southwark, showing that when they first appear in twelfth-century records, their sites were near the markets and the port. The thirteenth century, however, saw a marked swing towards Westminster and the road to it (the Strand outside the city boundary, Fleet Street within it); first to settle here, before 1225, was probably Ralph Neville, bishop of Chichester and Chancellor, whose palatial property later became Lincoln's Inn. By the end of the medieval period nearly 200 'Inns' of this kind can be identified in London or its immediate environs; their heyday was the thirteenth and early fourteenth centuries, and they must have been a potent mechanism for distributing luxuries from the capital to the countryside and to lesser towns.

In the vast majority of cases where their plans can be ascertained, the houses of religious and noble leaders were of courtyard plan (Fig 3.5: Type 4). The hall of the property lay normally at the rear of a yard, though occasionally to the side on restricted sites, with a range of buildings (often separately let) fronting the street. Leaders of the merchant community in major towns, such as those who dealt in wine or some other aspect of royal service, also aspired to the style of house with a courtyard and an open hall of lofty proportions. Pantin saw the type as one species of 'parallel' house, in which the hall lay parallel to the street, and described fourteenth- to sixteenth-century examples from Exeter, King's Lynn, London, Norwich and Oxford.

By the fourteenth century, when they can be discerned a little more clearly, the three diagnostic chambers of the noble residence, at least in London, were the hall, undercroft and occasionally a tower. The large hall of stone (and later, of brick) and undercrofts, often sited below the hall or other principal buildings, survived into later centuries to be recorded. In London, secular towers are known at several fourteenth-century houses, in documentary record or in the panoramas, though none has yet been excavated. It seems that lords, despite the comparative absence of clan-fighting which governed the domestic architecture of cities such as Siena or Genoa, still had sufficient influence and apparent need to build or maintain such towers. Crenellations, presumably largely on the hall, were infrequently licensed during the fourteenth century and were largely decorative and symbolic; although most large houses had gateways, they were made of stone in only exceptional cases. Parallels for these houses may be found in the Home Counties, for example in Kent, at rural houses of standing such as Nettlestead Place (*c.* 1250–60), Old Soar, Plaxtol (*c.* 1290), and Penshurst Place (late thirteenth century in parts); or further afield, a good parallel is found at Little Wenham Hall, Suffolk (1270–90). It is reasonable to transport the plan form and architectural detail of Little Wenham Hall into the larger towns and the capital in the thirteenth and fourteenth centuries. We must correct any impression that religious and lay lords lived exclusively in rural manor-houses; there was a flourishing urban society in medieval Britain, but we now have few traces of it.

A town with a good number of surviving medieval buildings, such as Salisbury (RCHM 1980), or a corpus of house-plans such as those of properties in London in 1607–14, provided by the surveyor Ralph Treswell (Schofield 1987), both demonstrate a variety of forms of medium-sized and smaller houses, but two main types may be proposed (Fig 3.5, Types 3 and 2). In this typology, for the moment, we are concerned with buildings on restricted sites towards the middle of towns; in peripheral or suburban areas, where plot width allowed the house to stand side-on to the street, further designs were possible.

The Type 3 house (filling a whole property, and of three to six rooms in ground-floor plan) did not have a true courtyard with a formal gate to the street, though it might have a yard with buildings along one side, or an alley running the length of a long, narrow property. The latter arrangement is illustrated most clearly by properties on waterfront sites, such as in King's Lynn or south of Thames Street in London. Many had an alley down one side, and in consequence buildings were usually arranged down the side of the plot behind the street-range which commonly comprised shops, sometimes let separately. Along, usually at the side of, most waterfront properties ran the access alley from the street to the river and the main water supply. This originated for the most part as a private thoroughfare, in some cases becoming public through time and custom.

Pantin (1962–3, 228–39) divided 'right-angle' houses into either 'narrow' (i.e. filling the tenement) or 'broad' (i.e. leaving space for an alley); it would have been better if these terms had been transposed, thus applying to houses rather than apparently to properties, and thus his terminology is not followed here. The studies of Pantin and others (e.g. Parker 1971 on King's Lynn) show a great variety of arrangement within the Type 3 band.

Smaller, and more uniform in its characteristics, was a house with two rooms on three or more floors (Type 2). This type is known from documentary and archaeological evidence in London from the early fourteenth century. In several cases such houses form a strip, two rooms deep, fronting, but separate from, a larger property behind. Examples have been excavated on the New Fresh Wharf site (Schofield 1977; 1994, Fig 79), and houses of this type at Abchurch Lane in London, used as the examples in Figs 3.5 and 5.4 (on p. 137), may have been those built on the site shortly before 1390. In Type 2 houses the ground floor was a shop and warehouse, sometimes with the two rooms thrown together to form one, or a tavern. Because the ground floor was given over wholly to trade, the hall lay usually on the first floor at the front, overlooking the street. In the late fourteenth-century examples at Abchurch Lane, the kitchen was a separate building across a small yard; but elsewhere in the capital the kitchen was often placed above ground in the main building, as structures occupied every inch of the tiny plots. Pantin traced the Type 2 form in the post-medieval period in Oxford (Pantin 1947, 136–8) and it is also found in other towns such as Exeter and Norwich from

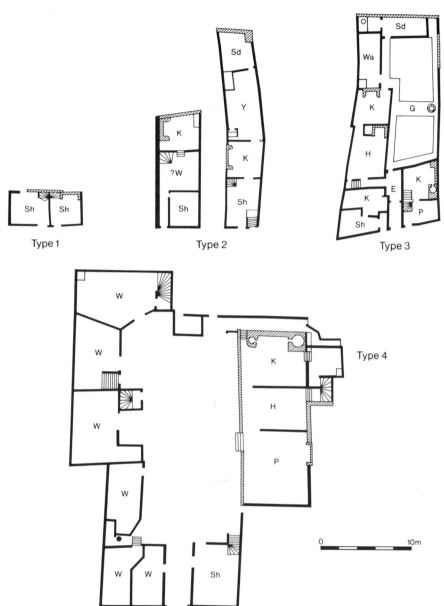

Figure 3.5 Types 1–4 of house-plans from the London surveys of Ralph Treswell in 1612 (Schofield 1987). Room and space functions for Figures 3.5 and 3.16: B buttery; Ch chamber; E entry; G garden; H hall; K kitchen; P parlour; Sd shed; Sh shop; St study; W warehouse; Wa wash-house (for scouring yarn); Y yard. The buildings were mostly timber-framed; hatching indicates brick walls

around 1500 (Portman 1966, 5, 25–6). A less compact form had a hall forming the back ground-floor room and rising through two storeys, e.g. 20 Jordan Street, Coventry (Pantin 1962–3, 220–1).

The houses of the medieval poor have largely been destroyed without trace in almost every town. These humble dwellings did not survive into the era of engraving, and as they commonly lay along street frontages, archaeological excavation has not uncovered them because of later street-widening and the digging of cellars, especially in the nineteenth century. Sometimes the existence of buildings, probably forming continuous facades and one room deep, are inferred from the absence of rubbish pits near the line of the street, as has already been noted; such spaces are found near major streets in eleventh-century London (Horsman, Milne and Milne 1988). One-room timber-framed houses of thirteenth- or early fourteenth-century date have been excavated at Lower Brook Street, Winchester (Biddle 1967), and more substantial examples in stone of the fifteenth century at St Peter's Street, Northampton (Williams 1979). Others are examined in the case study of Alms Lane, Norwich (see below, pp. 76–7). Work in Perth has uncovered graphic evidence of poor lifestyles, in single-room buildings with walls of posts and wattle which were probably both living and working space for cobblers and other artisans (Holdsworth 1987).

In back streets of larger towns, and even along major streets of smaller towns, houses could also stand with their long sides or eaves to the street. Examples are provided by the Norwich and Northampton sites, and sometimes there is a mixture of buildings with their gables or sides to the street, as at Flaxengate, Lincoln. Sometimes a throwing together of two properties, after an acquisition, would result in the building of a street frontage which was, in effect, two properties wide and which would be roofed parallel to the street. We should never assume that the outlines of properties seen in towns today, or on nineteenth-century maps, were the original medieval outlines. The golden rule for the archaeologist is: check it on the ground.

A distinctive form of house, called the Wealden by modern students, is found throughout rural south-east England and in some of its towns. The first-floor chambers are jettied at one or both ends of the central, open hall, to give the hall itself a recessed appearance. Nine form a rent of Battle Abbey, *c.* 1468 (Martin and Martin 1987, 16–17); other examples include 3 Church Street, Canterbury, fifteenth/early sixteenth century (Pantin 1962–3, 212–13); and 55 Spon Street, Coventry, fifteenth century (ibid., 216). One at 49–51 Goodramgate, York, is a hall range at right-angles behind a street frontage, a configuration also likely, but not yet documented, in London streets. The form dates from the late fourteenth century to perhaps the 1530s, when jetties began to go out of fashion.

Another book in this series deals in greater detail with medieval houses, with greater emphasis on standing structures (Grenville, in preparation).

Other types of building with domestic characteristics

There were other types of secular building which often looked like houses, and usually grew out of them.

In medieval towns, there were three main types of victualling house: in ascending order of size and status, the alehouse, the tavern and the inn, though the distinctions were often blurred. As a rough analogy, in a sample of Canterbury drinking-houses of 1560–1640, alehouses had a mean number of 4.8 principal rooms, taverns 10.0, and inns 14.0 (Clark 1984, 5, 64).

The brewing industry developed during the fourteenth century and prominent London brewers could maintain one of the earliest recorded company halls, bequeathed to them in 1408. The introduction of hops for the brewing of beer, from at least 1420 in London (Salzman 1923, 295–7), made it necessary to incorporate storage areas into brewhouses, since, unlike ale, beer made with hops could be stored and transported. Brewhouses of the fifteenth century were evidently sometimes large establishments: in 1463 the Saracen's Head in Aldersgate, London, included a well-furnished brewhouse, a hall with two glazed windows, two privies and three refurbished stables. The largest examples contained horse-mills, to grind the malt, but otherwise brewhouses were evidently similar to dyehouses in the character of their installations, since there are cases of dyers and brewers using the same lead troughs and vats. In the next section of this chapter will be discussion of a small tenement which may have functioned at least partly as a brewhouse at Alms Lane, Norwich.

Taverns were drinking-houses where wine was drunk. Taverns are known in undercrofts by the early fourteenth century in London and Oxford (Keene 1985a, 1990; Salter 1926, 155–6). Some undercrofts were evidently built to be drinking-places from the start. The Peter and Paul tavern in Paternoster Row, London, rebuilt in 1342, comprised an undercroft provided with fireplaces and therefore presumably for drinking, and drinking-rooms or partitioned areas on both ground and first floors (Salzman 1952, 432–4). During the fifteenth century the main drinking areas seem to have spread to the ground floor of buildings, and then the cellar was abandoned; the Cheapside area in London was thick with taverns which must have had a frequent trade in company meetings and feasts, possibly in special chambers. On the other hand, smaller late medieval taverns, with their drinking-rooms at ground-floor level, often resembled private houses and modifications from one function to the other were probably minimal.

Inns were naturally extensive establishments, and provided accommodation of some comfort. By 1345 a guest could obtain a single room, at least in London; in 1380 the custom of the realm, it was noted, was that the keeper of a hostelry was responsible for the goods left by the guest, who should also receive a key to a single room. Inns were to be found in numbers immediately outside gates, where custom concentrated and where long properties could incorporate stable yards, or near other major entry points to a city, such as from the Thames into London at St Paul's Wharf, where in 1390 a nearby inn could offer a suite of rooms comprising hall, chamber, buttery and kitchen. Archaeological work on inns has often been based on surveys of standing structures, such as at Canterbury, Newark and Oxford (Munby 1992; 21 inns are known in the town by 1400).

From shortly after 1300, the word *Row* is used in London and other towns to describe blocks of shops or houses-cum-shops which must have had some kind of unified architectural character. A surviving example is Lady

Row, Goodramgate, York, built in 1314 (Short 1980); two storeys high, jettied on the first floor, and with simple living accommodation above a ground-floor shop. Three London contracts of 1369–73 indicate the nature of unitary blocks of shops in the later fourteenth century; these also appear to have contained living accommodation in the form of halls or solars (Salzman 1952, 446–8). Such blocks or rows were often built by institutions such as religious houses, both those in the town and outside in the countryside, seeking an income from rented premises in the towns. These blocks contained both domestic and trade accommodation. The design and function of shops and buildings whose sole function was trade are considered below in Chapter 5.

Excavated sites: Norwich, Hull and Hartlepool

The typology of urban houses outlined so far is based on a combination of standing buildings, which tend to be the superior sort of construction (they must have been, to survive to the present day) and post-medieval plan evidence. How much is this typology corroborated by medieval archaeological sites? The following examples are taken from three towns in eastern England where survival of medieval houses and their yards was extensive.

In Norwich, a site at the junction of Alms Lane and St George's Street, north of the river Wensum, was excavated in 1976 (Atkin 1985). Until the mid-thirteenth century the area was waste ground on the margin of settlement, used for rubbish dumping and quarry pits. In the first of three periods considered here (Period 4, c. 1275–1400), a building interpreted as a brewery was established on the Alms Lane frontage, with the rest of the site occupied by an iron-working complex (Fig 3.6). On the Alms Lane frontage, a clay floor lay around a large hearth (Building A1); ground into the floor was ash and large quantities of germinated, burnt barley. South of this lay another building (A2) with a similar hearth (H922); a later small smelting furnace (H871) and deposits of slag indicate that iron-working was going on here. Slightly later, on pottery evidence, Building C1 was built at right-angles to St George's Street to the east. It comprised two rooms, was possibly tiled, and had two possible smithing hearths in it. A third room was added in a period of rebuilding. Towards the end of this period Buildings A1, A2 and C1 were allowed to become derelict, and a malting oven (1479) and hearths and furnaces (H1404, H470) constructed to the north.

The industrial, as opposed to residential, character of the structures is mirrored in the pottery from this period: there was a higher proportion of local unglazed bowls in comparison to cooking-pots. Though much of the pottery was local, there were already (around 1300) imports from Holland and Langerwehe on the Rhine. Smallfinds included blacksmith's tools (including some from later demolition layers, but thought to originate in this period), and a block of sandstone, unique to the site, which may have been used for sharpening them.

In Period 5 (c. 1400–1450), the site was divided into three tenements, with clay-walled houses on each property (Fig 3.7a); these divisions may have been inherited from the earlier periods. The occupation was now in part domestic, though strata still contained much iron-working waste and coal probably from smithing activities. On property B to the east lay two buildings, B1 and B2. As its strata contained Langerwehe stoneware from Germany, B2 was probably constructed later than the buildings on property A (the imported pottery is conventionally dated nearer the middle of the century in Norwich). On property C, to the south, small traces of a further building (C2) were also recorded. Here were also several fragments of a pottery vessel which may have been part of distilling apparatus. Buildings B1 and B2 produced implements used in domestic crafts, such as a bone spindle-whorl, and dress ornaments.

In Period 6 (*c.* 1450–1500), houses extended along St George's Street, and there is the first evidence of buildings with upper storeys, by adaptation of the existing structures (Fig 3.7b). This sign of increase in status is underlined by better contemporary pottery. The appearance of Raeren stoneware in this period dates the period to the end of the fifteenth century; other imports were Dutch redwares. The standard of house fittings, personal implements and jewelry (nail-cleaner, strap-end and pin from a brooch) was higher now than previously. For this site documentary evidence is available but limited from about 1290, and makes no useful contribution to the interpretation of the structures.

The second example is from Hull. As part of a campaign of investigations in the 1970s, two sites in the south-east part of the old town were excavated, in High Street and Blackfriargate; we are concerned with that in Blackfriargate, a site now beneath an orbital road (Armstrong and Ayers 1987). The excavation lay within a single medieval property on the north side of the street which led from the medieval market-place and butchery (Marketgate, Queen Street) on the west to the High Street in the east and, as a continuation of the street, to Rottenherring Staith on the river Hull.

Six periods of activity (called phases by the excavators) account for the years between about 1250 and the end of the fifteenth century. Phase 1 (mid-thirteenth century, after 1250) consisted of flood strata and a gully. Phase 2 (late thirteenth/early fourteenth century) comprised a three-bay building along the street, its bays shown by padstones which would have supported the main structural timbers, and a number of pits within the property, though their investigation was terminated by the flooding of the present river Hull during the excavation. This was probably the property of a Simon Wytelard in 1293. In Phase 3 (first quarter of the fourteenth century) the buildings were rebuilt, furnished with hearths and extended, and more pits were dug behind the buildings.

Phase 4 (second quarter of fourteenth century, before 1352) saw a major rebuilding after about two generations (Figs 3.8 and 3.9). The buildings, based on padstones, were replaced by new ones with sills of brick, a new material being used elsewhere in the city wall and the church of Hull, and timber frames. They formed a central bay and an entrance parallel to the street with two wings at right-angles, filling the street frontage of the property (Fig 3.9). The eastern wing comprised a hall with central hearth, and the western wing included what was probably a kitchen or outhouse, provided with a succession of ovens.

By this phase the tenement boundaries had been fixed, partly by stone

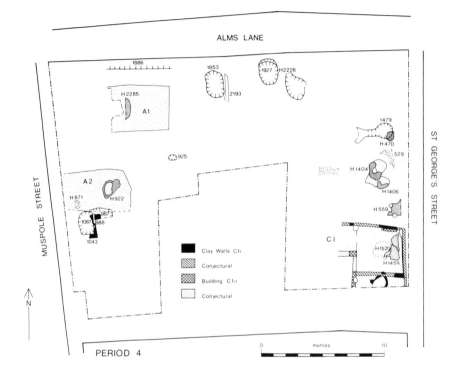

Figure 3.6 Alms Lane, Norwich: Period 4 plan (Atkin 1985)

walls; they survived to the twentieth century. This fixing reflects the increasing stability of life within Hull as an urban place. The excavators argue that highly skilled brick building was taking place on many sites in Hull during the first half of the fourteenth century; models may have been taken from continental northern Europe. Far from being a second-class substitute for stone, 'brick in England was used positively and for prestige' (Armstrong and Ayers 1987, 266).

The buildings of Phase 4 were probably owned by a Robert de Swanland in 1347. He divided and sold the property in 1352. This division was also shown in the archaeological record as Phase 5 (mid/late fourteenth century, after about 1350), when the large building of Phase 4 was subdivided to make two smaller dwellings (Fig 3.10). This changed the former gateway or entrance and a room next to it, interpreted as a shop, into small rooms with identical central hearths of brick. The division of 1352 is also very useful for pottery-dating studies in Hull, as it provides a fixed point or *terminus ante quem* for the styles and vessels found in the Phase 4 layers: local and North Yorkshire wares, and imports from Saintonge, the Low Countries and Spain. In Phase 5 further imports appear, including Siegburg and Langerwehe wares from the Rhineland. In Phase 6 (fifteenth century) the building to the west was repaired and possibly incorporated small-scale industrial facilities, but that to the east was dismantled.

In this case, the writers of the excavation and finds report do not bring out

Figure 3.7 Alms Lane, Norwich: (a) Period 5 plan; (b) Period 6 plan (Atkin 1985)

Figure 3.8   Blackfriargate, Hull: the Wytelard property in the early fourteenth
century (Phase 4) looking south (with the exception of the extended wing on the right
which is an addition of Phase 5 in the mid to late fourteenth century) (Armstrong and
Ayers 1987)

the significance of the many objects in stone, fired clay, glass, iron, copper,
lead, wood, leather and textiles from the site described and from a nearby
site published with it. The reader must work from individual finds in
catalogues to contexts on the site. It would have been useful to know if the
excavators thought, for instance, that the few fragments of medieval
window-glass from the site might have indicated glazed windows for the
houses there. A small number of decorated floor tiles were found in layers of
the Phase 3, Phase 4 and Phase 6 buildings, and probably came from use in
them. The tiles were of types made in Nottingham, but the occurrence of two
fragments of tile kiln waste on the Wytelard property, one in a layer behind
the Phase 3 buildings, corroborates documentary evidence that East
Midlands tilers were working in Hull in the fourteenth century.

To travel further north for the third example, at Hartlepool, excavations
at Church Close in 1984–5 found Anglo-Saxon monastic occupation
immediately north of St Hilda's parish church, and after a distinct break in
occupation marked by deposition and cultivation of a sandy soil, a number
of properties were laid out in two periods: the first possibly part of the initial
founding of the medieval town in the late eleventh and early twelfth
centuries, and the second in the mid/late thirteenth century (Daniels 1990).

The earlier phase comprised two properties with buildings of slot- and
post-hole construction, said here to be another rural tradition which went
well with signs of cultivation in their backyards. During the twelfth century
and up to about 1250, these buildings were extended and the yards became
enclosed, dug with pits and hearths; urban lifestyle was spreading on to the
site. By the end of this period some of the buildings were on sills of stone. In

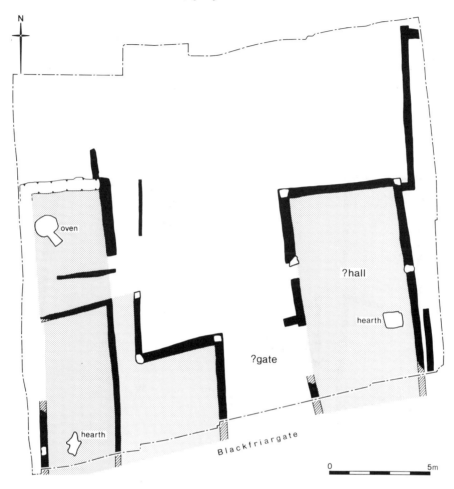

Figure 3.9 Blackfriargate, Hull: Phase 4 plan of the Wytelard property, early fourteenth century (Armstrong and Ayers 1987)

the second period (Fig 3.11), three long stone buildings (II, IV and V) were erected on the northern property, their individual rooms reached by two alleys and with a common yard at the back. From the absence of tile on the site, they must have had thatched roofs. A similar building (III) was constructed on the southern property, much less of which lay in the area of excavation. This building preceded the others, and may have served the church to the south.

Building II, from its stouter construction, may have been of two floors, with the others only having one ground floor. A number of sill and jamb stones from it suggest it had freestone door- and window-frames, though the windows were, in the main, not glazed. From the suggested sitings of doors (Fig 3.12), it seems that Building II also had an alley to itself, whereas the other two buildings shared an alley. Building III on the southern property had been demolished in the mid to late fourteenth century. The buildings on

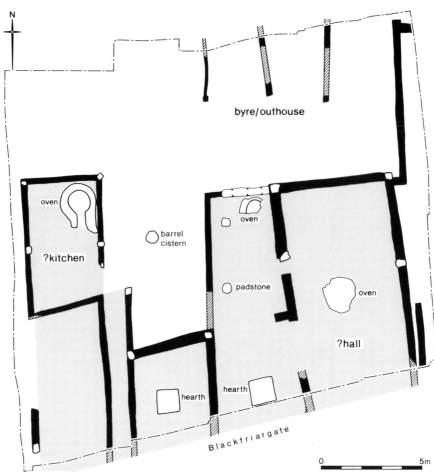

Figure 3.10 Blackfriargate, Hull: Phase 5 plan of the Wytelard property, mid to late fourteenth century (Armstrong and Ayers 1987). The new buildings presumably indicate a greater density of occupation along this part of the street

the northern property shared a history of adaptations, in the form of room expansions and contractions, the insertion or removal of hearths, and movement of partitions and doorways until the late fifteenth century, when they were demolished and ploughsoil once more covered the site.

On this site the excavator has attempted to analyse the function of the various rooms in the three parts of the northern property, which on structural grounds we can call individual tenements (Buildings II, IV and V). Their front rooms (not completely excavated because of proximity to the modern pavement, as is usual in urban excavations) had drains which ran into the medieval street; presumably they were shops (i.e. workshops). Building II had a larger number of domestic items in its component strata than the other buildings. The remains suggest that the house comprised a shop (room E), a hall with central hearth (A), a service room (B) and kitchen (C). Though Building II was thus domestic in function, several of the quickly

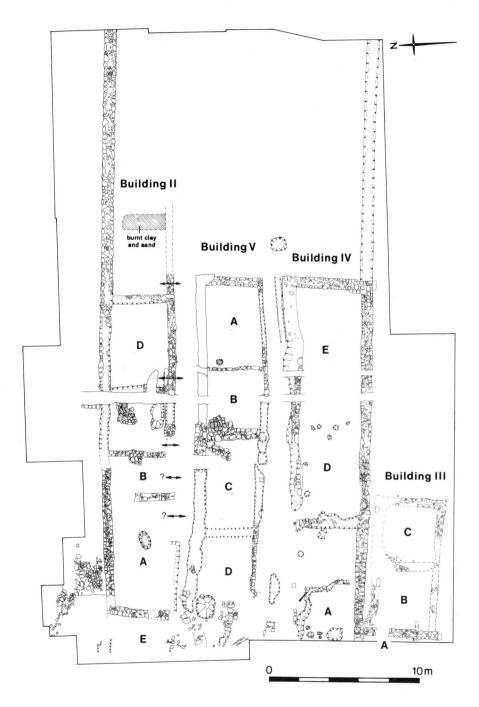

Figure 3.11 Church Close, Hartlepool: plan of medieval tenements in the late thirteenth century (Daniels 1990)

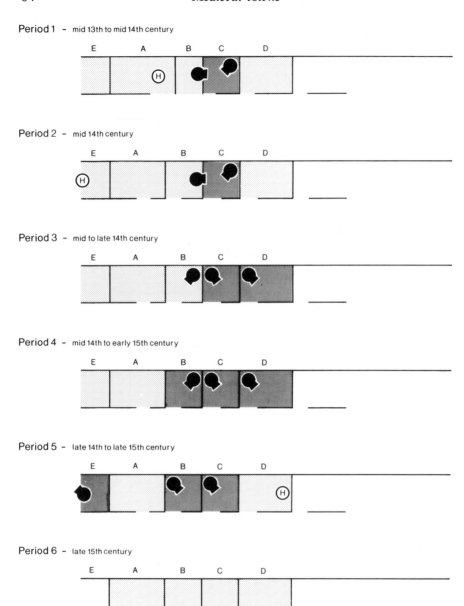

Figure 3.12 Church Close, Hartlepool: diagram of tenement use of Building II from the mid-thirteenth to the late fifteenth centuries (Daniels 1990)

changing phases of its use included ovens which may have had industrial purposes, and many stone containers were found in and around the building; these are shown diagrammatically in Fig 3.12. They appear to have been at first domestic in scale, for baking already processed food (the only seeds found around the ovens were of heather, used as fuel) and possibly processing fish; quantities of herring and whiting bones were recovered. When, however, ovens were built first in room D and then in room E, it is possible that food preparation had reached commercial proportions on this site. Buildings IV and V had a similar mix of domestic and industrial features, but they were more on the industrial side: in the mid to late fourteenth century the yard behind IV was the site of a lime kiln, a rare feature in Hartlepool where none of the domestic buildings so far known had mortared walls. Much more domestic refuse probably lay in the rear parts of the medieval properties, but these strata had to be removed by machine in order to examine the Saxon levels beneath.

These three examples of excavated sites show that there was great variety in the forms of medieval secular buildings, in the way they were laid out on plots, and especially in the ways they changed shape and position over quite short periods. When stone buildings were erected, the changes might thereafter be slower, but they still occurred. Thus, there is a danger in seeking an over-rigorous typology of house-plans, and it is better to explore the range of shapes and sizes while keeping in mind the broad categories outlined above as Types 1–4, or those described by Pantin.

The third part of this chapter looks ahead to the ways in which archaeological study of secular buildings in medieval towns can be developed. Three important topics can be summed up in the questions: (i) what can be deduced about the physical nature of the built environment in towns, from the materials and other factors influencing construction of secular buildings?; (ii) what parts of houses were influenced by social factors such as the needs of trade, or the contrasting desire for higher standards of living?; and (iii) can archaeological investigation in the medieval town throw light on more personal matters, such as the developing wish for privacy, or the way in which the house might be more subtly divided between public and private areas, or even male and female domains? To explore the second and third questions, it is necessary to examine the extent to which the use of individual rooms and spaces, and communication routes through buildings, can be detected by archaeological means.

Built environment, construction methods

The nature and quality of the built environment was influenced largely by three factors: the variety of building materials, the technological sophistication of construction methods, and urban building regulations.

Houses in medieval towns were built out of four basic materials: timber, stone, brick, and earth. The range of materials available had a profound influence on the types of building possible, on decoration and on lifespan of buildings. The sources and species of wood were largely local, even in London (exploitation of timber is discussed below in Chapters 4 and 7). The

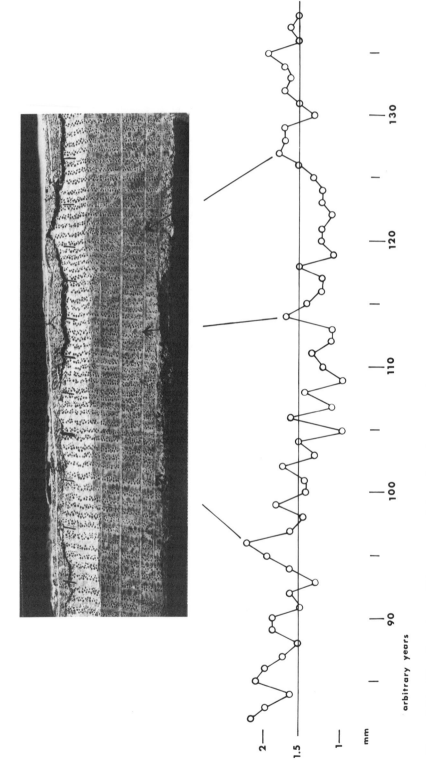

Figure 3.13 The edge of a twelfth-century oak board used in a waterfront construction at Seal House, London; the vessels forming the annual growth rings can be seen (Museum of London Archaeology Service and University of Sheffield)

stones used in medieval buildings in towns were almost totally from the immediate region; former Roman towns had a great stock of Roman building material within their walls, which was dug out and reused, especially up to the end of the thirteenth century and occasionally later. Houses largely of stone were always the prerogative of the rich, and seem to have been a feature of the thirteenth and fourteenth centuries, as shown by the number of arched foundations of stone found on archaeological sites. Thereafter, however, houses of stone are rare, except in towns near good quarries. Brick was imported from the late thirteenth century and locally produced during the fourteenth century, but was in general use only from the early fifteenth century (Smith 1985). The use of the new medium to build new and larger houses in Hull has already been noted; it had a superior overtone. It may be significant that the spread of brick buildings somewhat later in London coincides with the adoption of brick in royal and episcopal palaces, of which there were a great number in the area. Further study of the sources and chronology of use of brick in Britain is required; as an example of what might be done, in a town such as Nijmegen (Holland) a major archaeological study of the houses between 1300 and 1500 relies on a chronology which interweaves historical evidence, stratigraphy, pottery types, and at least seven brick sizes (Clevis 1989).

One of the main potential contributions of archaeological study in the medieval period, as in previous periods, is increasing knowledge of construction methods in buildings of timber, stone and brick; that is, in foundations, walls, roofs, and internal details such as doors, windows and tiled floors.

The structural character of foundations of domestic buildings from the eleventh to the fourteenth centuries in London has recently been examined in detail, in the light of excavations both in the area around the northern end of London Bridge and around Cheapside. Twenty-eight early medieval timber buildings have been divided into three main types: (i) earthfast; (ii) ground-level; and (iii) foundation-bed (padstones, rubble platforms or mortar-capped rubble or gravel-filled trenches) (Horsman et al. 1988). The stone buildings introduced from the twelfth century were sometimes greater in area than the largest timber cellars which preceded them, and in every case much heavier. New foundation techniques were employed: the use of piles and, from perhaps the mid-thirteenth century, arches in stone. Three different types of foundations were developed, and the period of use or fashion of each can increasingly be specified by the dating of archaeological examples: (i) chalk and gravel foundations without mortar, sometimes with piles (in use before the eleventh century, to sometime in the thirteenth century); (ii) arched and mortared foundations (from the mid-thirteenth century, rare by the sixteenth century); and (iii) mortared foundations without arches (from the twelfth century onwards) (Schofield et al. 1990, 163–7). Thus a type-series of foundation styles is being developed, covering the tenth to sixteenth centuries.

Timbers, whether from standing buildings or from waterlogged deposits on archaeological sites, can often be dated by dendrochronology (Fig 3.13). Timbers with at least 50 annual rings are preferable, but this need not mean timbers with large cross-sections; some only 80 × 50 mm. in cross-section

have contained more than 50 rings. The best timbers for tree-ring dating fall
into two categories: those with the longest ring sequences which are used to
construct a site master curve, and those with bark and sapwood, which are
important in providing precise felling dates. Though the main species used in
medieval constructions, and the main focus of study, has been oak, the
scientists are eager to extend their chronologies for elm, fir and beech.

Many standing medieval buildings in both towns and rural areas have had
their parts dated by this means. Every year a list of new datings is published
in the journal *Vernacular Architecture*. In 1985–91, for instance, dates have
been provided for cathedrals (Angel Choir roof, Lincoln; Ely nave roof;
Salisbury crossing vault), castles (Great Hall, Leicester Castle arcade; Martin
Tower, Tower of London), prominent civic buildings (Exeter Guildhall; The
Governor's House, Newark, roof), inns (The New Inn, Oxford, jetties; Cross
Keys Inn, Leicester, roof), as well as rural buildings such as barns and
farmhouses. The date range is throughout the medieval period, and the
number of twelfth-century dates, at least from the larger buildings, is
encouraging, since so much of the evidence for the early centuries of the
period has disappeared above ground. We have already noted the increasing
contribution of archaeology in the form of timbers reused in waterfront
constructions; these often provide details of construction of buildings
formerly standing on land. Similar dendrochronological studies of standing
buildings in towns are taking place elsewhere in Europe: according to a
recent list, towns in the southern German state of Baden-Wurttemberg and in
Switzerland have produced eleven domestic buildings dating to before 1300,
and another 52 from the period 1301–1350 (Lohrum 1993).

The built environment is also partly a product of building regulations in
the town. From about 1200 the Assize of Building of London laid down
requirements for party-walls, roofing materials (i.e. tile roofs), and made
rules governing drains and disposal of sewage. Thus we can study the effect
of civic control on secular buildings, especially on wall construction (walls
3 ft thick, as required by the regulation, are commonly found on City sites
dating to after about 1200) and roof design.

In the absence of alternative evidence it has been suggested that thatch was
the main covering medium for Saxo-Norman buildings in London. Other
possibilities are shingles and boards; late Saxon shingles are occasionally
found in pits. Two different ways of roofing buildings with ceramic tiles were
evident in London during the twelfth century. One involved the use of
flanged and curved tiles together, in the same manner as Roman *tegulae* and
imbrices. The second system, introduced at around the same time, involved
the use of pegtiles with 'shoulders'. In both systems the crest of the roof was
covered by either curved tiles or specially manufactured decorated ridge tiles.
Both the flanged/curved and the shouldered pegtile systems seem to have
fallen out of use in the late twelfth and early thirteenth centuries when
standard medieval pegtiles were introduced. The civic regulations banned
reeds, rushes, straw or stubble, and required roofs to be covered with tiles,
shingles, plastered reeds or boards, and it therefore seems likely that tiled
roofs became more common during the thirteenth century.

The use of stone and brick in domestic buildings in Britain was probably
influenced both by availability (more bricks being made in the fifteenth

century) and by social approval of the material, prompted or reinforced by civic and royal practice. Stone and brick also brought a measure of stability. Buildings constructed of such durable materials or having stone foundations beneath their timber frames survived to form relative points of permanence within the more rapidly changing surroundings formed by timber buildings. Thus the main buildings of some of the larger houses were a link with former topographic arrangements.

The majority of secular constructions, however, were of timber; and certain developments in building construction in timber may be attributed to factors at work in the crowded town. Jettied buildings are recorded in London in 1246, and these appear to be the earliest certain occurrences in the country; by 1300 jettied buildings were common in the streets of many English towns. Engravings show that jettied buildings were also formerly common in towns of the upland zone and in Scotland, but the passage of time has almost totally removed them. The exploitation of the roofspace, another need arising from density of living, is shown by the development of dormer windows in the early fifteenth century and of the side-purlin roof, presumably at the same time. The technology of the timber frame allowed easy expansion of building units to handle changes in circumstances, such as more functions within the domestic complex or more occupants. As we know from standing buildings in smaller towns, by 1500 new houses had the roofspace partitioned for chambers (e.g. Paycocke's House in Coggeshall (Essex): Hewett 1969, 134–7). Overall, in at least English towns, the best use was made of town plots by increasing sophistication of carpentry rather than use of stone or brick, and archaeological study should reflect that importance.

Social environment: parts of houses and of properties

The second area for development in studying secular buildings is the extent to which the social environment of houses in the town (the influences of wealth, status, and ethnic group) conditioned the way rooms and spaces within houses were used, and how communication between those rooms and spaces was ordered. Here we can see changes in the composition of the house over time which were probably also a result of urban life.

In some towns, standing buildings survive from cellar to roof, and may be examined, but their interiors will have usually been changed, often drastically, over the centuries of their use, so that the intended functions of rooms in the medieval period is lost to us. Whole parts of the house have often been rebuilt, or chimneys, doors and stairs inserted or moved. Thus, a standing building is often rather like a very ragged manuscript which is difficult to read. There are two general ways of recording standing buildings currently in operation: the first tends to record the frame and details of carpentry (for general principles, Hewett 1969; 1980); the second analyses a building as a three-dimensional block of stratigraphy, giving context (layer) numbers to individual beams, areas of masonry, brick or plaster, doors and windows (e.g. Carver 1983). Though the first technique is appropriate for rapid survey, especially of buildings not under threat, the second method is to be preferred in rescue archaeology.

In many towns, however, the medieval buildings have long disappeared, and the archaeological strata are all that are left. Occasionally, documentary evidence can reconstruct the buildings above archaeological remains. The following paragraphs consider what parts of medieval houses are usually seen by archaeologists, and what might be inferred about use of the rooms or spaces from artefacts and other evidence found within houses.

The position of the cellar or undercroft within the property seems often to reflect a need for easy access to the street; and here the expense laid out on vaulting (and presumably other kinds of colourful decoration) may have been intended to encourage business in or off the street. One type of undercroft with its bays arranged in only a single row or aisle, lay along the street frontage, presumably beneath small shops, or occasionally down the side of a property with one end (and its entrance) by the street. This position with one end against the street had been established by some of the twelfth-century stone buildings. On prestigious properties a stone building in this position, on an undercroft of two aisles with columns down the middle (Gisors' Hall, London; Clifton House, Queen Street, King's Lynn) was presumably the hall or focus of the tenement. A third site was beneath the hall of the property, usually towards the rear of a wide tenement, but cellars in this position may have been vaulted far less often. The vaulted cellar was more usually tied to the street and, as a result, was often let separately from the buildings above and around it; a stone house in London had a cellar which was sublet before 1200, and at Chester streets of undercrofts or cellars, many of them probably separately let, formed the famous Rows during the late thirteenth and fourteenth centuries (Fig 3.14; see also the book on housing by Jane Grenville in this series).

Though some vaulted undercrofts lay below ground-level shops, and may have functioned with them, other examples were associated with the storage and distribution of wine. Cellars involved in the wine trade in London are known in the Vintry from the late twelfth century. Here archaeological evidence for buildings and use of pottery illuminate each other. The increased traffic with south-west France is also shown in the ceramic evidence of the period, for during the late thirteenth century pottery from northern France rapidly fell out of use in the city, to be replaced by wares from Saintonge and other centres in south-west France (Vince 1985, 59).

During the fifteenth century, perhaps as a result of the many economic troubles then being experienced by towns, undercrofts went out of use as places frequented by people coming in off the street. In Southampton, the thirteenth- and fourteenth-century undercrofts combined the function of shop and warehouse, but undercrofts of the fifteenth century were for basement storage only, and their architecture reflected this change (Platt and Coleman-Smith 1975, 72), as they became simpler, less embellished structures. This would appear to be the pattern for other towns, except for large public buildings such as town guild halls which occasionally had vaulted undercrofts of great splendour (e.g. the guild halls of King's Lynn, London, Norwich and York, all of the first half of the fifteenth century). We do not know why undercrofts went out of fashion as shops, and why the function was taken over by ground-floor shops. Perhaps there was less

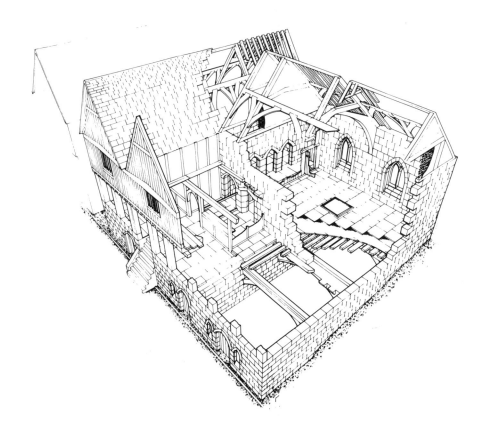

Figure 3.14   Chester Rows: cutaway drawing of undercroft with house above, 38–42 Watergate Street (Brown et al. 1987)

hoarding of goods in prestigious town-houses; and there is a notable concomitant development of the above-ground warehouse (especially for cloths) in larger centres in the fifteenth century. Cloths would suffer if stored in damp cellars, unlike the wine which needed cool temperatures. So perhaps the increase trade in draperies demanded, or at least influenced, a partial abandonment of the cellar and the increase in size of shops and warehouses at ground level.

Architectural historians of the post-medieval period sometimes assume that internal fittings of buildings are 'generally better indicators of changes in lifestyle and taste than are external features, since they were more readily adapted or added in response to variations in prosperity, social requirements or fashion' (RCHM 1987, 215). In societies like medieval towns where, on the whole, many functions took place in rooms which were not specialised structures, the fittings and furnishings take on a special significance, since it is from these that we must deduce functions and activities (Rapoport 1990 for parallels and discussion). House-fittings sometimes survive in and around excavated buildings; we can also attempt to deduce room or area functions from artefacts.

In reports from British archaeological sites there are few instances where room function can be deduced from or suggested by fittings or artefactual evidence. This must stem from medieval houses, like their Roman predecessors, being composed of spaces which could be easily adapted for different purposes; in the ancient and medieval world there was a fluid mixture of domestic and manufacturing functions within houses, but the processes rarely left structural traces. In addition, few rooms are excavated with their finds in their original places; even finds from dump layers which form floors are secondary, being broken and reused as building rubble and therefore of no use in reconstructing the function of the rooms themselves. Some suggestions have been made about room function from fittings such as hearths and ovens, as in the Norwich and Hartlepool cases already cited.

More certain advances in this subject have however been made on American sites, such as the *pueblos* or settlements of the natives of Arizona in the fourteenth century, which provide interesting parallels. Study of the Grasshopper ruin, for instance, which consists of over 500 one- and two-storey buildings, has shown that previous methods of studying such complexes from their architectural characteristics are limited – similarities in construction, such as room size, may be due as much to the availability of suitable timber as to overt styles. An alternative approach is to examine the activities which took place in the rooms by studying the artefacts in undisturbed contexts, of which there were many at this site. Even so this analysis was confined to the surviving ground floor of each building, which was often a subsidiary storage area; in fourteenth-century Arizona, as in contemporary European towns, life's main events took place on the first floor. Ciolek-Torello used the statistical technique known as factor analysis to suggest five statistically significant causes of variance, of which the first three can be readily interpreted: in decreasing order of magnitude, (i) manufacturing activities (shown, for example, by tools or waste), (ii) storage of food and other non-perishable items (e.g. jars), and (iii) food preparation and cooking facilities (Ciolek-Torrello 1984, 136–8). In other words, these were three important activities which directed or influenced the way the people of the *pueblo* erected fittings in their buildings (mealing bin, cooking hearth, storage box) or discarded artefacts or manufacturing waste (tools and raw materials). Environmental analyses such as those of pollen and animal bones (e.g. by flotation of samples from floors around hearths) would provide further information in this kind of analysis.

We are not aware of many examples of intact medieval British sites where this kind of analysis has yet been possible. More commonly, some progress could be made in making basic suggestions about plot or property use, rather than the function of individual rooms within the house. It may be found, as in the case of eleventh- to twelfth-century pits on central sites in London, that artefactual evidence (pottery, crucibles, objects of wood, leather and bone) does not indicate different functions for properties, and that whole streets or parts of them might be characterised as 'small artisan' dwellings

Period		Tenement C	Tenement B	Tenement A
X 4/2	1600 1475	BRONZESMITH stone mould for bronze casting many bronze objects	BRONZESMITH outdoor hearth	BRONZESMITH (Bell-maker) kiln for moulds
X 4/1	1475 1400	BRONZESMITH bronze lumps bone off-cuts	BRONZESMITH bowl furnace bronze objects	?
	14thC	Site frontage levelled and lowered; City wall built at rear		
X 3/3	1330 1300	BONE/BRONZE-WORKER timber-framed house crucible antler off-cuts	? bone off-cuts	BONE/BRONZE-WORKER timber-framed house well, pebble yard bronze lumps
	c. 1300	Site frontage levelled and lowered		
X 3/2	1300 1250	Residential ? timber-framed house	BONE-WORKER clay tile and window-glass	Residential pebble yard
	c. 1250	Site frontage levelled and lowered		
X 3/1	1250 1100	Residential ? timber-framed house	BONE-WORKER bone, horn and antler off-cuts	Residential ? timber-framed house
X 2	1100 *c.* 900	Residential ? timber-framed house (shown by space)	Residential large oak timbers cesspit	Residential post-holes, daub

Figure 3.15 Sidbury, Worcester: archaeological summary and interpretation of three properties excavated in 1976 (Carver 1980)

(Schofield et al. 1990). But in certain other cases, when several properties have been excavated, analysis of the finds provides some clues to differences, as at Sidbury (Worcester). Here, medieval properties, particularly away from street frontages, were relatively undisturbed because they had not been subjected to the need for basements or large buildings (Carver 1980, 155–220). The post-Roman use of the site began in the tenth century, when it is assumed that timber-framed buildings were erected at right-angles to Sidbury, the street which led to the cathedral. Three narrow properties or tenements (labelled A–C) are indicated (Fig 3.15). From structural (bowl furnace, outdoor hearth, kiln), artefactual evidence and the few available documents, it is suggested that by the twelfth century there was a bone-worker carrying out his trade on the central Tenement B; bronze-workers were active on all three properties in the fourteenth and fifteenth centuries. In 1976 Tenement A still had the first floor of its timber-framed front building, of around 1300, to be recorded. Figure 3.15 shows how these conclusions, largely based on archaeological excavation, enable us to see the three properties being subjected to pressures which changed their character as a group, first from residential accommodation to bone-working, and then to bronze-working. It would be illuminating to know if this reflected the history or needs of the nearby cathedral and its large community.

Some rooms, such as the shop, warehouse and especially the vaulted cellar or undercroft, changed their size, importance and perhaps function over time, presumably as a result of market forces which demanded different patterns of wholesale and retail trading. The chronology of the changing forms of these trade-related buildings can probably be seen as indicative of changing emphases in the organisation of both local and long-distance trade. This might be related to geographical shifts in the epicentres of trading networks, which would result in shifts in organisation and perhaps design of the buildings which served those networks (Dodgshon 1987).

One particular continuum or dimension has proved a useful method of studying the medieval house and property: trade vs. domestic uses for space. It is likely that the larger medieval house, in the town at least, was organised to reflect this dichotomy or progression (we would expect trade rooms near the street and domestic accommodation behind or above). A good number of house-plans of early seventeenth-century London have survived, and given the conservatism of both building styles and the merchants who used them, even in the capital, it is probable that some of the arrangements perceptible in 1611–12 were in place before 1500 (Figs 3.16 and 3.17). Here the ground-plan of a large house in the centre of the city, in Needlers (later Pancras) Lane, is analysed according to four general functions: commercial, domestic, storage and service rooms (kitchen and buttery). It divides neatly and significantly into these four zones or parts, with the commercial nearest the street, and a point (marked 'x' on Fig 3.17) where the visitor decided which of the three other parts to enter. This house was carefully ordered in its spaces and in the matter of access between them; the only access between the four parts at ground level was via the central space (there may have been a communication route formed by upper chambers, since there were two staircases). Presumably this planning was deliberate.

If this were an archaeological site, without the benefit of a drawn survey, the excavator might have worked out these zones. Archaeology can distinguish the trade function of buildings, and their domestic or comfort characteristics. Trade features would include evidence of there being a separate or lock-up shop; a cellar, either under the front room or elsewhere on the property; and if so, whether that cellar had a door to the street. Domestic or 'comfort' characteristics would include the number of fire-places, whether the property has a garden, and whether the buildings include rooms which may have functioned as a hall, parlour, kitchen, larder and buttery. A further measure of comfort (at least to modern eyes) is whether the privy was inside the building or outside, in the courtyard or at the end of the garden.

Figure 3.16 Plan of house in Needler's Lane (later Pancras Lane), London, in 1611; room and space functions are keyed as in Figure 3.5 (Schofield 1994)

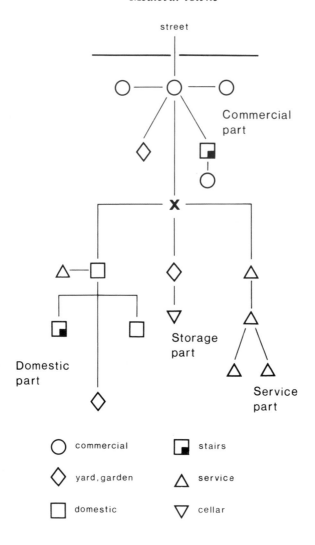

Figure 3.17 Access diagram of the plan in Fig 3.16, showing the clear division into commercial, domestic, storage and service areas. The symbols are those used in a similar analysis of this site by Derek Keene

Communication, perceptions and privacy – gender studies

Communication within properties was provided by courtyards, alleys and stairs. The origin of the internal court and the smaller alley, both of which could in time become public by custom, can be traced back to the early twelfth century and was no doubt older. In waterfront areas during the twelfth and thirteenth centuries, alleys grew in step with properties to articulate the space bordering the river (Fig 3.18). When properties were subdivided, alleys which began at the former entrance to the tenement were

Figure 3.18 A river gate and stair at Skeldergate, York (York Archaeological Trust)

formalised and extended to reach the new sub-units. In some tenements the alley went through to a second gate of the property, and thus became a common thoroughfare. Thus, over time, the private parts of major properties became more accessible to public infiltration. This led to the building of separate dwellings on the backlands of properties, and the formation of satellite communities down the alleys. Thus, the development of housing on medieval plots can be studied from another dimension, public vs. private space.

Many of the smallest properties, however, had no adjacent private space, or very little, and were forced to grow upwards. This was especially true of the many houses which formed frontages to the street, with larger and separate houses behind. Stairs and staircases were developed to articulate this growth.

Can archaeological recording tell us about notions of privacy? The value of privacy in the home was developed by the thirteenth century in London; glass windows which were broken, and had therefore lost their opacity (for early glass was cloudy), were to be reglazed. In 1293 the earl of Lincoln, having acquired the first residence of the Blackfriars in Holborn, granted a plot of ground next to his gate into Holborn on condition that the building to be erected contiguous to his own residence would have a wall 10 ft high and with no window, arch or opening in it. From similar references in the Assize of Nuisance (Chew and Kellaway 1973) for the fourteenth and fifteenth centuries, it is clear that the preservation of privacy was a concern, and it may have influenced the design of medieval houses, but comparatively few complete house-plans are so far known for the period up to 1600.

Besides privacy of the family from observation by other households, a concern with privacy of the individual within the household may be traced, though sketchily for the same general reason, in the multiplication of bedrooms and of chambers generally in the London houses of prosperous merchants from the fourteenth century (Thrupp 1948, 132–5). When the survival of wills and deeds allows us to generalise (i.e. from about 1300), there seems to have been more desire for small extra sitting-rooms (parlours) than for privacy in sleeping quarters. An inventory of a grocer's house in 1390 refers to only one bedroom for the couple and five children, two of whom were daughters. There might be a separation of sleeping accommodation between family and servants, but not otherwise. Even in the mid-fifteenth century, a wealthy mercer, his wife and seven children slept in one room, but by this time, among his social class, this may have been unusual. Before 1400 a vintner's house had four bedrooms, and other city merchants had similar amenities in the next century. It is possible that noble households were ahead of their more conservative merchant neighbours.

Material remains, such as the building itself and any associated artefacts, might display areas of the domestic unit which were used or occupied by one sex or the other. In this matter, so far, archaeological work and the related evidence of surveyed plans (which generally date to the late sixteenth century and after) are silent. Medieval women, at least in prosperous medieval London households, were often educated and given training in a trade; there were also independent women householders among all classes (Thrupp 1948, 169–74; Power 1975; for contrasting views, see now Yentsch 1991, Gilchrist 1994). The medieval woman's contribution to the home economy has been outlined for rural England (Hanawalt 1986) but not in detail for towns. It may be that medieval and Tudor town-houses were not significantly ordered, explicitly or otherwise, into male and female areas.

4 Crafts and industries

This chapter examines one of the most characteristic elements of a medieval town, its wide range of crafts and industries. Indeed, the association of towns and industry is so clearly fixed in our minds that it is important to remember that many medieval industries were rural-based, taking advantage of the availability of fuel, raw materials, water power and low land values. Medieval industries in general must have been labour-intensive, smelly, and, at a time when the bulk of urban housing was constructed of timber, a fire risk. Why were artisans allowed to operate within a town rather than, say, on the border of a Royal Forest where fuel, labour and water were at hand and there were fewer people to be offended or threatened by their activities? Among the possible reasons must be that towns, through the size of their resident population, were large consumers of goods. Furthermore, towns provided access to trade routes and merchants.

These would have been important not only in the marketing of finished goods but, for some crafts, for the purchase of raw materials. In addition, several medieval industries would have involved the investment of substantial capital and this too may have been more readily available in towns than elsewhere. The way in which artisans and their customers reacted to these conflicting forces provides one of the main interests in the archaeological study of industries, especially in those cases where the opposing pressures were evenly matched, so that a slight change in raw materials or technology might have a significant effect on the location and organisation of an industry.

From the thirteenth century onwards the majority of our information about the distribution of urban industries comes from documentary sources, mainly in the form of personal names (Reaney 1967, 176–91). Indeed, many occupations are recorded as personal names which have left no archaeological evidence whatsoever. Nevertheless, caution must be used when using this type of evidence. A 'plumer', for example, could be a dealer in plumes or feathers but might instead be a plumber.

As an example of the contrast between archaeological and documentary evidence we will look at the Wigford suburb of Lincoln where a recent survey of published and some unpublished but transcribed documentary records, dating mainly from the twelfth to the fifteenth centuries, revealed very few direct references to industry, not surprising considering that the sources were almost entirely concerned with land transactions and therefore with property owners who might not necessarily be occupiers (Vince 1993). Occasionally, the occupation of an owner, or the owner of a neighbouring property, might be recorded but, in the main, occupation has to be inferred from personal names, with all of the pitfalls that this type of evidence presents. Nevertheless, repeated occurrences of occupational personal names revealed a not unexpected pattern. The suburb of Wigford, on the southern fringe of the city and with easy access to water, was the home to workers in the leather industry (23 per cent of the 110 industrial personal names), the

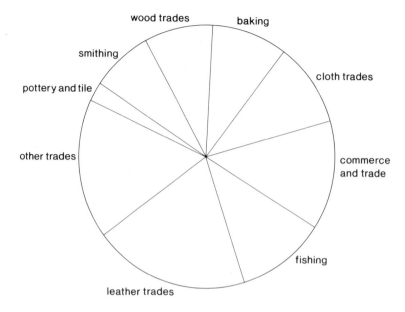

Figure 4.1 Medieval industries in the suburb of Wigford, Lincoln: the proportions of groups of trades, based on a sample of 128 references drawn from a large range of documents (Vince 1993)

wood trades (10 per cent), fishermen (13 per cent) and the cloth trades (12 per cent) (Fig 4.1).

The archaeological evidence, gleaned from about half a dozen excavations of moderate size carried out in Wigford over a period of 15 years, is less able to stand statistical examination. The leather trades are only obliquely represented in our archaeological record, through the related industry of horn-working. This is to be expected since tanners, who were the most numerous representatives of this industry recorded in the documents, would have dug their tanning pits at the rear of properties whereas archaeological investigation has concentrated on street frontages. Horn-working, however, is less noxious and the horners may well have operated in workshops incorporated into the frontage properties. Fishing is possibly represented by wicker enclosures erected on the river foreshore to confine fish. The cloth trades are again only tangentially represented, by sherds of pots which were probably used to dye yarn with madder (cf. Pritchard 1991, 168–9). Professional baking, which accounted for 11 per cent of the documentary references, was probably not represented at all archaeologically. All the excavated hearths and ovens are likely to have been for domestic use. The absence of archaeological evidence is because the bakers of Wigford were concentrated in a small area of the suburb, extending to the north of the river Witham. The sites of their ovens have almost certainly been totally destroyed by the nineteenth-century and later construction of deep cellars for department stores and banks.

Conversely, evidence for non-ferrous metalworking was present in some quantity on at least one excavation but is not represented in the documentary sources, where metalworking is perhaps indicated by what is however more likely to be the family name of 'Marshall' (which originally meant 'smith'). Pottery and tile production is represented by only three documentary references, while the archaeological evidence for this industry is extensive, consisting of a pottery kiln and tile kiln from one site and two recorded discoveries of pottery waste. Neither the archaeological nor the documentary sources for Wigford have been exhausted and it is quite likely that further work on both will show a wider measure of agreement. One thing is clear, however. The archaeological evidence will always be detailed and particular while that from documentary sources is likely to be extremely brief in particular cases, with a bias towards the wealthier sections of society, but wide in extent.

Archaeological evidence, when interpreted cautiously, can therefore both provide useful confirmation of the range of crafts and industries being practised in a town, and extend our knowledge beyond the documentary sources. In addition, it can produce a body of data on the raw materials used, the range of processes being carried out, the tools and workshops and, perhaps, the organisation of the craft which is far more detailed and with a greater chronological depth than that likely to be available in written sources.

Before we can use archaeology to study crafts and industries, however, we need to define the terms of study more closely. Both the terms 'craft' and 'industry' imply the production of goods on a large scale, more than can be used within the household. This is certainly the way that the terms are used here. However, adopting the criterion of production for sale or exchange as a distinguishing feature introduces the first of many problems encountered in the use of archaeological evidence in the study of medieval crafts and industries. Whereas in the present day one might reasonably expect to be able to distinguish amateur from professional industry through the material evidence (for example by looking for a permanent workshop, looking at the scale of production, investment in equipment and so on), this may well be an inappropriate way of looking at much medieval industry where we can expect there to have been less division between workplace and domestic accommodation, smaller scale output and less investment in equipment than in the equivalent crafts today.

To take one example, the bases of 'ovens' (i.e. hearths with evidence for a surrounding superstructure) are relatively common finds on medieval sites. Presumably the majority of these ovens were used for the domestic production of bread, pies and the like. Despite this, we know from documentary sources that professional bakers existed in towns and that their ovens were sometimes significant enough to warrant specific mention in property deeds. However, was that significance brought about by their size (in which case an archaeologist should have little difficulty in recognising one) or their number (in which case only extensive excavation would prove the previous existence of professional bakers on the site). Even more worrying is that there appears to be little direct evidence in most of these archaeological finds for the original function of the oven. What is found within them is the last remnants of their fuel, not their products. If, in the end, the only way that the function of these features can be identified is through the presence of documentary sources, then surely archaeology is either providing incidental detail to the historical record or, worse still, making no significant contribution at all to our knowledge of medieval industry? Let us therefore now examine the archaeological evidence for the production of raw materials and fuel, manufacturing processes and the organisation of urban industries with a critical eye.

Raw materials

The raw materials of some industries were used in bulk and were therefore processed close to their source. An example would be the production of charcoal, which remained, until its demise in the early twentieth century, a woodland industry (Foard 1991). At the other extreme, some raw materials were rare within Britain and had to be imported. Gold, silver, precious and some semi-precious stones, ivory and furs were certainly within this category but so were hard, fine-grained rocks suitable for hone-making. From the time when towns began to thrive and goods were routed through them, a goldsmith would have to have had easy access to a town to obtain his raw materials. In between the extremes, the decision as to whether to place an industry closer to the source of raw materials or closer to the markets would have had to be faced. Major factors would have been the bulk of the raw material, the quantities which would be used and perhaps other factors such as the decrease in bulk involved in production and the quantity and nature of any waste.

Inorganic raw materials

A wide variety of raw materials was extracted from the ground, of which building stone was perhaps the most widely used, in those areas where suitable sources occurred. Rural buildings might have been constructed using locally available materials (although it is now recognised that often they were not, Dyer 1986), but in a town the opportunities to find suitable building materials within the confines of a normal tenement were limited. Stone quarries themselves are rarely located in towns, although many sites on the outskirts of the Bail in Lincoln have evidence for quarrying in the medieval period since that part of the city lies on an economically important bed of limestone which was used extensively in the town. The most common evidence for the craft of masonry is the presence of layers of stone chippings, a by-product of the dressing of ashlar. These are most often found (or at least recognised) on the sites of major constructions such as castles and religious houses, but at Baynard's Castle, City of London, a spread of chippings is interpreted as evidence for a commercial mason's yard next to the public wharf, the east watergate, in the mid-fourteenth century (Webster and Cherry 1973, 162–3). A characteristic feature of urban excavations, however, is the robber trench, often of considerable size, dug to extract as much stone as possible from previous foundations. The reuse of building materials could also follow on from the demolition of a building, and while there must have been a continuous trade in second-hand materials, this

10mm

Figure 4.2 Baynard's Castle, London: pieces of uncut amber from a fourteenth-century waterfront deposit not far from Paternoster Row by St Paul's – where rosaries or paternosters, which used amber beads, were sold and perhaps made (Museum of London Archaeology Service)

would have produced more potential raw material at some times than others. Towns with Romano-British antecedents would have had access to large quantities of Roman building materials when first re-occupied in the late Saxon period. The White Tower in the Tower of London, for example, was built at least partially from reused Roman building material and such material appears to have been regularly used in the city down to the end of the thirteenth century. Eventually, however, this source of raw materials would have dried up, although the amalgamation of some urban parishes in the fourteenth and fifteenth centuries and the subsequent decay and demolition of parish churches would have again given opportunities to reuse large quantities of building materials, in this case not only ashlar and other stone but also floor tiles and window glass. This explanation is often put forward to explain the presence of decorated floor tiles in small quantities on secular sites of no apparent pretensions. Finally, the reuse of material from religious houses dissolved in the 1530s is starting to receive attention (Stocker 1990).

Stone was also used for smaller artefacts, either for use in the home or as personal ornament. Surprisingly perhaps, there is evidence that in some cases the raw material was transported to a town to be worked. For example, at St Alban's House, City of London, an assemblage of waste from the production of shale finger rings was found in a late eleventh- or early twelfth-century deposit (Pritchard 1991, 154–5, Fig 3.38). The raw material was not local to

London. Although it could not be reliably provenanced, the two potential sources for these London finds were Kimmeridge in Dorset or Whitby in Yorkshire, each of which implies the transport of raw materials over a considerable distance. Amber, too, must have been widely traded as raw material since debris from bead manufacture has been excavated at Trig Lane, City of London (Fig 4.2) while the potential sources are the east coast of England and, more likely, the Baltic. A third example consists of honestones, which had to be made from a hard yet fine-textured stone. From before the Norman Conquest the major source of such rock, at least in northern and eastern England, was Norway. Schist from the Eidsborg region of southern Norway was exported in a semi-finished state, to judge by deposits of large quantities of waste flakes thrown into the backfill of the city ditch at Ludgate, London, in the late thirteenth century. How much of the trade in Norwegian schist was controlled by London artisans is unknown, nor is it yet possible to chart accurately the inland distribution of these hones. Stone mortars, by contrast, were fashioned at the quarry. These vessels were used to grind herbs, spices, medicines and so on, and were an essential part of the medieval kitchen. They are found sporadically in excavations but their rarity is probably due partly to the usefulness of a broken mortar as building stone or hard core. There is no archaeological evidence for the manufacture of these vessels and they were probably finished at the quarry site, or at least nearby, since there are typological differences which correlate with the petrological identity of the stone. For example, mortars of Purbeck Marble with pierced handles are known from sites as far apart as Winchester in Hampshire and Ribe in Denmark (Dunning 1977, 326). Finally, mineral pigments were used in painting. Almost all would have had to be brought into the town, either from the surrounding countryside, as with ochres, or from farther afield, as with cinnabar.

A further common use of stone in towns was to provide lime mortar. Medieval lime kilns have been excavated in towns, as at Bedford, and it may be possible to identify the source of limestone used if the lime had been incompletely heated (Baker et al. 1979, 46–50). The Bedford kiln was situated close to Bedford Castle and it is likely that its primary function was in the production of mortar for the castle complex. Lime was also used in the tanning process and another kiln from Bedford, from St John's Street, was found just inside the defences of the southern half of the town, an ideal location for tanning being on the outskirts of the settlement and in a part of the town with easy access to running water.

Metalworking was commonly carried out in towns but it is often difficult to establish the scale of the enterprise and the actual processes being carried out (Fig 4.3). The smelting of iron from its ore is likely to have been primarily a rural activity, governed by the location of the ore sources. However, smithing too produced large quantities of slag and in towns with a substantial iron-working industry smithing slag was common enough to be used as road metalling, as at Gloucester, London and Worcester. Copper alloys were produced from copper, zinc, lead and tin, each of which would most often have arrived in towns in the form of ingots, either of a single metal or already alloyed. Ingots of lead were found in a twelfth-century pit

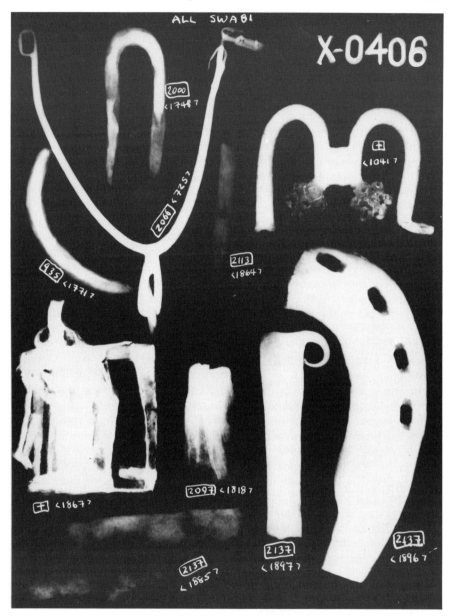

Figure 4.3 Metal objects from the waterfront excavation at Swan Lane, London, revealing their details on an X-ray photograph. Since most metal objects have corroded, the X-ray enables identification and careful conservation (Museum of London Archaeology Service)

in the City of London, perhaps destined for use in the manufacture of lead or pewter artefacts. More often, the raw materials of non-ferrous metalworking are represented by small offcuts from ingots, and moulds from the production of ingots. The latter are usually small and may represent a stage in the production of copper alloy artefacts on site, through remelting or beating, rather than the production of ingots for re-export. Chemical analysis of copper alloys shows that relative proportions of the major constituents were determined by the intended method of manufacture of the artefact so that cast, beaten and drawn items have differing compositions. Silver and gold were also worked in towns but here the raw materials have even less chance of entering the archaeological record than non-precious metals. Evidence for their use comes mainly from residues found within crucibles.

Glass-making is a rare urban industry and, indeed, a rare industry in' the British Isles until the end of the medieval period. Even simple decorated window panels could be imported from Flanders in the fourteenth and fifteenth centuries. Nevertheless, there is both archaeological and documentary evidence to show that the craft was practised. Raw materials for glass manufacture include fragments of broken vessels or windows, known as cullet, small cubes or tesserae of coloured glass, quartz sand, a source of alkali (sodium or potassium) and finally colouring, or decolourising, agents. Medieval technology did not allow for the production of blue and red glass (coloured respectively by cobalt and reduced copper) which were therefore most often imported as small tesserae or cakes for re-melting. Both documentary sources and analyses suggest that blue glass was produced by recycling Roman glass and since the latter was made with sodium rather than potassium as a source of alkali there is a difference in preservation. The blue glass often survives in much better condition.

One source of alkali was from wood ash, used not only in glass production but, more importantly, in the manufacture of soap. Wood was also required in large quantities as fuel. Suitable supplies of quartz sand, which had to be relatively free of impurities, were also needed. All of these requirements lead to the glass industry developing most often in wooded areas, often at some distance from towns. Late medieval London, for example, was usually supplied with window glass from sites in the Weald. Nevertheless, in the sixteenth century and later, urban glassworks became more common and, with the replacement of stoneware bottles by glass vessels in the mid-seventeenth century, the industry was usually associated with towns. In this case the balance between production at source and production at the market was tipped by a change in the demand for glass and, perhaps, by changes in technology.

Clays were used in a variety of ways in medieval towns. Depending on the local building traditions they could be used for walling, in the form of daub or bricks, flooring (again either fired or not), and roofing (as fired tiles). Clay was used to line pits and other features to make them waterproof and clays were also, of course, the basis of the pottery industry as well as having a role in other industries in the form of crucibles and kiln structures.

The majority of clays used in towns required no special properties and could be obtained either from clay pits on the edge of the settlement or even by quarrying within each town. All that was required was a clay in which the quantity of inclusions was not so great that the clay could not be moulded to shape or lose its cohesiveness. Petrological studies of burnt daub have consistently shown that this material could have been obtained locally although within the town there would undoubtedly have been some trade and movement of clay.

By contrast, clay for use in pottery production was definitely imported to some towns. This can be demonstrated where the characteristics of the clay can be matched with a known geological outcrop or, more negatively, where a survey of local clay sources shows that none shares the same characteristics. Examples are the use of shell-tempered clay in Lincoln in the tenth century. Similar clays were used at the village of Potterhanworth by the fourteenth century but a survey of clays in and around Lincoln leads one to conclude that the clay was imported to the town, albeit probably only from a few kilometres away (Woods 1989). Clays with a low iron content which produced off-white bodied vessels when fired could be found in association with the Coal Measures and appear to have been imported for use in urban pottery industries at a number of places, including Bristol and Nottingham, in the later medieval period (Dawson et al. 1972). Longer distance transport of raw clay can also be demonstrated in the Thames valley in the thirteenth and fourteenth centuries. Surrey Whiteware pottery was manufactured from clay quarried from the Reading Beds, which occurs as a narrow outcrop around the rim of the Thames Basin, and yet in the thirteenth and fourteenth centuries kilns producing whiteware were operating in Kingston-upon-Thames and wasters from late fourteenth-century whiteware production have been found on the south bank of the Thames at Bankside (Pearce and Vince 1988). By the fifteenth century, however, both Kingston and Bankside had ceased production and the whiteware industry in the Farnham area, a rural industry which had existed earlier, expanded production to supply a large area of the lower Thames valley. Here too, presumably, the competing forces which previously had favoured transport of raw clay to the urban market shifted in favour of rural production.

The raw materials used in brick and tile production can be studied using the same techniques as pottery. Here too there is a pattern discernible behind the detail of individual circumstances. Brick and flat roof tile were used in the medieval period mainly in the south and east of the British Isles. This may be partly because along the west coast and the south-west peninsula slates could be used instead; the latter could be cleaved to form a much thinner (and therefore lighter) roof covering without the expense of digging, preparing and firing clay. Until the later fourteenth century bricks seem to have been mainly imported from the Low Countries but roof tiles were being made and used in large quantities. An area occupied by the Beverley tile industry, at Grovehill, has recently been excavated by the Humberside Archaeological Unit and petrological analysis of the products has confirmed that they were made from local clay sources. At Bristol, however, the same Coal Measure clay was used to make ridge tiles and pottery, although the tile fabric is often much less well prepared. It seems that ridge tiles were often made by potters, using the same methods and raw materials, whereas when brick and flat roof tile manufacture started in the west of England (in the sixteenth century) new, more local, sources of clay were exploited.

Refractory clays, used to make vessels which could withstand heating in a furnace, have a more limited natural distribution than clays suitable for pottery, brick or tile production. However, several of the white-firing clays used for pottery, such as Stamford ware and Surrey Whiteware, were also suitable for use as crucibles and in these cases the crucibles, like ridge tiles, were produced by potters alongside other forms and sold to the metal-workers.

Organic raw materials

Many of the raw materials required by urban artisans would have been of organic origin. As such, they rarely survive in the archaeological record and even when they do they are difficult to provenance. Nevertheless, the increasing quantity of material recovered from anaerobic deposits, especially waterfronts, is leading to developments which offer the promise of much more detail in the near future. Prime among these materials is wood, required for house-building and other structures, furniture, machinery, as well as for smaller, portable artefacts.

Environmental archaeology shows that towns supported a wide flora, including trees and shrubs, but it is doubtful if any urban artisan could have existed using solely local material. Indeed, both archaeological finds and documentary records show that structural timber was being imported from far and wide. London Bridge, for example, was repaired using timber from the Baltic. Such imports can be recognised archaeologically either by identification of the species, if that species has a restricted distribution, or by dendrochronological analysis, which can show the likely source area of a timber (or more likely a group of timbers) by computing its similarity to tree-ring sequences of the same date from different regions. Most wood used, however, will be found to have come from species which could have grown locally in the medieval period. Much work is being undertaken by specialists in ancient timber on the range of species used, whether or not there were preferences for particular species for particular purposes and the way in which the pattern of timber use changed through time. Tall, straight oaks grown in dense forest conditions, for example, seem to have become unobtainable in England even before the Norman Conquest. Documentary sources show that tree bark was used in tanning, and that the bark was harvested from living trees rather than felled timber. Once collected, the bark was pulverised. Tanning mills which must have been employed in this process are known only from documentary sources, for example at Newbury and Okehampton (MacGregor 1991). Fragments of bark itself have, however, been found on an excavated late medieval tannery at Gallowgate, Aberdeen.

Withies and reeds were required in large quantities in towns, for use in basketry and matting, as well as being used structurally, in thatch or as a backing for plaster. To date, archaeology has demonstrated (or confirmed) that basketry and matting were used but has not provided any information about the sources of raw material or location of production. It may be that artefacts of these types were brought into town in a completed state, although obviously the raw materials were also being imported for use as walling and floor covering.

Tanners required quantities of urine for the preparation and tanning of leather but the only archaeological evidence for its use is the presence of ceramic urinals, and jugs which appear to have been used as urinals. These vessels occur on domestic sites, however, and there is no evidence to show for what purpose, if any, the urine was being collected. Dyers also used organic materials, such as woad, madder and other plants (Hall et al. 1984). The plant remains themselves can be recognised if preserved through anaerobic conditions, in addition to which, the use of madder can be recognised by the characteristic staining it produced on the inside of vessels used as dye pots. Theophilus, writing *c.* 1122, recorded that madder was heated with lye in a 'raw pot' but under his description of its use for staining ivory or antler (Hawthorne and Smith 1979, Ch. 94). By the late medieval period there is documentary evidence for the large-scale processing and distribution of organic dyes, but the presence of pollen from such plants would be the only secure archaeological means of demonstrating that dye-plants were being grown within a town. Mosses, on the other hand, have very specific habitats and those used to stuff late medieval shoes from London have been identified as woodland species (Grew and de Neergaard 1988). Given the abundant evidence for shoe-making and repairing in the Thames waterfront deposits, it is more than likely that these mosses were being imported as raw materials.

The production of cloth from the fibres of the flax plant, linen, was a widespread and regionally important industry by the medieval period (as, for example in the north-east of England, Higham 1989). This is shown not only by documentary references to the industry, but also by the presence of the element 'Lin–' in place-names (Ekwall 1960, 298–9). Flax seeds are a common component of botanical residues found in soil samples taken from urban deposits but, as with dye-plants, this is not necessarily to be taken as evidence that the flax plant was grown in towns as well as in the countryside. It could well have been imported in an unprocessed state to be retted (softened by soaking in water) leaving the required fibres. Several excavated structures have been postulated as being associated with flax retting (for example at St Aldates, Oxford; Durham 1977) but positive archaeological evidence for the location of flax-production in towns, in sharp contrast to that in the countryside, is lacking.

Animal products were another major source of raw materials for urban artisans. Bone was utilised for the production of a variety of artefacts (for example, a pair of spectacles found in a fifteenth-century dump at Trig Lane, London, Fig 4.4) and waste materials, such as the sawn extremities of longbones or shoulder blades with holes left where circular blanks have been drilled from them, are easily distinguished from normal food debris. Some artefacts, such as pins made from pig metapodials, use the whole bone, and therefore leave no manufacturing debris. It would probably never have been necessary to import bone as such to a town since the activities of butchers would generate more than enough raw material. Hides for conversion to

Figure 4.4 Fifteenth-century bone spectacles from Trig Lane, London; an important find in the history of optics (Museum of London Archaeology Service)

leather were, however, sometimes traded, although here too towns with a large population would have generated a large number of hides through butchery.

Documentary records show that pelts were imported from Scandinavia and the Baltic for the manufacture of furs but the only evidence for this trade seems to be the occasional finding of bones from the extremities of fur-bearing animals which were left on the pelt after skinning. Even here, apparently, there is the possibility that the animals were of British origin (O'Connor 1991, 259). Beaver bones may also be evidence for a trade in furs and, in this case, the species appears to have been nearing extinction in England well before the Norman Conquest (ibid., 256).

Antler, like fur, was also used in a number of industries. In the eleventh and twelfth centuries it was used principally for the production of combs. Later medieval combs seem to have been made more commonly from wood while antler, although still used, declined in importance. Herds of deer were maintained for hunting in deer parks throughout the medieval period and if the base of the antler is found it can be seen whether it was shed by the animal and therefore collected seasonally or whether it was removed from the dead beast, as a by-product of the hunt. In either case, it is clear that antlers are over-represented in urban archaeological deposits in comparison with deer bones and were therefore imported to towns as raw material for antler-workers.

Cattle horn was used for several purposes, including the manufacture of combs, lanterns and windows. Horn itself rarely survives, except in anaerobic conditions, nor is it possible to determine the origin of the cattle from which it came. Deposits of horn cores, however, are a relatively common find, at least in early post-medieval urban excavations. There has been some discussion about the significance of these deposits, in most of which the horn cores have been utilised to line pits, but it seems clear that whatever their final function these horn cores were the by-product of horn-working (Armitage 1982; Armitage 1989; Levitan 1985; Robertson 1989). Since both horners and tanners used by-products of butchery in their crafts, these two industries were often to be found together.

Wool formed the raw material for the weaving industry and because of its economic importance there is substantial documentary evidence for the organisation of the cloth manufacturing process in the medieval period, at least from the thirteenth century onwards. The manufacture of cloth involved many discrete stages recently described and discussed by Crowfoot et al. (1992, 15–25). In between each of these stages there could be a change of artisan and location. First, the shorn wool was collected from the farms where it was produced, often areas of limestone upland. Then the wool was made into yarn. The yarn was woven into cloth. The cloth was fulled, then dyed, and finally made into clothing or furnishings. Each stage of this process was sufficiently distinct to give rise to its own occupational name: spinster, weaver, webster, fuller, tucker, tailor and the like. Similarly, it is possible to recognise archaeological type-fossils for almost every stage.

The collection and transportation of wool is perhaps the least archaeologically visible of these processes, although a structure at Fountains Abbey has been identified as a storehouse on the basis of its heavily barred and shuttered windows (Coppack 1986, 53). In view of this building's later use in the fulling and finishing of cloth, it is possible that wool was being stored in it in the twelfth century when it was first built. The second stage, that of the production of yarn, is represented by carding combs and spindlewhorls. Yarn for worsteds was prepared from long-staple wool prepared using a wool comb. Such combs were used to align the fibres, thus producing a smooth yarn. Fragments of wool combs have been found on urban archaeological sites and the iron teeth from wool combs (also known as 'heckles' or 'hackles') are sometimes recognised among collections of iron nails. Yarn for woollens, however, was prepared from shorter-stapled wool by being fluffed up so that all the fibres were randomly aligned. Initially, this process was carried out using the prickly heads of teasels (also used later in the process to dress the finished cloth). By the fourteenth century, however, hand-cards were used instead. These were like large square brushes with a wooden base on to which were attached pieces of leather which had nails (later wire) inserted (Ponting 1957, 13). An early eighteenth-century example with wire bristles was excavated at Gloucester in 1974 (Goudge 1983, No.

47). The combed or carded wool was then spun into yarn. Initially, this process was carried out using a distaff or spindle of wood. Medieval examples from England rarely survive, although there are a number known from Norway, but the bone, fired clay, lead or stone spindlewhorls, used to give the spindle momentum, are common finds.

From the thirteenth century onwards there is evidence from manuscript depictions for the existence of the spinning wheel, but hand spinning clearly continued to the end of the medieval period and the latest datable spindlewhorls known were manufactured in Raeren stoneware, a type not produced until the late fifteenth century. These late spindlewhorls are rare, however, and it is clear that by that date the spinning wheel had robbed us of information on the distribution of the process. Until the eleventh century the process of weaving using the warp-weighted loom involved the use of two characteristic artefact types which survive in some numbers; loom weights and 'pin-beaters' (Pritchard 1984). After that date changes in technology meant that loom weights and 'pin beaters' were not needed. These new looms were much more massive, involved a higher investment in manufacture and maintenance and sometimes required more than one person to work them (Fig 4.5). However, almost all parts of these looms were made of wood and therefore rarely survive in archaeological deposits. The clearest evidence for their use is likely to come from the fact that quite sizable workshops were required to house the loom and that the former existence of such workshops may well be recognisable from the ground plan of medieval tenements.

The next major stage in cloth manufacture was the finishing of the cloth. Evidence of surnames in medieval documents and street names such as Walkergate in Lincoln show the former existence of fullers, or 'walkers', who removed the grease and dirt from cloth by trampling it under foot in troughs with water, soap and fullers earth. The mechanisation of the fulling process, which had started by at least the late eleventh century, led to a movement of the industry out of the towns and to the fringes of upland districts, where adequate supplies of water to run the fulling mills could be found. The fulled cloth could then be dyed, if indeed the dye had not already been applied at the yarn stage, as seems likely until the middle of the twelfth century, and the cloth then could be marketed.

Although most dyestuffs were of vegetable origin, one was obtained from an insect: the kermes shield louse, a native of the Mediterranean littoral, was used to produced a vivid scarlet colour for cloth. There is archaeological evidence for the use of this dye, and documentary evidence for its importation but, as yet, no evidence for the location of any workshops where it was used (Walton 1992, 200).

Silk weaving was practised in at least one town in the British Isles, London, and raw silk has been found on archaeological sites, albeit in small quantities (Pritchard 1984; Crowfoot et al. 1992, 82–126).

In general, where raw materials were of high value, and used in small quantities, they were imported to the towns where they were used. Where raw materials could be processed at the point of production or extraction, and especially where there would be a reduction in their bulk by doing so, this was done. However, within the medieval period there are a number of

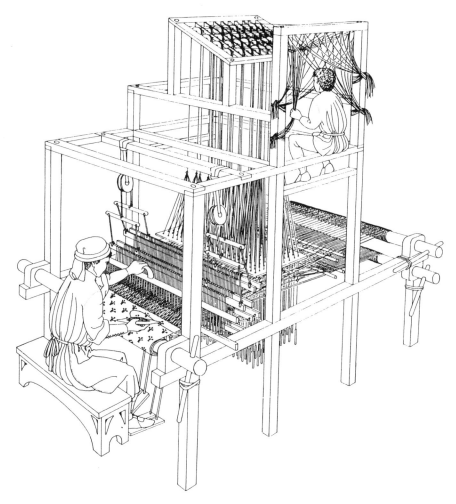

Figure 4.5 Reconstruction of a drawloom as it might have looked in the fourteenth century (Christina Unwin, in Crowfoot et al. 1992)

instances where an industry changed from being a rural industry to an urban one and vice versa. The most widely quoted example is that of fulling where documentary sources have been interpreted as showing that the industry gravitated to rural areas with good possibilities of water power following the introduction of the fulling mill. However, if the technology of the fulling mill was already known on the continent in the later eleventh century, then this can only be a partial explanation. A more complex interpretation might have to involve a consideration of the social position of fullers in urban communities, the willingness of rural landowners to invest in fulling mills, the relative claims of other artisans to the power source, the contemporary economics involved in distributing the finished cloth and the changing demand for fulled cloth. In such cases, where archaeological and documentary evidence shows that the location of an industry was not governed by strict geographical determinants, there is a middle ground in which archaeologists and historians can work, elucidating the reasons why industries were located where they were and why they moved.

Fuel

Heat was a necessary element in many medieval industries. The way in which it was used, or at least the archaeological evidence for this use, is considered below. As with raw materials, the fuel would have had to be imported to the workshop, or the workshop located where the fuel was. Here, too, there were complex factors determining which option to take. In addition, there was the added problem of fire-risk and the nuisance caused by smoke and fumes. Analysis of ashes from industrial processes can identify the nature of the fuel. In the main, domestic fires utilised a range of fuels and probably consumed much wood and organic waste. Industrial processes may, however, have required the use of special fuel. Coal, for example, can have a high sulphur content which may affect its use in metalworking, while documentary sources tell us that early post-medieval glassworks used pre-heated bundles of beech wood to fire their furnaces. Fragments of unburnt or charred coal or wood can be identified. In addition, the age and condition of the timber can be determined; in one case from Lincoln, charred woodlice were found within the ash. It is probably not possible to distinguish charcoal ash from wood ash since they derived from the same source. Straw has been identified as the fuel used in some ovens (probably bread ovens) and the range of seeds found within another sample has led to the suggestion that spoiled animal fodder was used as the fuel (Jones et al. 1991).

Peat was widely used as a fuel, to the extent that large areas of the Norfolk Broads consist of flooded medieval peat workings, and it should be possible, perhaps through identification of plant remains within the ash, to show that peat was the fuel used in a particular industry.

Analyses of ashes has also been carried out using X-ray Diffraction to see if it is possible to use the range of minerals present in the ash as a means of determining the firing temperature. This work showed that the method was promising, although more primary research is needed to establish the accuracy of the method and to refine procedures for sampling and analysis (Middleton 1984–5).

Manufacturing processes

In some industries a craftsman would carry out all the processes from preparation of the raw materials through to the sale of the finished goods, but in others varying degrees of specialisation took place. Archaeology can sometimes reveal the range of processes involved in an industry and, by study of tools and waste products, which processes were carried out at which sites. Many industries used distinctive tools, although the humble knife could be used for numerous purposes, for example, holes in medieval roof tiles and jug handles are of the same wedge-shaped cross-section and size as those of domestic knives. Where a specialised tool is used in an industry, the archaeological discovery of that tool is potentially significant. Tools are, however, rare finds. Even today there is a market for secondhand tools and tools were often recorded as bequests in medieval wills. Two classic examples of the conservative nature of medieval artisans are to be found in the bell-making and tile-making industries. A set of moulds used to produce the lettering and decorative stops on inscriptions has been identified by the impressions left on surviving medieval bells. This set was first used in London in the fourteenth century, was passed from father to son in London and finally emerged in Exeter, where it was used some 200 years later (Waters 1912).

Studies of medieval floor tiles have shown that it is quite common to see cracks in the dies used to stamp the tiles, showing that the dies were used as long as possible, but in one case the tiler has gone to the trouble of adding extra wood to two sides of a set of dies so that they could be used on tiles of a larger size (Eames 1980, i, 124–5). Naturally enough, therefore, many urban industrial sites produce no actual tools. There are, however, a number of tools which have been broken or are small enough to be lost on the floor of a workshop. Leatherworking needles, for example, have a distinctive triangular cross-section which distinguishes them from those used on cloth and would be lost quite easily. They must also have broken often during use. Crucibles too were to some extent expendable. If a crucible was thought to be cracked it would be discarded, even while still complete, since if it broke during use the value of the lost metal would be much greater than the value of the crucible. The Museum of London houses a large collection of complete Stamford ware crucibles of varying sizes, all of which are unused and complete. They were found at Old Jewry, off Cheapside, and may well have been discarded because they were thought by the metalworker to be suspect. Industries requiring other pottery and glass vessels also produced relatively large quantities of waste. Vessels used in distilling and assaying, for example, sometimes occur with other, domestic, refuse but occasionally they are found in deposits of industrial waste. To date, however, such finds have mainly been from the sites of large establishments such as castles (as at Sandal, Yorkshire) or religious houses, where they may either have been used in alchemical experiments or in the production of medicines (Moorhouse 1983).

Waste products are a common residue of urban industry. Metalworking in particular produced large quantities of waste whose study can be used to investigate the processes carried out. Slag is the most voluminous waste product, as noted above, but off-cuts and spills of metal are also found. These can be used to distinguish metal casting from the working of sheet metal. Other industries which produced off-cuts as a waste product were leatherworking and woodworking. The recyling of leather is revealed from the number of medieval shoes found with their uppers cut away for reuse. Since these are found alongside scraps and off-cuts from fresh hides, it is clear that shoemakers, at least, used a mixture of fresh and recycled materials. Studies of surviving medieval buildings too reveals evidence for the reuse of materials, in the form of beams with pegholes and mortises which could not have been functional in the beam's present position. Buried evidence for woodworking is less common, although probably originally accounted for a significant proportion of medieval urban archaeological deposits, as is indicated by excavations in Norway, where the climate has led to a greatly reduced speed of decay. There, wood chips form a significant element in most archaeological deposits and can even form the majority of the bulk of a deposit (Herteig 1991). Where woodworking debris survives it can demonstrate the use of the pole lathe, which gave rise to characteristic waste products, the spinning-top shaped cores left over from the production of wooden bowls.

Fuller's earth has been found on sites in the City of London identified as dyers' workshops. It is a naturally occurring clay, formed by the weathering of volcanic ash, which, when boiled up with wool, will remove the natural oils and greases, which bind on to the clay minerals. This material would make an ideal subject for organic chemical analysis since clay minerals have been shown to bond so tightly to organic compounds that the compounds resist the degradation which normally takes place within archaeological deposits.

Unfinished artefacts are another rich source of information about urban industries. They can reveal details of manufacture removed from the finished product, such as casting seams, and can show the stages of production. Moulds too can reveal much detail of manufacturing processes. Stone moulds, made of fine-grained limestone or mudstone, were often reused. It is not uncommon to find several generations of moulds cut into a single block. Clay moulds, on the other hand, were less highly prized and in most cases were designed to be used once and had to be broken to extract the moulded object from them. Because of their size, bells and cast metal vessels gave rise to large quantities of mould fragments. Their study cannot only reveal the type of object being cast – bell, cauldron, skillet, laver or whatever – but also, through organic chemical analysis, the nature of the wax used to make the initial model. Study of bell-mould fragments from Winchester has shown that wax from the Sperm Whale was used in the moulding process. Despite the undoubted value of industrial waste in the reconstruction of medieval urban industries, in many cases the only evidence for the industry comes from the finished products. Here, of course, one has to be wary of drawing the unwarranted conclusion that if an artefact was found in a particular town, that was where it was made. Nevertheless, if artefacts of stone or fired clay can be shown by petrology or other characterisation methods to be of local origin, then their study can at least reveal the previous existence somewhere in the locality of workshops where they were produced and of the processes carried out there.

Examples of the sort of evidence which can be revealed are the metallographic study of metal artefacts and the study of earthenware vessels. A metallographic section through an iron edge tool, for example, can show the number of metal bars used in its manufacture, their composition, their hardness and any treatment that they may have received (Wilthew 1987). Sections through copper alloy artefacts can distinguish cast from beaten or drawn metal and, again, can reveal the existence of treatment such as annealing. Study of a pot can show whether or not the potter's wheel was used in its manufacture, and whether separate pieces of clay were used, and, if so, how they were assembled. Tools such as knives, roulettes (roller-stamps) and stamps of various kinds can all be identified from their impressions on the finished product.

Workshops and industrial areas

In many cases, the evidence for craft activity comes from typical domestic refuse deposits. Is this association a true indication of the way in which these industries were carried out, as yet another activity within the domestic household? Spindlewhorls, for example, are common finds on urban sites and reflect the way in which the spinning of yarn was carried out as a domestic task by women, to the extent that being a spinster was synonymous with being an unmarried woman. In other cases, however, there must have been large-scale movement of the waste products (for example wasters from the rural kiln-site at Danbury, near Chelmsford in Essex, have been found widely in the surrounding area, including the town of Chelmsford). It is therefore important to recognise the remains of workshops to establish beyond doubt that an industry was being carried out on a site, and to establish something of its scale and organisation. In many cases, however, such evidence does not survive. By the late medieval period weaving, for example, was usually carried out in long upper chambers provided with good lighting in the form of numerous windows. These chambers can only be recognised if the buildings themselves survive. The ground plan of such a building may hint that it housed a weaver's workshop but the point may be incapable of proof.

Rope-making similarly leaves little artefactual or waste evidence but may be identified from the distinctive nature of its workshops. Rope, made from bast derived from tree bark or from hemp fibre, was important in the shipping and fishing industries and consequently most medieval ports and riverine towns would have had a rope walk. The location of these rope walks is often shown on early maps or may survive as a place-name, as in the Ropewalk in Lincoln. In northern climates the whole operation had to be carried out indoors, so as to protect the hemp from damp. In most British towns, however, the rope walk itself was an open area, which needed to be *c*. 6 m. wide and *c*. 300 m. long. From the early seventeenth century onwards the rope was spun using a large tread wheel and the finished rope, by the post-medieval period, was coated in tar which required a tarring shed to house large hearths over which copper cauldrons filled with molten tar sat. Naturally enough, these establishments were hazardous and were often located at the edge of settlements. In London, however, the Hanseatic League had a rope walk in the middle of the City, at the Steelyard (Harris 1985, 144). Clothmakers also required large open spaces to stake out their cloths so that they could dry under tension. These tenter's yards are often recorded in place-names (as in Tentercroft Street, Lincoln) but at least one has been excavated, in Bristol – a distinctive find, apparently consisting of copper alloy pins. The cloths would have been tacked on frames using tenterhooks, a type of iron staple.

Urban salt production is known from excavations at Droitwich, in historic

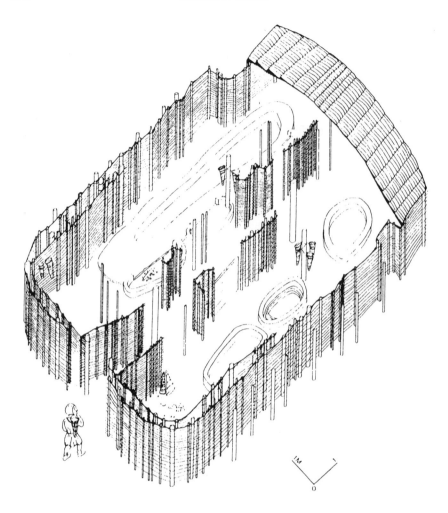

Figure 4.6   Nantwich, Cheshire: reconstruction of a twelfth-century wich house from excavation. This lowly building displayed building traditions as old as the ninth century (McNeil 1983)

Worcestershire, and Nantwich in Cheshire (McNeil 1983). Remains of twelfth- and thirteenth-century wich houses were excavated at the latter site and revealed clay- and timber-lined rectangular troughs within a wattle superstructure (Fig 4.6). This distinctive type of workshop may be expected throughout the extensive outcrop of rock salt in the north-east midlands, as indicated by the distribution of '–wich' and 'Salt–' place-names.

Most other urban crafts did not require distinctive workshops and many are therefore archaeologically invisible. We are left, therefore, studying those industries whose processes required the provision of heat, or abnormally high quantities of water or other unusual conditions. Even here, it is clear that in many cases the archaeological evidence is capable of many interpretations and it is perhaps documentary evidence which is being used to determine which industry particular structures were associated with. Hearths, of course, are common finds on medieval urban excavations but most will have had a purely domestic function. Even the proliferation of hearths in a structure need not imply an industrial function. Excavations at Bartholomew Street, Newbury, Berkshire, revealed two rooms, tentatively identified as a hall and kitchen, where a large proportion of the floor space of the room had at one time or another been used as a hearth. Vat bases would have had a similar plan to bread ovens but instead of the circular area forming a dome, it would have formed a cylindrical or slightly tapering chamber over which the copper cauldron or vat would have sat (Evans and Tomlinson 1992). A group of such structures was found at Swan Lane, City of London, where they dated to the late twelfth and early thirteenth centuries and are interpreted as having been used for dyeing cloth or yarn (Figs 4.7 and 4.8). Similar bases were still being used in Exeter in the eighteenth century (Henderson 1985, Fig 10), while a sixteenth-century example preserved at Lacock Abbey in Wiltshire was used for brewing. Clearly, a range of evidence is required before the function of such features can be positively identified from archaeological evidence alone.

Another major class of industrial feature found on medieval urban excavations is the pit or trough. There is no doubt that most holes in the ground ended up as convenient places to dump rubbish. However, they may well have had other functions, of which the most obvious is the storage or disposal of liquids. Post-medieval tanners workshops are known from several towns, for example Gloucester and Exeter (Heighway 1983; Henderson 1985). By this time tanners were using pits to contain slaked lime, used to remove the fat and hair from fresh hides. Further pits were needed to hold the hides while they were being tanned. However, unlike the lime pits these would not leave any obvious traces of their original function. Perhaps the best way to identify tanning pits is to look for groups of pits set within or just outside a structure, instead of at a distance from it, and where the pits were backfilled at the same time. Shallow rectangular troughs are often associated with metalworking and may have been used in annealing.

Dry material also required heating. Malt was produced by spreading out barley and leaving it until it started to germinate. Then the barley would have been gently heated to stop the germination process. By the early post-medieval period malting kilns were huge affairs, taking up the top storey of a building, while a hearth occupied the lower level (Stocker 1991). Malt was widely used in beer production and documentary records show that it was widely produced at a variety of levels: production in larger households for home consumption, production by brewers and production for export. To date, the physical evidence has not been recognised. One hearth or vat base looks very much like another and further evidence is needed to identify the function. Charred grain ought to identify debris from malting but few deposits of germinated barley are known, and none in association with structures which might be malting ovens.

The location of pottery and tile kilns is normally revealed by the large quantities of waste found within and around them. Kilns with a wide range of sizes and shapes were used. The earliest post-Roman pottery kilns to date are those from Cox Lane, Ipswich, which are of eighth- or ninth-century date

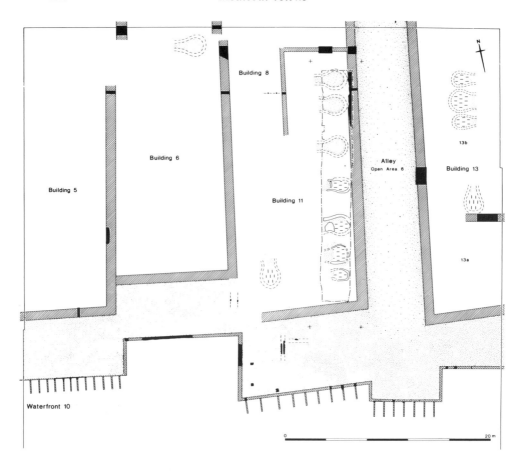

Figure 4.7 Swan Lane, London: thirteenth-century buildings and waterfront revetments. The first part of the excavation was a narrow trench in the basement of a functioning multi-storey car park, which found many hearths or vat bases; the wider watching brief found fragments of the surrounding buildings and revetments (Museum of London Archaeology Service)

(West 1963). Later tenth- and eleventh-century pottery kilns were of similar size and are mainly found in towns. Later in the eleventh century, however, pottery-making began to shift from town to countryside, although there were several major, urban potteries in the twelfth and thirteenth centuries – for example at Worcester and Doncaster. In many cases, however, the exact location of even major pottery industries is still unknown. This is the case with London-type ware which, at its height, was being traded widely across the North Sea and along the eastern seaboard of the British Isles. Some late medieval urban potteries are known, for example at St Mark's East in Lincoln (Chitwood 1988; Hooper et al. 1989), but most pottery by then was produced in the countryside, often, as in the Surrey/Hampshire border industry, in marginal scrubland (Pearce and Vince 1988). The St Mark's East kiln is typical of the latest medieval kilns, having a much larger cross-

Figure 4.8 Swan Lane, London: one of the vat bases. Such installations may have been for a number of industries, including dyeing and brewing (Museum of London Archaeology Service)

sectional area than earlier kilns and with multiple flues replacing the single or double flue/stoke hole of the earlier kilns. These multi-flue kilns were the ancestor of the post-medieval bottle kiln (so-called from its shape, not its function) which had, in addition, a covered surround or 'hovel'. Tile, by contrast, seems to have always been fired in rectangular kilns. These kilns had a raised floor, supported on arches, often themselves made of tile.

Potteries and tileries consisted of much more than the kiln itself. A workshop was needed for the potter. The potter's wheel needed to be secured on a strong pivot. Clay would need to be stored. Pots would need to be dried prior to firing and stored afterwards. Finally, fuel had to be stored. In many cases, however, these functions can only be surmised if one already knows that the site is a potter's workshop and what the range of activities carried out at a medieval pottery would have been. Tileries had similar requirements, although their storage needs were probably greater than those of potteries, while the tiles would have been produced outside on a yard surface rather than at a wheel.

Blacksmiths' workshops must have been common in every town, and in many rural settlements too. A smithy was found in excavations at Six Dials, in Saxon Southampton, situated at the junction of two streets and dating to the eighth or ninth centuries. A later example was excavated at Winchcombe, Gloucestershire (Guy 1986). The floor and surroundings of a rural smithy excavated at Burton Dassett in Warwickshire were extensively sampled by Dr G. MacDonnell to determine the distribution of hammer scale. By this means, the location of the forge itself was confirmed and details of the way in which the smithy operated could be recovered. Such methods are much more difficult to apply in urban situations, principally because it is less likely that the whole of the contemporary medieval surface would survive to be sampled.

The organisation of urban industries

Archaeological evidence may be used to establish details of the organisation of urban crafts and industries. Baking, for example, could be carried on at a domestic level, but we know from documentary sources that professional bakers were present in towns from at least the early thirteenth century. If the remains of an oven are found, how can we tell the status of its user? Only by observing a pattern, perhaps that ovens are not found on the majority of urban tenements, or that there are a range of sizes in which the largest might be those of professional bakers and the smaller ones those of private individuals. Many other crafts may have been carried out on a casual, part-time basis, especially if the equipment and raw materials were inexpensive. Thus, the simplicity of lead-casting, or the re-melting of glass, should lead to caution in the interpretation of traces of these activities within an urban tenement. Furthermore, the quantities of slag produced by iron-smelting and the large volume of mould fragments resulting from the casting of bells, cauldrons and the like, both make it difficult to be certain whether deposits containing these materials are the result of industrial activity on site. The carrying out on a site of many industries, on the other hand, can be completely invisible archaeologically. An example of this must be leather-working. Waterlogged or otherwise anaerobic sites may produce abundant evidence for leatherworking, in the form of off-cuts, but with no other evidence for the craft. If those sites had not been anaerobic, in common with the deposits on most urban excavations in the British Isles, there would have been no indication of this activity at all (Figs 4.9 and 4.10).

The presence of crafts and industries which required the use of expensive raw materials or machinery is more easy to establish, although it may prove impossible to determine which of the many industries that required the heating of large vats or ovens a particular structure may have been associated with. In these cases, too, it is reasonable to assume that the activity was carried out on a full-time, professional basis. The provision of workshops, all equipped for the same industry, can even be used to demonstrate the investment of capital in urban industries, so long as evidence can be found to show that the workshops were within a single property. Documentary sources provide many details of apprenticeship and guild structures by which entry into a craft was governed and professional standards upheld. There are instances where even this type of information can be retrieved from archaeological data, for example where the relationships between individual craftsmen can be established through a close study of their products. However, it must be admitted that, where it survives, the documentary record provides detail which is different from that found archaeologically, although the advantage of archaeology is that it can provide data where no documents exist. It is, for example, impossible to use documentary evidence to study urban crafts and industries in the eleventh or early twelfth centuries, and it is much clearer from archaeology than from documents that the mid to late twelfth century was a period of change in the organisation of a number of industries, among them potting, tile-making, dyeing and non-ferrous metalworking.

A common feature of twelfth-century and later urban industries is their nucleation. Not only do some industries occur in towns but not in the surrounding countryside, but there are distinct zones within towns. The existence of these quarters in the twelfth century can be demonstrated both by street names and by the concentration of certain types of industrial waste, such as large brass-melting crucibles and bronze-casting mould fragments from certain areas of the City of London. Sometimes this zoning will be explicable in terms of the requirements of the industry. The fringes of a town will always be attractive to those industries which require large areas for storage or preparation, for example timber yards and tanneries. The borders of rivers were especially popular as industrial zones, as demonstrated in London (Egan 1991) and Norwich (Ayers 1991). There may also be a symbiotic relationship between pairs of industries. Horners and tanners would have shared raw materials whereas the bark discarded by carpenters as waste could have been used by tanners as a raw material. Bladesmiths and scabbardmakers may similarly have found it convenient to work nearby. Collection of archaeological data on the range of industries represented on urban excavations ought to test and expand this short-list as well as elucidate more of the detail of the inter-relationships of different crafts. Were different crafts thrown together by chance and mutual needs or did they seek each other out?

Technologies and styles of manufacture

Medieval industry was not efficient. First, there was an expensive wastage of resources. Fortunately for modern archaeologists, thousands of items of

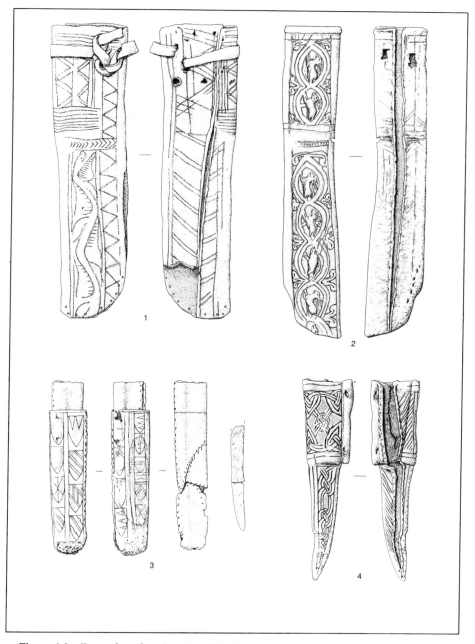

Figure 4.9 Examples of medieval scabbards from waterfront excavations in London. Some were made from a single piece of leather stitched together with flax thread. Thongs that survived were complex knots at the top (no 1). The scabbards were decorated with engraving (no 2), stamping, incising and embossing. Some have additional inner sheaths (no 3) (Cowgill et al. 1987)

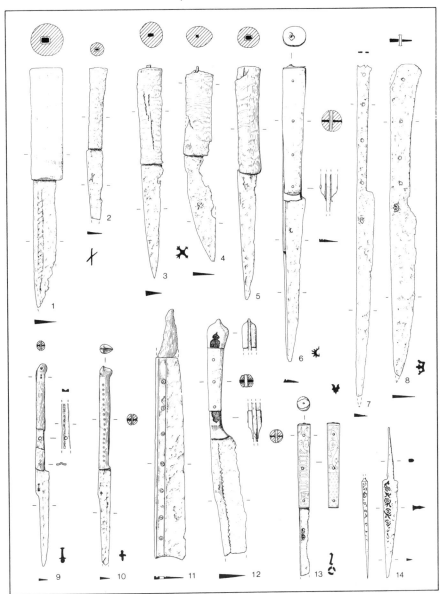

Figure 4.10 Examples of medieval knives from the excavations in London. Early twelfth-century knives represent the end of the Saxon tradition of wide blades with an angle on the back, sometimes decorated with pattern welding (no 1). Late in the twelfth century these were replaced by more triangular blades embellished by a greater range of techniques, such as scrolls of silver wire (no 14) or a single letter stamped into copper-alloy discs inserted along the blade (no 11). In the fourteenth century there is an increased diversity of forms, coinciding with the introduction of 'scale-tang' handles, in which two plates were riveted together on either side of the iron tang (no 6). Previously, handles were simply fixed on a spike (no 2). This new development allowed finer decoration. During the century also makers' marks became common (no 8). Their use reflects an increase in the organisation of the guilds which controlled the trade, but they cannot yet be identified with any London cutlers (Cowgill et al. 1987)

metal were discarded in towns with no thought of recycling or reuse, even though metals were often imported from far away in foreign countries. Secondly, some of the methods of manufacture seem labour-intensive to modern eyes. Several everyday dress accessories, for instance, were assembled from different elements, occasionally using different alloys, where there is no apparent decorative or functional advantage over using a single piece of metal. Punched decoration was occasionally added to cast fittings (Egan and Pritchard 1991, viii).

At present there are some, though not many, significant technological advances or innovations in the medieval period. In the pottery industry, which has been most studied, changes such as the use of lead glaze, the use of the wheel or of up-draught kilns were either introduced before the Conquest or were adopted from other crafts (McCarthy and Brooks 1988, 79–80). A recent study of artefacts from the extensive excavations at Winchester suggests that there were a number of technological developments in some industries, but stagnation in others. The warp-weighted loom was displaced first by the vertical two-beam loom and then by the horizontal loom. Wire-drawing and the associated craft of pin-making emerged during the thirteenth century (on the detection and definition of the medieval pin-making industry, see Caple 1991). Candles with wicks of cotton in place of flax replaced the open oil lamp; milling by the hand quern was replaced by machine milling, possibly following the introduction of the windmill in the late twelfth century. On the other hand, there was only limited change in the metalworking trades (Biddle 1990, 70).

When a large number of artefacts are recovered, developments of style and workmanship can be traced over long periods. Study of nearly 1500 medieval shoes from waterfront excavations in London has produced not only a summary of the main types in the period 1150–1450, but details of technical progress inside the manufacturing process (which in this case seems, from the abundance of shoemaking waste on many sites, to be local). In the twelfth century, rands – wedge-shaped strips of leather inserted between the upper and the sole – were introduced, perhaps to make the seams more waterproof. In the thirteenth century calfskin became the standard type of hide used in shoes, which were mass-produced in two pieces (the upper and the sole). Soles, in two pieces themselves, particularly on the long late fourteenth-century shoes called poulaines, would have made repair easier. In the middle of the fifteenth century the method of construction was changed, with the addition of heel stiffeners and an outer sole, in thicker leather, as a further component (Grew and de Neergaard 1988).

There is nothing yet to suggest strongly that these innovations occurred first in towns, though the sheer pressures of needs and availability of materials would make it seem likely.

Conclusion

In this chapter we have examined the archaeological evidence for medieval urban crafts. This evidence has been looked at sceptically since it seems to us that there is a temptation to latch on to certain interpretations and to make many assumptions which the evidence alone would not uphold. This is not to say that urban archaeology cannot answer questions about medieval urban industries, or that it can only be used as an adjunct to documentary research. Rather, we would argue for a critical approach to the evidence and for the more extensive and problem-orientated use of scientific analyses.

A large difference between medieval rural industries and those in towns derives from the increased pressure for space in the urban environment. There was a more rapid change of land-use in the town and more effort was taken to dispose of waste. There was also more opportunity to use waste products for other purposes. Medieval slag heaps may survive within the Weald or the Forest of Dean, while their urban equivalents have long since been flattened and their contents dispersed.

In addition to this methodological problem, we have also emphasised the geographical determinism which can lead to trite statements about medieval industries. The decision to locate an industry at the market rather than at the source of the raw materials seems to have been geographically determined in a minority of cases. In the majority, we see the medieval artisan balancing a number of economic, and probably social, forces. The later medieval history of urban industries is full of examples of town authorities trying to revive or foster crafts against the trend of social and economic forces. Changes in technology, population dynamics, the supply of capital and changes in demand all affected the final outcome. We see the study of this process as being one of the most fruitful areas of medieval archaeological research in this field. The other is undoubtedly the level of detail about industrial processes which can be extracted from a broad-based study of an industry.

5 Trade and commerce

Archaeology can be used to study trade and commerce through the characterisation of artefacts and the analysis of their distributions, and through study of the infrastructure required to facilitate trade and commerce, such as specific structures erected for the use of traders and, most notably, through the provision of coinage. The great challenge, however, is to produce a critical apparatus which will allow us to compare one town with another, to distinguish local, regional, national and international exchange networks and perhaps, finally, to use that data to address the question of the link between trade and the fortunes of towns.

Coins

Since at least the tenth century, towns were legally linked with both mints and trade: in 979, 53 English towns minted their own coins (Hill 1981, 131–2). Moneyers could only work in towns and traders were forbidden from trading except in a town. How far these tenth-century laws were obeyed is impossible to say. Certainly the trading laws were later relaxed and would, in any case, have been impossible to enforce. Moneyers, however, seem to have heeded the law. Since all coins from the late tenth century to the mid-twelfth century bore the name of the mint and the moneyer, this is not surprising. Moreover, the need for coin was much more closely linked with towns than was the mere exchange of goods. Foreigners were expected to exchange their coins for the local currency. This would allow control over the purity of the coinage as well as providing a source of income to the king, since every exchange benefited both the moneyer and the Crown. Coins were also required because of the lessening of social ties within the larger and more mobile urban communities. When buyer and seller are known to each other, and are neighbours often of long standing, then there may have been no need for immediate payment and, indeed, credit would be a favour to be returned in the future. When transacting with a stranger, however, payment for the goods and even witnesses to transactions are required. These simple requirements probably underlay much of the use of coins in medieval towns.

Coins did have other uses, however. All taxpayers would have needed to have access to coins, no matter how remote their farm or how well they knew their neighbours. Furthermore, the provision of services and goods in return for land seems to have been commuted to a money transaction over much of England by the thirteenth century and it is probable that much of this transaction was carried out using coins.

We should therefore expect to find that coins were used more frequently in the larger towns than in the smaller ones and more frequently in the smaller towns than in their rural hinterlands. Nevertheless, finding evidence to support even this simple proposition is not easy. Coin recovery on an excavation depends on rubbish disposal; rural rubbish was spread on the fields whereas urban rubbish was more often buried in rubbish pits on the site in the eleventh to thirteenth centuries but disposed of communally later on. Coin loss would also have been related to the number of transactions that took place; presumably more took place in towns than villages, because of the higher degree of activity. Medieval villagers may well have had coins but, if they only used them at markets or for paying tax, there would be fewer opportunities for coins to be lost. A Wiltshire barber in the fourteenth century was helping to bury one of the sarsen stones at Avebury when it toppled over, crushing him to death. When his body was uncovered it was found that he had been carrying coins in his purse but whether this was because he was going to spend them that day, or whether he felt it was safer to carry his money with him, or whether he had just been paid is, of course, unknown. Despite these difficulties, it is important to continue to collect data on coin loss from different classes of settlement and, in some way, to establish the frequency of coin loss. This may be relatedly to the quantity of earth excavated or to the area of the excavation, or as a ratio to other finds. It is also important to use metal detectors (on authorised excavations) or sieves to recover coins in order to establish the recovery rate.

Coins themselves were adapted for a range of transactions, most notably for smaller sums. The use of metal detectors on sites in the City of London has shown that from the eleventh century onwards coins were often cut in half or quarter to form small change (Fig 5.1). Naturally enough these small fragments are difficult to spot by eye and were not often incorporated into hoards. The extent to which they were used may therefore have been underestimated, and we are ignorant as to whether or not the use of small change of this sort is more common in towns than in the countryside. At present the evidence would suggest that this is the case, but so few sites have been systematically screened that this is by no means conclusive. Until the reign of Edward I no denominations smaller than one penny were minted, but from that time on both halfpennies and farthings were produced, perhaps as a response to the use of cut halfpennies and farthings. It may be significant that these coins were apparently not produced at all of Edward's mints and, to judge by modern dealers' prices, provincial pieces were much more scarce than those produced in the London mint. This might of course be merely a matter of fiscal policy, but it is as likely to reflect a greater need for small change in the capital. Edward I also produced a higher-value coin, the groat, which was worth four pence. However, surviving pieces had been mounted and gilded at some time in their histories, suggesting that they were not a commercial success. Certainly, no further groats were produced until the fourth coinage of Edward III, in 1351. From then on, both groats and half-groats were minted in quantity. In addition, a gold coinage was introduced. Although at times during the fifteenth century the supply of gold faltered, this pattern of minting continued to the end of the century when the Renaissance-style profile coinage of Henry VII introduced the testoon, worth one shilling. Only a very small number of coin lists have been published from later medieval towns or from rural settlements. Nevertheless, the potential interest of such data is now belatedly being recognised.

Figure 5.1 Two pennies, a halfpenny (one side folded over) and a quarter-penny or farthing, from the excavation at Billingsgate, London, 1982 (Museum of Archaeology Service)

There are approximately 112 medieval towns in England and Wales which at one time or another had a mint. The significance of having a mint seems to have varied. In the tenth and eleventh centuries royal policy was to distribute the minting of coin at towns throughout the kingdom. Some of the late Saxon mints operated on a large scale, with up to a dozen moneyers known to be working at a time. Most late Saxon mints, however, seem to have been operated by a single moneyer and, in the case of some mints in Wessex, one moneyer seems to have been able to serve more than one town. While it is possible that there were strategic reasons for the existence of certain mints, it is likely that a large element of the business carried out by these moneyers was connected with local trade and the availability of ready cash for recoining. Many of these late Saxon mints were situated in places which seem to have had small populations and, even before the Norman Conquest, there were places which were losing their mints.

One reason for having a local mint was the policy of recalling all the coins in circulation at regular intervals and replacing them with coins bearing the current design. This policy continued under the early Norman kings but finally collapsed during the anarchy of Stephen's reign in the middle of the twelfth century. Distinct coin types which could be easily checked were replaced in Henry II's reign by first the Tealby and then the short-cross coinages. Short-cross pennies issued by Henry II are similar in appearance to those issued by John and to those of Henry III. Once in circulation it would have been very difficult to recall these coins and it does seem that late twelfth-century pennies were still legal tender and in circulation when this coinage was finally demonetized in 1247. There are therefore good reasons why it might have been advantageous for some of the smaller mints to be closed down and, by the late thirteenth century, when Edward I introduced his new 'sterling' coinage, not only the small market town mints had been closed but many of the large regional mints as well. Exeter, Chester and Lincoln had been important mints since the tenth century and all were closed during the reign of Edward I. For the rest of the medieval period the kingdom was supplied with coin from a handful of mints, principally those at London, York, Durham and Canterbury, which were supplemented at times of major reissuing of coins by temporary mints such as those at Bristol, Norwich, Coventry and Southwark.

Tokens and jettons

Tokens and jettons made of non-precious metals (tin, lead alloy and copper alloys) were also used in trading. That lead alloy tokens were used in the medieval period in London and other large medieval towns (such as Paris) has been known since the middle of the nineeenth century. Their study was quickly obscured by the presence of fake pieces, termed Billy and Charlies after two of their most notorious producers, which were inspired by these early finds. The use of tokens as unofficial currency was suggested by the character of their designs, many of which have simple symbols on one or both faces. These symbols were taken, by analogy with seventeenth-century trade tokens, to represent the alehouse where they could be redeemed (Fig 5.2). The study of these tokens revived in recent years following an exponential increase in the number of finds, both from controlled excavations and from the metal detection of spoil from waterfront sites in several large ports, notably London and Dublin. The concentration of finds of tokens at large international ports may or may not be significant. No such pieces were recovered from Colin Platt's excavations in the thriving medieval port of Southampton (Dolley 1975), but excavations at Montgomery Castle on the Welsh border did produce a couple of pieces (Knight 1983). Here, too, much more information is needed about the type of sites where these pieces were used and about their relative frequencies before one can determine the way in which they were used. For example, the presence of tokens on a castle site might suggest that they were used in gaming or gambling rather than for exchange.

The function of jettons is, by contrast, well understood. These copper alloy

Figure 5.2 Late thirteenth-century tokens from Billingsgate, 1982: they were probably used as fractions of pence, prior to the issue of official halfpence and farthings (Museum of London Archaeology Service)

counters were used with the reckoning board (properly called a *counter*) as a means of accounting. Each jetton placed in a particular column on the board represented a corresponding sum of money, and additions and subtractions could easily be followed, even by the illiterate.

Production of these jettons seems to have been limited to a small number of centres. The earliest pieces found in the British Isles can be dated to the early fourteenth century since they were sometimes struck with the same dies used to make official silver coins. There is no indication, however, that these jettons were ever intended to be used for exchange. Some, indeed, had a hole punched through the centre to make it quite clear that they were not coins. Later in the fourteenth century supply in England was supplemented and later probably surpassed by supply from France and the Low Countries. There too the influence of official coinage on designs can be seen. In the late fifteenth century German manufacturers took over the supply and by the middle of the sixteenth century the market seems to have been dominated by makers in Nürnberg.

Jettons are widely distributed on medieval sites, both rural and urban. Strangely enough, considering that they would have been used in sets, they seem to occur in small numbers as a part of general refuse deposits. There are no known instances where a complete set was discarded or lost. One would postulate that the use of the reckoning board would be limited to the middle and upper classes since the majority of the population had no need for accounting. However, there is no overwhelming concentration of jettons on middle or high status settlements (although they are common on castles and monastic sites), nor on particularly wealthy or commercial tenements in towns. Again, it is probably only the collection of quantified data from a variety of types of site which will enable patterns to be seen.

Guilds

The trader's tools were cash, credit and weights and measures, along with standards of calculation exemplified by the jettons. The trader's workshop, his centre of distribution, was the town. Although every medieval town retained a strong agricultural element, its atmosphere of liberty came primarily from the privilege to make things and sell them. The organisation which upheld and often jealously guarded these privileges was the gild merchant or guild (Salzman 1964, 71–82). The first evidence that survives for the urban guild dates to the late Saxon period and it is suggested that its original function was to be a substitute for the social life which a man lost when he moved from a village to a town. The guild, therefore, was an institution which would organise feasts, and take part in religious festivals and other public events. These, however, were perhaps only the most obvious trappings of the guild. They also looked after a member throughout his life. They would take responsibility for the widow and children of a dead member. They would organise his funeral and might arrange for mass to be said for his soul and that of his family. It is for this reason that guilds have been termed 'artifical kin'.

From the twelfth century onwards we read of specialised guilds whose members were involved in a particular trade or occupation. This coincides with the first archaeological evidence from London for the concentration of industries in particular quarters of the town, although it seems that Winchester, and doubtless other towns too, had already reached this stage in their development before the Norman Conquest (Biddle and Keene 1976, 335–6). Guilds could also be specialised in terms of their religious activities, perhaps existing primarily to honour a particular saint. In short, by the end of the medieval period guilds existed for a plethora of reasons and covered functions which today might be catered for by clubs and societies (such as the Rotarians or Freemasons), unions, friendly societies, chambers of commerce and others. A man might belong to more than one guild, although trade guilds were keen to preserve their influence by restricting their membership and took strong action to ward off other trade guilds which they percieved as encroaching on their rights and privileges.

The archaeological evidence for guilds consists almost entirely of the physical remains of guild halls. In plan and function there is little to distinguish the hall of a guild from the hall of a magnate (e.g. for London: Schofield 1984; 1990). In both, the prime use of the hall and its ancillary buildings was to house large groups of people for feasts and other public events. A hall complex would often contain the main hall, a chapel, a kitchen, stables and a yard, as well as smaller rooms for storage, garderobes and perhaps some private quarters for a porter, bailiff or other official in charge of the safety and upkeep of the building. Other halls were on the first floor of prominent buildings (e.g. the Peacock Inn at Chesterfield). Artefactual evidence tends, on limited excavated evidence, to be unhelpful. The

Tanners' Hall at Gloucester has been excavated but its original ground floor had been almost entirely cut away by seventeenth-century tanning pits (Heighway 1983). St Mary's Guildhall in Lincoln may be an example of a complex taken over by a guild after construction in the mid-twelfth century as the urban residence of King Henry II. So far as one can see, this change of function did not entail any obvious structural alterations to the building (Stocker 1991). Artefacts from the building included a large but unexceptional assemblage of early to mid-fourteenth-century pottery from a pit in the courtyard, fragments of fourteenth-century painted window glass from a tracery window in what is interpreted as a chapel, a near complete Valencian lustreware bowl, found walled into an alcove with a complete ceramic money box, and two boat-shaped, stamped iron ingots. These finds indicate occupation by people of moderately high status and wealth but without the documentary evidence would happily have been accepted as the refuse of an individual wealthy citizen rather than a guild. One might have expected that animal bone assemblages would be more useful in identifying sites where elaborate feasts attended by the middle and upper classes of medieval urban society were held. However, in this case at least, there was nothing exceptional in the medieval levels. Another Lincoln guild met first in a building which was given to the Franciscans in the mid-thirteenth century to form part of the site of their friary. They later met in a chamber above one of the main gates into the city. This chamber, totally rebuilt in the early sixteenth century, is still used for meetings of Lincoln City Council.

Churches and commerce

Documentary sources make it clear that the church, too, was often closely associated with trade and commerce (see above, Chapter 2, pp. 51, 56). These links could be of many sorts. For example, there are records of people who, while continuing to work as merchants or traders, had dedicated their lives to God and a particular monastic order. A church could also, through its patron saints, both sponsor and protect trade through international fairs. The major international fairs of twelfth- and thirteenth-century England were, without exception, under the protection of a saint. At Lincoln, for example, it was St Hugh who protected the fair held on the outskirts of the Butwerk suburb on a site which today is a public park, the Arboretum. Naturally enough, the fair would have coincided with a religious festival on the saint's day, but the primary function of the fair was to facilitate trade.

In many towns churches also provided the only stone buildings which could be used as treasuries and strong rooms by wealthy travellers, most of whom would have been merchants. Not only would money and other valuables lodged with the church have been physically protected but, as with the fairs, the patron saint of the church and the sanctity of the church as a whole would have protected the goods against theft. A large number of late Saxon and early Norman hoards have been found in churchyards. Partly, presumably, this is because access to the churchyard was not restricted and disturbed ground would have been a common sight, but there is also the possibility that those people concealing their goods in a churchyard also knew that robbers would be less likely to risk eternal damnation by stealing from consecrated ground.

Shops

The erection of a permanent building for the primary purpose of retail trade is likely to have been common in the larger towns by the twelfth century (e.g. in London: Keene 1990a). Such structures are rarely mentioned in the type of documentary records available, and until this time timber was almost universally used as the main building material, so it is doubtful if the origin of the medieval shop can be proved to predate this period; although, when evidence is found for craft activity on properties fronting the cardinal streets of a town, there is a strong likelihood that the goods manufactured on that site were also being sold from it. If so, then there were probably shops in tenth-century Gloucester and Lincoln. We should, however, be wary about the term 'shop' (*schopa*, a term used from at least 1080); it also meant *workshop* throughout the medieval period, since many artisans made and sold their wares in the same place. When a London document of 1422 refers to 'my lane with 20 shops in it', it is not an early shopping mall, but an industrial alley.

The Norman House at the junction of Steep Hill and Christ's Hospital Terrace in Lincoln is a good example of a building in which shops of some kind were an integral and original part of the design (for its setting immediately outside the South Bail Gate, see Fig 5.3). The house is known through thirteenth-century and later documents as the urban seat of a succession of minor country gentry, one of whom achieved some notoriety by being murdered by his wife's kin (Johnson and Vince 1992). It was originally occupied and probably built by one of Lincoln's Jewish community, Moseus of York, from architectural evidence in the third quarter of the twelfth century. It contains an undercroft, a row of shops on the ground floor and a first-floor hall; originally it was part of a larger complex of buildings. The shops had no original access to the rest of the complex and must therefore have been designed to be let out to shopkeepers.

Shops in the modern sense would have been a common feature of the larger towns from the beginning of the medieval period onwards and by the end of the period would have been found in small towns. If a room fronts on to a main street, has no evidence for access to other rooms behind the frontage and has no evidence for a hearth used for cooking, it is likely to have been a shop. Variants to this general scheme exist; it was also possible for a shopkeeper to rent a storeroom or workshop on the street frontage where there was a connecting door, the lock of which was only usable from the owner's side. Furthermore, the sale of cooked foods would have required the existence of hearths and ovens within the shop. In towns where medieval buildings survive, traces of fittings and partitions which indicate shops are often recorded, sometimes during refurbishment to meet the shopping needs of the present century. Documentary and plan evidence tells of a variety of

Figure 5.3 The South Bail Gate of Lincoln, *c.* 1200, showing the medieval position of the Norman House immediately outside the gate (D.R. Vale, Lincoln Archaeological Unit).

shop forms by the opening of the seventeenth century (Fig 5.4); many were simply the front room of a domestic building, that is the living-place of the shopkeeper.

Traders and merchants

We can define a trader widely, as anyone who earned a living by the exchange of goods or services, or we can be more restrictive. Documentary sources make it clear that there was much blurring of roles, and yet there was a wide difference between, say, Aaron the Rich, the late medieval Jewish merchant/financier from Lincoln, and the general run of tinkers and hawkers who are rarely recorded by name but whose activities are reflected in the distribution of mundane, mass-produced goods (such as pottery or copper alloy dress-fittings) often over large distances.

Identifying merchant communities as discrete entities in medieval towns is extremely difficult using archaeological evidence. The houses of native rich merchants were largely indistinguishable from those of nobles or prominent churchmen, and they did not usually congregate together, but lay dispersed through the town behind facades of smaller buildings (see Chapter 3, above). However, documentary sources, place-names (especially names of streets) and church dedications sometimes do preserve evidence for the existence of foreign communities in a medieval town. These quarters could occur through

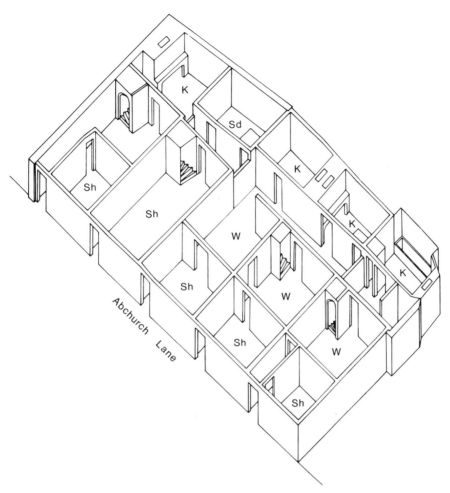

Figure 5.4 A variety of forms of shop *c.* 1600, in Abchurch Lane, London; from the Treswell surveys (Schofield 1987). This block may have been built about 1390. For key, see Fig 3.

the natural tendency of immigrant groups to stick together, especially, as with the Jews, when they were under constant threat of persecution. In other cases, as in London, legislation was passed restricting the areas where members of these groups could live. In yet further instances it was the occupation of the immigrants which caused them to cluster in certain areas. Flemish weavers, for example, lived in a suburb on the south-east side of Beverley.

Urban archaeologists have discussed the practicalities of identifying the domestic quarters of immigrant groups, and especially merchants, through their retention of a distinct material culture. It may be that details of diet and dress will prove to be the most sensitive indicators. Figs, dates and grape pips (which could either be from locally grown grapes or imported sultanas) are regularly found preserved in medieval cesspits, but there is no indication yet that they were eaten more often by one section of the community rather than another (see further discussion in Chapter 7 below). Further indications of mercantile traffic, if not of merchants' homes, are specialised market buildings called cloth halls, found in several medieval towns such as Norwich, where the surviving fifteenth-century Dragon Hall in King Street dates from 1436. It stands next to the River Wensum and has an arcade facing the river, for ease of transport (Fig 5.5).

Foreign traders of lower status and wealth may not have been able to indulge any desires for exotic food or clothing, nor may they have wanted to draw attention to their differences from the native English. However, one aspect of medieval culture which does seem to be related to ethnic group is the use of pottery vessels. In Wales and Ireland, for example, use of pottery is seen as an Anglo-Norman trait and is thought to be more common on the sites of the planted English towns, castles and monasteries than on contemporary native settlements; even those where other aspects of Anglo-Norman culture, such as the construction of castles from stone and mortar, were adopted. Use of coins was also perhaps a specifically Anglo-Norman practice in Wales in the thirteenth century (Knight 1983). Cooking vessels may be particularly sensitive indicators of cultural differences since, even if the same ingredients were used by native and immigrant groups, differences in preparation may be reflected in the type of vessels found. Small cooking pots with handles, termed pipkins (if they would sit on a surface), or ladles (if they would not), are a case in point. The earliest vessels of this type found in towns in the British Isles are imported ladles from the Rhineland (Blue-Grey or Paffrath ware), found in the later eleventh and twelfth centuries. By the later twelfth century pipkins were being produced in London, perhaps because the type of cooking with which they were associated had been adopted by the English. It is also possible to explain the distribution of eleventh and twelfth-century Blue-Grey ware ladles in terms of access to a cross-channel port rather than the presence of Rhinelanders; with one exception, a deposit found at Dowgate in London, a site known from the twelfth century as the location of the Steelyard, the headquarters of the Hanse in England (Dunning 1959). A high proportion of the pottery from this deposit was of Rhenish origin, not just the ladles. A detailed study of this assemblage by John Cotter showed that a high proportion of the vessels bore signs of use; the ladles were sooted from use over a fire, while the frilled bases of beakers and pitchers of Pingsdorf ware showed signs of chipping where they had been used at table. Here perhaps we have the tableware of the German merchants, who (at least in later decades) lived a withdrawn life, guarding their morals and trading secrets behind a high wall which enclosed living quarters, a dye-house, wine cellar, and gardens (Fig 5.6). The main hall of the Steelyard, now beneath Cannon Street railway station, has recently been sampled during redevelopment.

Relatively high quantities of imported pottery are also found in some thirteenth- and fourteenth-century pits and cellars in Southampton, and in one case the identity of the owner is known. Without this documentary evidence one might have postulated that the owner was French. However, unlike the case of the Dowgate pottery, the forms and presumed functions of

Figure 5.5 Interior of the Dragon Hall, King Street, Norwich, built 1436 (Norfolk Archaeological Unit)

Figure 5.6 The Hanse Steelyard on the London waterfront, as recorded by Hollar in 1647. The London Steelyard resembled its colleague at King's Lynn, and they both lack any overtly foreign features

the Southampton pottery were no different from those of locally made wares although the pottery was of better quality. High-quality imports could enhance the status of their owner whether he or she was English or foreign. In sum, therefore, we can identify broad trends, such as the foreign culture of the thirteenth- and fourteenth-century burgesses of Wales and Ireland, but would find it difficult to identify the presence of small numbers of foreigners within English towns through archaeological means alone.

Two examples of trading networks: building-stone and pottery

By recording and excavation in a number of towns, the archaeologist can chart the distribution of types of artefact. Each type must have travelled from its point of origin or manufacture along a land or water route; and a map of those final resting-places will therefore indicate a trading zone or network over which a trader operated, or over which a particular artefact was exchanged and found its way. In the cases of artefacts in metal or leather, we may have to chart only their style of manufacture or decoration, since the object will carry little evidence of a particular place of origin in its material. But with building-stone and pottery, geological analysis of the material can pin down the point of production.

From numerous building accounts we know that prestigious, often royal, projects such as castles, palaces, cathedrals and abbeys ordered British and foreign stone from a remarkable number of places. This would have stimulated land and water transport, when transport often account for up to two-thirds of the cost of the stone (Pounds 1990). Study of the use of building stones in Canterbury has further claimed that because of changing political and economic conditions, and because some quarries either dried up or their access was cut off (by war or silting), different types of stone were used in buildings at different times; the only exception being that Caen stone from Normandy was always available (Tatton-Brown 1990). This suggestion is based on observation of standing and ruinous medieval buildings, and on the rich documentary evidence for building dates in Canterbury. Thus, apart from the reuse of Roman material and local flint and other stones, the buildings of Canterbury in the late eleventh and early twelfth century used newly imported cut stone from Caen in Normandy, Quarr from the Isle of Wight and from Marquise near Boulogne; the Norman cathedral at Winchester was also built of Quarr stone. Though the largescale building programmes continued almost without stoppage from the mid-twelfth century there is no Quarr or Marquise in evidence, but much 'marble' shafting using Purbeck from Dorset and an onyx marble which may come from North Africa or even the Middle East. In the thirteenth century, the Surrey quarries of Reigate and Merstham were much used for work in London, and these stones appear in quantity in Canterbury buildings; Kentish ragstone, from round Maidstone, appears later. Thus, regional and foreign trade and transport systems were energised by the needs of major building programmes.

The variety of building-stones in a town shows the pulling-power of its money or influence. By contrast, distribution maps of individual pottery wares show how commodities were traded to and through towns. Our examples are some of the most important English wares which served medieval London. From the late twelfth to the early fourteenth century, a whole range of pottery items – not only jugs, cooking pots and dishes but aquamaniles, watering-pots, lamps and roof finials – were produced at an unknown site near the City of London (Pearce et al. 1985). Perhaps because many of the jugs sported contemporary (and fashionable) French decoration, this 'London-type' ware is found in the late twelfth century at east-coast ports and along the Scottish coast at Perth, Aberdeen and Inverness; and further to Bergen and Trondheim in Norway. In the Scottish and Norwegian cases, the lack of a contemporary native production of pottery probably emphasised its novelty. London-type ware also reached Hereford, Gloucester and Exeter, and the area of distribution in south-east England shows the trading network of London in the thirteenth century. Presumably these pots from London are only the surviving traces of a range of commodities, including textiles or wine, which came via the capital; and perhaps they were traded because of their French-style decoration, in some cases so good that archaeologists have difficulty telling apart genuine French jugs from London imitations (ibid., 6).

From about 1250 pottery industries producing whitewares began in Surrey. Three main industries can be distinguished: Kingston-type ware, made along the south bank of the Thames from Kingston (nearly 30 miles upstream) to Southwark, from the late thirteenth century to the end of the fourteenth; Cheam, from the mid-fourteenth to possibly the early sixteenth; and a 'Coarse Border' industry in north-east Hampshire and west Surrey, in existence by 1250, but starting to supply London in quantity about 1350. At this time it grew to become the largest pottery source in south-east England, and so it continued until the early 1500s (Pearce and Vince 1988).

The pattern of findspots of Kingston-type ware (Fig 5.7) suggests that in the period 1275–1325 the main market was London itself; and the pattern for Cheam ware which followed it was largely the same. These two industries concentrated mostly on tablewares, whereas the Coarse Border pots were largely to do with cooking and storage. Their distribution (Fig 5.8) shows that they were marketed over a much larger area, through Berkshire and Hampshire to Winchester. One suggestion might be that the more refined, thinner-walled Kingston-type and Cheam wares were a sign of metropolitan fashion, whereas the stouter Coarse Border wares, used in the kitchen and buttery rather than at table or for show, were common to a large part of the surrounding countryside.

The quantity and range of foreign imports into towns distinguishes their peculiar trading contacts. The frequency of northern French pottery, for instance, is much greater in medieval Southampton than in London, where a main French partner must have been Rouen. In the late thirteenth century, through to the early fifteenth, fine jugs from Saintonge near Bordeaux were common in both places (Fig 5.9). From the middle of the fourteenth century, however, London increasingly received its foreign pottery, along with much else, from the Low Countries and the Rhineland.

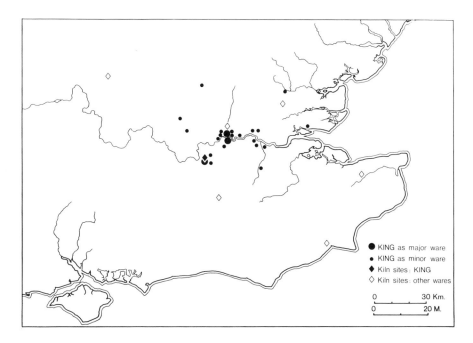

Figure 5.7   Map of findspots of Kingston-type ware (Pearce and Vince 1988)

Discussion

Archaeology can be used to study medieval trade and commerce most successfully when looking at broad patterns. The distance over which particular goods travelled is an ideal example. Providing that the goods can be characterised, one can study the decline in interaction between a source of goods and the consumer of these goods wherever those goods survive. Not only does this information often access classes of society for which documentary sources are rare or absent, but it also applies across continuous stretches of landscape unaffected by the survival of documentary sources.

One clear conclusion from this type of study, whether the data come from the study of pottery, other artefacts or coins, is that there are very considerable differences between what was the norm in the twelfth century and the situation four hundred years later. At the beginning of the period the principal sources of pottery had been established by the middle of the eleventh century, as were the mints. These can be seen as variations and developments of a late Saxon system. By the end of the thirteenth century goods were more often being produced at a smaller number of centres than in the previous century and, as a consequence of this, they tended to be transported over larger distances. We know from documentary sources and could have surmised from archaeology, that this change involved changes in the organisation of trade with the development of the trades of chapman and carter who would act as middlemen between producers and their customers. A feature of the material culture of this period is an increase in its quantity.

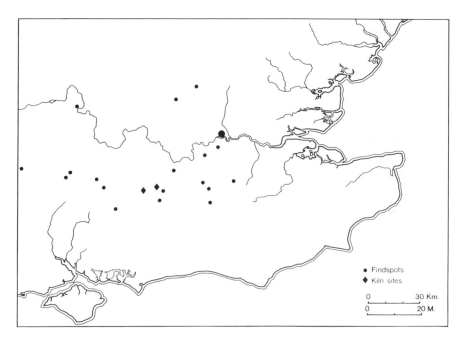

Figure 5.8 Map of findspots of Coarse Border ware, suggesting it was distributed predominantly by land routes (Pearce and Vince 1988)

There were more goods around *c.* 1300 than in the previous century, and considerably more than in the late eleventh century. By and large, however, patterns established at the end of the thirteenth and beginning of the fourteenth centuries survived, fossilised, until the end of the fifteenth century. The outline of this change of organisation is clear but the detail needs to be established. Some parts of the British Isles were outside of this network; but, in contrast, one result of the research excavations at Wharram Percy on the Yorkshire Wolds has been to show that the inhabitants of this village, now completely deserted and isolated, were in regular contact with the outside world and were not, as might have been thought, a self-sufficient community. Coal and deep-sea fish were both finding their way to this small community, almost certainly through the medium of trade with the neighbouring towns of Beverley and York.

Despite the changes described above, there remained several ways in which a producer could get his or her goods to the consumer. Most simply, the producer could take his or her wares to town, where they would be purchased by town-dwellers and people from the hinterland of the town. Documentary sources indicate that bread and ale were distributed in this fashion. Most goods, however, would have been passed to at least one middleman before reaching the customer, while some goods, such as spices and high-quality textiles, would have passed through a whole series of hands.

Naturally enough, as one travelled up the scale from simple to complex transactions, there was also a decrease in frequency of activity. Certain goods

Figure 5.9 Saintonge Polychrome jugs from London. These distinctive jugs were produced in the Saintes region of south-west France in the late thirteenth and fourteenth centuries. Their distribution in the British Isles, especially in ports, is closely correlated with that of the Gascon wine trade (Museum of London Archaeology Service)

were required daily and these would have been supplied through the shop or tavern. Others were required regularly but not every day. Such goods were probably distributed mainly through a weekly market. Pottery and metalware, cloth and clothing are all likely to have been distributed in this way. Hawkers and tinkers would have been less regular visitors to a town and may be the source of some of the small metal trinkets and exotica found on medieval urban tenements. Finally, there were the annual fairs and direct trading relationships through which professional merchants distributed their goods and services.

To return finally to the point raised at the start of this chapter, archaeology should be capable of answering questions about the role of towns in trade and, broadly speaking, it does do so. As the number and size of towns grew in the twelfth and thirteenth centuries, so does the evidence for increasing complexity in the marketing of goods and a general rise in the availability of such goods. When towns in general ceased to grow in number and many declined in size, in the fourteenth and fifteenth centuries, there is evidence for the continuation of earlier modes of distribution and production, although not a return to earlier, simpler patterns. In fact, both in pottery studies and in the minting of coin, there is evidence for a continued concentration in fewer and fewer places. This is true in the Severn Valley, where Bristol became the only mint (and even then only intermittently used), and the Malvern Chase, the only pottery production centre, and in particular for London. The two pottery types found on late medieval and early Tudor sites in the Severn Valley which were not locally made were whiteware cups from the Surrey–Hampshire border and Rhenish stoneware. Both are likely to have been marketed through London. The growth of London in late medieval times is also reflected in the coinage, and an interesting project would be to chart the distribution of goods made in the hinterland of London or imported via London and compare it with the relative frequency of coins from the London mint in hoards and loose finds. Throughout much of lowland England and even Wales it is likely that London would completely dominate both archaeological patterns.

6 *Religion in towns: churches, religious houses and cemeteries*

The social order of the medieval town was pervaded by a set of religious beliefs which was given its official form by churchmen in the thirteenth century, and which infused the language, ritual and even fabric of urban life until much of it was swept away at the Reformation. Thus the history of the manifestations of religious belief in towns in our period is of great interest. Churches are not only buildings for a specific function – worship – but they may have acted as mirrors to the communities they served, and because of comparatively little disturbance over the centuries in comparison to secular sites (apart from the cataclysm of the Reformation) we may still be able to see those reflected images.

A distinction must first be made, in terms of numbers, between pre-medieval towns and towns founded in the medieval period. By 1200, towns both of Roman origin (such as Gloucester, Exeter, Winchester or York (Fig 6.1)) and of Saxon origin (such as Ipswich, Norwich or Thetford) possessed many parish churches. In 1300, for instance, a person walking the 1¼ miles from one side of the City of London to the other would pass the doors of sixteen churches (out of a total of over one hundred); there were even greater concentrations, by square mile, at Lincoln (32 churches by 1100), Norwich (57 by 1200) and Winchester (57 by 1300) (Morris 1989, 172–5; Biddle and Keene 1976, 329–35). The high number of churches reflects a great period of church-building by secular patrons in these towns during the tenth and especially eleventh centuries. By 1300, and especially after 1400, the number of churches was in fact declining slowly, particularly in smaller towns. In addition, towns founded after about 1100 normally had only one church; so that more than 50 per cent of the English places which were urban at the time of the Norman Conquest contained more than one church, but only 4 per cent of the boroughs founded in the following two centuries (Morris 1987).

In Wales, also, older foundations had more churches, though on a smaller scale, Chepstow had three churches besides the priory, Haverfordwest had three, and Cardiff had two churches and a chapel at the entrance to the castle (Soulsby 1983, 45–6). As noted in Chapter 2, several pre-existing Celtic or early Anglo-Norman churches were instrumental in determining the sites of Welsh towns and English boroughs. Scottish burghs tended to have only one church, strongly linked to the lives of the townspeople (Ewan 1990, 10–11).

We can therefore make an easy but crude distinction between older towns like London or Winchester, where there were many usually small churches, and newer towns, particularly those which flowered in the late Middle Ages,

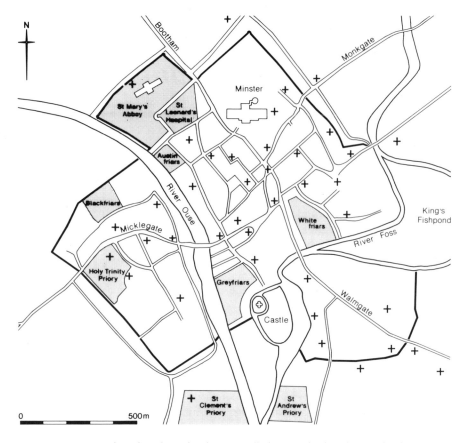

Figure 6.1 Map of medieval York, showing all the parish churches and religious houses (after York Archaeological Trust)

which have one large and fine church. There were also towns such as Hedon, Stamford and Reading which lie somewhere in between.

Archaeological assessment of churches

First, is it possible to recognise a church on purely archaeological grounds? The answer is usually yes, for the church as a building or as a complex of stratigraphic units (layers, walls, floors) has a distinctive character. Both inside and immediately outside the church will be human burials; and, by comparison with sites of secular buildings, the small finds will include large numbers of floor-tiles, fragments of decorated window-glass and moulded stones (Fig 6.2).

A *church* can be either a parish church for a town or village, or the building specially used for worship within a wider complex of buildings occupied by a community of people dedicated to a religious life (monks, nuns or friars). Larger churches in towns might have communities of priests

Figure 6.2 St Nicholas Shambles, London: late medieval walls often contained moulded stones from earlier phases of the parish church (Museum of London Archaeology Service)

attached; cathedrals, the seats of bishops, would normally have several other buildings adjacent to the church or nearby. The archaeological assessment of the church itself as a building can pick out features which are found in many or all of these types.

Churches are usually extremely long-lived sites. Of 24 English urban parish churches excavated in recent years, only three or four might date in origin from after 1100 (Morris 1987, 181–3). Further, the earth within a church is a particularly rich and complex archaeological site, the layers inside it (apart from burials) are often crisper than those outside the building, due to lack of animal action or leaching. Four categories of archaeological evidence can be identified: the structural development of the building; the evidence of construction methods (scaffolding, mortar-mixing areas, bell-founding pits); floors, furnishings and fittings; and burials (Rodwell 1981, 105–29). Following a similar approach, the first part of this chapter is concerned with the growth of the church in its various stages and their reasons, the relationship of archaeological strata to medieval liturgy (i.e. practices of worship), the interaction of church and society as demonstrated by patronage of embellishments such as stained glass and monumental brasses, and the several kinds of information to be derived from the siting and care taken over burials (human skeletons as illustrative of health and disease among medieval town-dwellers are considered in Chapter 7).

The growth of a church and its various uses

What light does the excavation report from a typical urban church throw on these questions? Let us take an example, St Mark's, Lincoln (Gilmour and Stocker 1986). Excavations of 1975–7 after demolition uncovered what remained of the parish church of St Mark's, on the west side of Lincoln High Street, about 450 m. south of the walled city in the medieval suburb of Wigford. The church and its graveyard were probably established between the late ninth and the eleventh centuries, with the mid-tenth century being the preferred date; a small rectangular timber building south of the later medieval church is probably the original church.

In the mid-eleventh century a new church of stone was built next to the timber church. It had two spaces or cells, the nave about twice the area of the chancel (Fig 6.3, Period I). It reused masonry from local Roman buildings in its fabric. The chancel was floored with flagstones, and the nave with beaten earth. Doorways in the walls of the nave on the north and south sides were indicated. Two north–south subrectangular robbing-pits inside the chancel may be indicators of successive positions of masonry altars; they were not dated, but the excavator suggests that they show a migration of the altar from the chancel arch (where the chancel met the nave) to the east end of the building, as is known in other churches and which seems to have been a product of the elaboration of the communion service during the twelfth century.

The church was probably burned in a city-wide fire of 1122. A western tower on massive foundations (Period II) was added shortly afterwards, presumably so that heavy bells could be hung and used. It is also possible that the tower was used as a baptistery, but evidence (in the form of a font or a special drain for the holy water) did not survive. Two generations later the ground plan was expanded by a rebuilding of the church with a new north aisle and an enlarged chancel (Period III). Here St Mark's demonstrates how phases of construction can be inferred when direct evidence such as foundations has been lost: reused in the foundation of the north aisle were moulded stones from a mid-twelfth-century door which joined with others found somewhere round the church in 1871. They probably came from the Period II north door of the church. Other blocks reused as rubble may have been from the chancel arch. The door mouldings are similar to others on the doors of Lincoln Cathedral of the 1150s or 1160s; naturally the style of the cathedral masons was diffusing among the smaller parish churches.

The need for a larger church could have stemmed from requirements for more space for processions, burial spaces for prominent parishioners, or the profusion of subsidiary altars. Traces of foundations or robbing trenches suggested that an altar stood at the east end of the north aisle, and that a rood screen divided the new nave and chancel, another common thirteenth-century development.

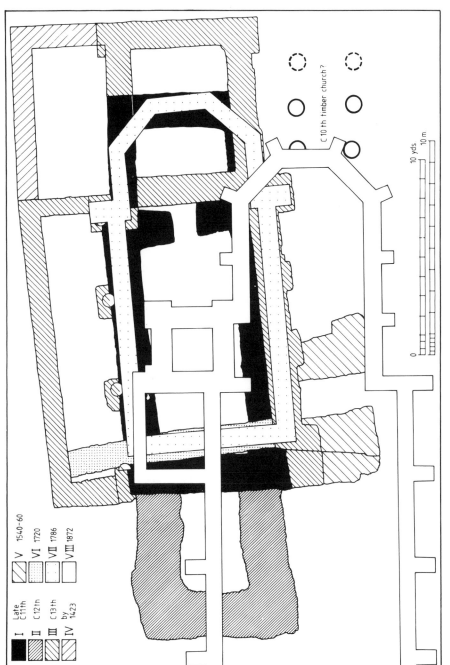

Figure 6.3 Development plans of St Mark's, Lincoln (after Gilmour and Stocker 1986, Fig 64)

After this substantial rebuilding, the church stayed much the same in form for the rest of the medieval period. This is typical of the Lincoln churches, whereas those in York and Norwich underwent thorough rebuilds in the fourteenth and fifteenth centuries. St Mark's did acquire a chapel, extending the north aisle, which was used as a mausoleum by a leading family of the parish in the early fifteenth century. The mortuary chapel sited on either the north or south side of the chancel is another well-known phenomenon in medieval parish churches throughout the country (examples from London are cited below). In the 1550s or 1560s a two-storeyed porch was added on the south side, built largely of reused graveyard monuments and architectural fragments probably from other sites, a vivid reminder of the destruction of many religious sites at the Reformation. Careful excavation and analysis of the results has therefore produced much about the growth and liturgy in a small suburban church, and a little about its use by prominent persons in the community.

In smaller towns and villages such a piecemeal history of building would be typical because of the sporadic availability of funds. The town with several, or many, churches provides further scope for ascertaining broad trends in church-building which would otherwise have to be sought over a wide region. Did the churches develop individually, or was there simultaneity in architectural development over the town? – did all churches get towers, or aisles, or lengthened chancels at roughly the same time? In larger towns such as London and York, the fully developed church with three aisles was common by the end of the fourteenth century, though in York in particular this was overtaken by further rebuildings in the next century; in Norwich, however, three-aisled churches appear to be rare before 1450. This would fit with a generally held view that Norwich's period of spectacular growth was in the late Middle Ages.

Internal arrangements sometimes reflected dual purposes for the church. Several larger conventual churches in towns doubled as parish churches: at Ely and Salisbury the parish used the nave, at St Paul's Cathedral the parish church of St Faith's, having been engulfed by the thirteenth-century expansion of the choir, lay in the basement, and at St Helen's Bishopsgate (also London), the parish and Benedictine nuns had two naves in parallel, separated by an internal wall.

Other patterns of use within the church were more the work of parishioners than of religious authorities. The fourteenth and fifteenth centuries saw the widespread establishment of chantry chapels, in which a prominent sponsor endowed the church to provide for a priest to say daily masses for himself and his family. Such chantries could take the form of a simple altar against a pillar, or the sharing of a chapel, or in exceptional cases screens of wood and even stone demarcated an area within the body of the church. Very exceptionally, the chapel was built at the sponsor's cost as an appendage of the church.

In the 658 wills surviving on the London Husting Rolls from the earliest example in 1259 to 1300, 59 perpetual chantries are recorded as being founded in parish churches. From 1300 to 1402, in the same series of wills, an average of 28 permanent chantries were founded every ten years. Often the endowment proved insufficient within fifty years, and the plethora both of under-funded chantries and of chantry priests led to the foundation of colleges for the priests. The singing of masses was, from the beginning, associated with the donor commemorated; so the mass might be said at a portable altar laid on the tomb, or even at a spot on the tomb itself marked by a consecration cross. Though it is rarely stated that the testator had improved the church, either in its architecture or by donating fittings or ornaments, it does seem likely that the period of the greatest number of chantry foundations, the fourteenth century, should also be the most likely period of architectural embellishment on that account. A similar development has been suggested for Florence, where the desire for private chapels was the major catalyst that brought about a boom in church construction after the mid-fourteenth century (Goldthwaite 1980, 12).

There have been two recent archaeological investigations in London which included the sites of what were probably chapels, rather than aisles. At St Botolph Billingsgate, excavations in 1982 found that a narrow space between the existing south wall of the church and an adjacent building, then secular, was filled in to form a south chapel, possibly that of St Mary in 1361. At a later date, possibly *c.* 1600, the chapel was incorporated into a south aisle on the same site. Secondly, excavation on the south side of St Martin Orgar (destroyed in the Great Fire) in 1987 uncovered a chapel at the south-east corner of the church, which may be that added in 1433 by William Crowmer, mayor.

While it may be commonplace for chapels to have been erected towards the east end of the parish church, some London churches show that the chancel area may have been embellished with chapels added to the north and south before the body of the nave was given aisles, to produce a winged effect in plan (examples are All Hallows Barking; St Alban Wood Street; St Bride Fleet Street; St Nicholas Shambles), probably during the fourteenth century. In two cases they were on special undercrofts with external entrances. This seems to be a peculiar tradition of large towns (Schofield in prep).

Town churches were also patronised by the crafts. At least ten medieval guilds are recorded in Stamford, for instance, and they were associated with seven of the parish churches. Most have left no physical record of their uses, but a prominent donor provided most of the expense for the surviving fourteenth-century north chapel of St Mary's church, which was probably used by the Corpus Christi guild (RCHM 1977, xlix, 24–5). In the early sixteenth century Holy Trinity, Coventry, housed not only the archdeacon's court but also eight chapels, three associated with trade groups: mercers, tanners and butchers (Morris 1989, 367). Chapels attached to several London parish churches, though they may have originally been sponsored by rich individuals, were taken over by the donor's guild and used to maintain and express a link with a parish church; sometimes guild equipment such as a chest for valuables or banners for pageants would be stored there.

The interiors of churches, especially the larger ones for which we have both physical remains and documentary records, tell much of the changing requirements in liturgy or the conduct of religious services (Draper 1987), though changes in architectural style in churches cannot always be attached to changes in liturgy. In larger churches with communities of canons or monks, the twelfth century saw the expansion and elaboration in architecture of the choir. From the late twelfth century, two developments were even more widespread. The need to provide more altars for the growing multiplication of daily masses and of the cult of the Virgin resulted in the focus of liturgy spreading out of the chancel area into transepts and chapels. Further, in the majority of the largest churches (such as at St Alban's or Chester), beginning in the seventy years after Canterbury Cathedral began the trend in the 1180s, relics became important generators of income from pilgrims, and a shrine would be inserted or added in a sacred area behind the high altar.

The altars formed stopping-places in elaborate processions which wound in and out of the church. In the thirteenth century, Salisbury Cathedral had seventeen altars; apart from two parochial altars in the nave, the others were in chapels along the eastern arms of the transepts (three on each side), in the extra choir transepts, and around the high altar (Draper 1987). These processional ways should be detectable in archaeological excavation (for an example from a Saxon church, Rodwell 1976).

Fittings, patronage and architecture

Archaeological study of churches, including the recording of changes to existing fabrics, is likely to include consideration of sculpture (Gardner 1935), woodwork (Tracy 1987; 1988), wall-painting (Park 1987), stained glass (Marks 1987), metalwork (Campbell 1987), monumental brasses (Binski 1987) and tiles (Eames 1980). Here the archaeologist holds discussions with the art historian, and whole new fields of enquiry are opened; but archaeological considerations may be illustrated by such rich material. Styles in sculpture and wall-paintings demonstrate both regional centres and continental, especially French, influences (for detailed studies, see the British Archaeological Association series on the art and architecture of cathedrals and their towns at Durham, Ely, Exeter, Glastonbury, Gloucester, Lincoln, Lichfield, London, Tewkesbury, Wells, Worcester and Rouen). At the other end of the scale, wall-paintings could be specific to certain locations within the church or its ceremonies: the Last Judgment over the chancel arch of a church, St Christopher by the door, or (rather pointedly) the wheel of fortune over a prominent seat such as that of a prior.

The interior of a parish church contained fixtures such as the rood, font, pulpit and pews; glazing and images (either paintings or statues); floortiles and monuments. Up to the twelfth century it was usual only for priests to be buried inside parish churches; noble and civic dignitaries were being buried in monastic churches from the later part of the century. By the middle of the thirteenth century effigies of knights are known in parish churches, and monumental brasses survive from the 1270s; latten images let into stone are recorded from 1208. Brasses of figures other than nobility (i.e. tradesmen, merchants) survive in towns from the middle of the fourteenth century (Evans 1949, 142). Two major firms of makers of brasses were probably working in London by the mid-fourteenth century; in 1352 a London hosier asked that a brass be set in his tomb (Sharpe 1889, 656–8). Alabaster seems to have come into use during the second quarter of the fourteenth century, and its frequency increased in the decades after 1350 (Gardner 1935, 328–84); it was carved into small reliefs, sometimes grouped in wooden frames to form reredoses or retables, and effigies.

These art objects display patterns of patronage. Glass-painting is a good example of a well-organised craft much in demand in major towns by the thirteenth century, and some of the masters are later known by name, for instance in York in 1339. Their patrons were generally the larger religious houses or prominent laymen; in the early fourteenth century windows in York minster were endowed by a wealthy goldsmith and bell-founder, Richard Tunnoc (the window shows bell-casting) and probably by vintners (other windows show wine-selling). From the late thirteenth century in York and London, donors were acknowledged by the appearance of their arms in the glass, or by the inclusion of discreet drawings of themselves at prayer.

Monumental brasses similarly demonstrate patronage of churches. From the late thirteenth century, brasses or simpler brass crosses could be ordered by all richer persons including prominent tradesmen; the workshops also produced monuments or monumental decorations in Purbeck marble (Blair and Blair 1991). The main production centre was London, with clients in southern England and East Anglia, capitalising on the growing population and an increasing preference for burial in the church. In the later medieval period (after about 1400) there was another fashion for prominent tombs within the aisled church, around the east end. To some extent, though not exclusively, this overtook the practice of building whole new chapels.

The most numerous artefacts available to the archaeologist are moulded stones: the individual carved blocks forming arches, doorways, tombs and pillars. Certain types of moulding can be dated to within twenty years, for example window tracery; studies forming data banks of mouldings, for instance at Warwick University, have correlated dated examples. Mouldings are now grouped by regions, and opinion is forming against the previous notion that architectural style was spread by itinerant masons following their patrons round the country. The position of the moulded stones in their strata can be significant, since the degree of articulation of stones forming a window or doorway helps interpretation of the demolition layers. Evidence for tooling on the stones is of limited value, since tools were long-lived and conservative in design; one or two tooling textures are roughly datable, for example the diagonal striations of the twelfth century (Stocker 1993). Regional groupings of mouldings are beginning to be noticed, and some geographical concentration of distinctive styles, such as the 'Yorkshire School' of twelfth-century parish churches. In this case a common repertoire of carvings showing literary themes (Labours of the Months and symbols of the zodiac) is shared by a number of churches which were in the hands of members of York minster chapter, the archbishop of York, or else were possessions of prominent religious houses (Morris 1989, 278–82, from work by L. Butler).

Burials

Much can also be learned about both the surrounding topography and about the management of the individual church and its land from study of the cemetery which nearly always accompanies the parish church (Rodwell 1981, 131–66). Here we are concerned with the rituals of burial, monuments and organisation of the cemetery.

In the eleventh and twelfth centuries, some burial practices, apparently of the Saxon period, lingered on in parish graveyards. The types of burial, and some apparent burial rites, can be illustrated by study of 234 articulated skeletons from the graveyard of St Nicholas Shambles, London (White 1988), with parallels from other excavated churchyards.

At St Nicholas, about half the burials were in the churchyard, and half within the confines of the church, though in the absence of horizontal strata it is possible that some of the internal burials were originally outside, to be covered by expansion of the church building. All burials avoided the first eleventh-century nave and chancel, confirming the prohibition known from documents against burial of laity inside churches until the twelfth century (Morris 1989, 292).

Most people were buried without a coffin, in an unadorned grave; in medieval times women were often buried in a shroud, for which the pin might survive near the bones, whereas men were sometimes buried in hairshirts woven from coarse two-ply yarn. Older men and especially older women might have stone pillows in the grave; often these stones lay to either side of the head perhaps as protection. Graves sometimes had simple trampled floors of chalk and mortar; slightly more prestigiously, dry-laid or mortared stone might line the grave in peremptory fashion. At York, in a priory cemetery, some people were laid in stone coffins which indicates that they were of higher status (Fig 6.4).

At St Nicholas Shambles there was evidence of two occasional burial rites. In three cases Roman tile was laid on the body, a practice noted at St Bride's in London and in Norwich in eleventh-century contexts. In five further cases a pebble had been placed in the mouth of a mature man and four comparatively elderly women (that is, over 38 years old; Fig 6.5). Even in the middle of the capital city, folk rituals, it seems, were still prevalent.

Burial statistics for the later medieval period may be of less use because of the practice of throwing disturbed bones into charnel houses. Much can still be learned, however, about monuments in the churchyard and routes through it. The finds from graveyard soil may be significant, since cemeteries in medieval towns were used as playingfields, places of work or assembly, open-air courtrooms and as markets.

Several London churches had *cloisters* around the cemetery, though it is not known what these comprised. The earliest reference is to cloisters at St Laurence Pountney in 1392. Several churchyards were arranged around a preaching-cross. Buildings in or encroaching upon the churchyard could include the rector's house, or a house for chaplains of the chantry endowed by a testator. Many churchyards had a well, sometimes built or endowed by a worthy citizen. Clearly there were many things going on in medieval churchyards which we only dimly understand.

Figure 6.4 Cemetery of St Leonard's Priory, York: some individuals were buried in stone coffins – presumably a mark of status (York Archaeological Trust)

Further questions about parish churches

Morris (1987, 184–5) identifies several objectives in the archaeological study of urban parish churches. First, there must be complete excavations of selected churches and their precincts (to ensure that earlier churches are not 'hiding offstage'), and to recover sufficiently large groups of skeletons to make a worthwhile contribution to population studies. Secondly, the difficult

Figure 6.5   St Nicholas Shambles, London: one of the cases of a burial with a pebble in the mouth (White 1988)

question of dating simple plan-forms and masonry must be tackled, for instance by typologies of foundation-types and further studies of moulded stone designs; this also requires more sites of short duration to isolate particular developments or snap-shot views of church development. Thirdly, churches had parts to play in urban environments: churches on walls (e.g. St Alphege in London, or St Mary Northgate, Canterbury; Tatton-Brown 1978, 80–1), at the doors of greater churches (e.g. at Westminster, York), buried deep within housing (St Pancras, Winchester) and especially on streets (e.g. in Colchester; Crummy 1981, 49). The relationship between church and market-place is considered in Chapters 2 and 5. The parish church must be studied on the same three levels as a secular building: as a structure, to understand its variety of form; as internal space, to understand the functions that went on in it; and as a leading component of a neighbourhood streetscape, pulling people away from their other pursuits.

To this list we would add a further research question concerning the origins of churches in the older centres. Here the majority of parish churches began life as parts of private residences in the tenth or eleventh centuries. This often governed their sites, which would be set back from the main medieval thoroughfare. What was the process of allowing public access to and use of this private place? It is another case, in parallel with changes to secular houses, where we might study the changing balance of private and public access. Archaeological and architectural evidence, for instance, demonstrates that Winchester parish churches were being extended as early as the late eleventh century, but the population was declining or at least static, and parishes did not increase in area until much later. It therefore seems likely that the increase in size represents the change or extension from

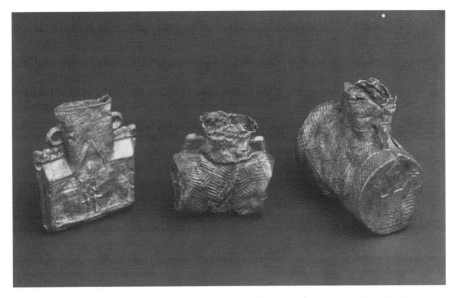

Figure 6.6 Ampullae (holy water containers) of tin – a souvenir of a pilgrimage to Canterbury. Becket is shown at the end, his hand raised in blessing. From the Swan Lane site, London, thirteenth century (Museum of London Archaeology Service)

private chapel to a wider and more public parochial function (Biddle and Keene 1976, 334–5).

Pilgrimages

A further aspect of medieval religious life susceptible to archaeological investigation is the pilgrimage. This was both an act of religious faith and, by the fourteenth century, a social occasion that combined tourism and religion. Pilgrims bought souvenirs of the shrines they visited, either in the form of metal badges worn on the hat, or ampullae, small tin or pewter containers of holy water, which were worn on a string around the neck (Fig 6.6). Many different types of souvenir have been found in foreshore deposits, both medieval and modern, in the City of London. Those from recent excavations, for instance, at the Swan Lane and Billingsgate Lorry Park sites, included a number of badges from the shrine of Thomas Becket in Canterbury (Egan 1985–6). Becket appeared on horseback or on a ship, and in the fifteenth century pilgrims could buy miniature copies of the sword that killed him, complete with scabbard. Other momentos include an elaborate madonna and child (Fig 6.7) and a badge commemorating the miracle-working image of the Virgin at the Whitefriars friary of Toulouse (Fig 6.8). Nor are these interesting finds confined to London. Watercourses in Salisbury have produced an impressive array of pilgrim badges from at least 31 places in England, as far apart as Finchale and Canterbury, and at least 22 places on the Continent, from Vadstena in Sweden to Compostela in Spain (Spencer 1990).

Figure 6.7 A madonna and child found in spoil from the Billingsgate site, London. The tabs at the sides show that this ornate badge was originally fixed to coloured cloth (Museum of London Archaeology Service)

Figure 6.8 Badge commemorating the miracle-working image of the Virgin belonging to the Whitefriars at Toulouse in France. Next to the Virgin, a kneeling figure is delivered of an evil spirit which emerges from its mouth, and a cured cripple discards his crutches; below, a friar kneels in prayer. From the Swan Lane site, London, thirteenth century (Museum of London Archaeology Service)

Religious houses

Another book in this series has been devoted to religious houses (Greene 1992) and therefore only five particularly urban considerations or features will be examined here: the numbers of religious houses per town and the relative importance of those towns; the placing of religious houses in towns and urban constraints on conventual precincts and their buildings; friaries; the study of internal space, for instance in nunneries; and hospitals.

Just as the number of parish churches in a town is one barometer of urban intensity (at least up to 1200), so the number of religious houses (including hospitals) may indicate regional centres, not all of them large towns today. We can also try to understand what factors influenced the placing of houses by each religious order.

At the Norman Conquest, urban religious institutions, often dominating their respective towns, were either Benedictine monasteries (Canterbury, Chichester) or secular colleges (Beverley, Ripon). Foundations continued, so that the largest number of urban religious houses in towns, by 1300, were Benedictine. From the early twelfth century houses of the Augustinian canons, and other minor orders of canons, spread through all kinds of towns. They undertook pastoral work and the care of souls, and therefore took responsibility for the sick and insane, and provided for the aged and lepers.

Some towns which are small today must have been formerly of greater significance, as measured by the number of their religious houses. A list of towns in Scotland which had two or three friaries and several hospitals each, for instance, identifies the political, ecclesiastical and academic centres: not only Edinburgh, Aberdeen, St Andrews and Berwick, but now smaller places such as Dumfries (seven institutions), Elgin and Haddington (six each) (Butler 1987, 169). In a study of the relationship between religious houses and Yorkshire towns, Palliser (1993, 3) suggests that foundations of hospitals and friaries are the better index of urbanisation, rather than monasteries as a whole; the former show the vigour and extent of twelfth-century towns, the latter reflect fortunes and intentions in the thirteenth century.

Thus a rough idea of relative importance between towns in an area may be gained by study of the parochial and ecclesiastical organisation together. In Dorset, for example, the ex-Roman and long-established Saxon towns had a complex religious apparatus. Dorchester had three parish churches, a chapel, at least two hospitals and a friary; Shaftesbury had a nunnery, twelve churches and chapels by 1300. Sherborne, never a borough but part of a bishop's manor, had its Benedictine abbey (a distinguished but now passed over Saxon religious centre), two parish churches, and several chapels and almshouse foundations. Later towns, as elsewhere in England, usually comprised a single parish, or part of a surrounding parish, especially when they were owned in some way by the established church (e.g. Abbotsbury, Beaminster, Cerne Abbas, all Dorset; Penn 1980).

Some major Saxon churches, often called minsters, survived to be major churches in towns, but others were replanned in such a way that their previous relationship to the inherited Saxon street-plan was destroyed. This is the case, for instance, at Wells, where the west front of the Saxon cathedral (now beneath the cloister) looked directly on to the market-place, but the present church and main buildings of the late twelfth- to early thirteenth centuries are aligned more strictly west–east by twelve degrees. Even so, probably by 1276, the old lady chapel of the former church, now severed by the east arm of the cloister, was rebuilt and enlarged on its former alignment. This skewed alignment was only destroyed when the chapel was replaced by a large new chapel at the expense of Bishop Stillington in 1476. Although this building is now gone, it has, in turn, left a scar in the form of its arcaded west end stuck to the outer wall of the cloister (Rodwell 1987).

Large religious houses within towns often had a delicate relationship with their townspeople. In medieval Canterbury, for instance, many of the inhabitants made their living out of the monks, either as servants, or as suppliers of luxuries, food, and building skills or labour (Urry 1967, 163–4). At the same time, riots and pitched battles between town and monks also occurred; in Canterbury in 1188, a difference of opinion between monks and the archbishop resulted in a year-long siege of Christ Church monastery (ibid., 165–6). Thus large religious institutions were commonly surrounded by high walls. In the late thirteenth century, as major towns put effort into their defences, so the major churches within towns fortified their precincts in stone – Norwich in 1276, York, Lincoln and St Paul's in London in 1285, and Canterbury in 1309. In the first half of the fourteenth century, these precincts were embellished or emphasised by prominent gates with a new architecture of octagonal turrets (the earliest probably that at St Augustine's abbey, Canterbury, in 1308). The crystallisation of the exclusive precinct was complete.

Within the close, the cathedral or monastic complex comprised many buildings, and their variety of detail will not be pursued here (for a study of monastic houses in this series, see Greene 1992). There are many archaeological and guide books which take the interested reader round monasteries, pointing out the function and appearance of the various buildings (e.g. Steane 1985, 68–73; Coppack 1990). A broad distinction can be made between monastic houses where all the associated domestic buildings of a resident community were necessary, such as Durham or Chester, and secular cathedrals, where the canons were not resident and buildings such as cloisters or dormitories were more formal than necessary, such as Wells, Salisbury or St Paul's.

An area of current interest concerns what happened in the outer courtyards of monastic houses and friaries, in that these would be the spaces where the house conducted the majority of its business with the outside world. A second yard or zone would have represented the storage and provisioning area of the monastery, where the food and other produce of the estates would be stored and processed. Urban precincts often included stables, brewhouses and accommodation for lay people. Sometimes, as in the small town of Waltham Abbey (Essex), excavation reminds us how many buildings must have crammed into the spaces between the stone structures we now see in cathedral closes. Excavations of 1970–2 near the Augustinian church of Waltham Abbey, in an outer monastic close called Veresmead and in the Grange Yard, uncovered twelve medieval and two post-medieval buildings (Huggins 1972; Huggins and Bascombe 1992). In the outer close stood a two-bay timber-framed aisled hall and a store; nearby stood two successive dove-cotes, and beyond a large fish-farm of ponds. In the Grange Yard were a twelve-bay aisled timber-framed barn near a dock, a hay barn, a brick building with stalls and a solar end; three successive farm entrance lodges and a forge.

Urban constraints, both on the site and on the form of buildings, were most severe in London. And yet recent work has uncovered remains of the finest priory in the city, and its inclusion here illustrates two further points of interest: how the topography of religious houses in towns can be illuminated by documentary and cartographic study, and how fragments can be preserved in new buildings.

The Augustinian priory of Holy Trinity was founded in 1107 or 1108 by Matilda, queen of Henry I, on a site where a small church already stood (Schofield and Lea in prep). The priory quickly grew rich due to continued royal gifts and donations of land; despite a savage fire in 1132 which damaged the new church, it was chosen as the burial place for two of the children of King Stephen, Baldwin and Matilda. Little is known about the subsequent development of the priory, but it can be reconstructed in some detail from a plan of about 1586, when it was dissolved and divided into several properties. A medieval arch, presumably from the church, survived into the post-war period by being part of one of these property boundaries, but otherwise the whole priory lay beneath several streets, almost forgotten.

The Aldgate area was spared both in the Blitz and in the first waves of post-war development, but during the 1970s and 1980s the character of the area changed dramatically as development sought out every available site. Two small sites had located parts of the priory by 1979, and archaeological work began on reconstruction of the priory on paper from the plan of 1586 (Fig 6.9). In 1984, however, the most significant part came up for redevelopment; a long narrow plot on the south side of Mitre Street, which bisected the site of the priory church. The excavation site incorporated the standing medieval arch, which is to be preserved in the foyer of the new building.

Besides 61 burials, the excavations at Mitre Street not only investigated the arch, but also found nearby the considerable remains of a chapel which would have protruded east from the south transept (Fig 6.10). It had survived 3.5 m. high not only because of its use as a cellar for later buildings, but because from at least the seventeenth century until 1984 it had been covered over by a cobbled yard. The coursed masonry was enhanced with corners and chamfers of cut stone; some of these blocks had twelfth-century masons' marks, several of an asterisk, and one of curving compass lines. The survival of the chapel was a surprise, but the developers decided to move it bodily to another part of the site, and to replace it in a special sub-basement back in its original position once the foundations of the new building had been laid (Fig 6.11). A few metres to the east, the surviving arch is interpreted as the entrance into a second chapel from the south aisle near the high altar. It now features beautifully in the building's foyer, to be inspected by clients waiting for the lift.

The urban order *par excellence*, and therefore in themselves an evidence of

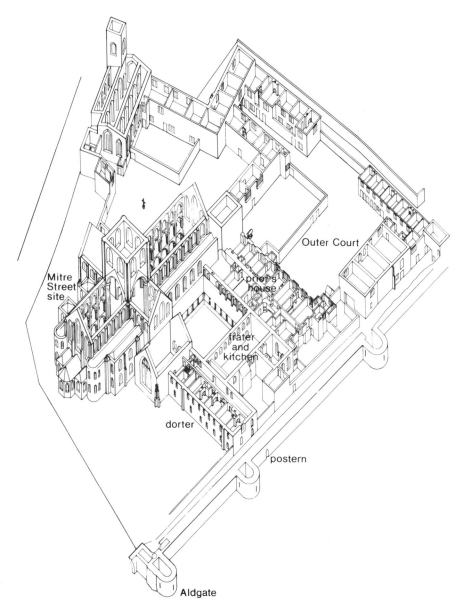

Outer Court

Mitre
Street
site

priors'
house

frater
and
kitchen

dorter

postern

Aldgate

Figure 6.9 Reconstruction of Holy Trinity Priory, Aldgate, by Richard Lea from the plans of John Symonds about 1586; the identifiable post-dissolution features have been stripped away (Museum of London Archaeology Service)

urban vigour, were the friars, especially the Dominicans (Blackfriars) and Franciscans (Greyfriars) (Butler 1984). The placing of their houses shows where they expected greatest spiritual (and financial) custom; besides the obvious larger towns, both orders had sites in medium-rank places such as Berwick, Lincoln, Norwich, Northampton, Oxford and Bristol. The

Figure 6.10　Holy Trinity Priory, Aldgate: the newly discovered chapel from the west (scale is 10 × 0.1 m. units) (Museum of London Archaeology Service)

Dominicans were also active in the far north, in Edinburgh, Perth and Aberdeen.

The formation of the Franciscan and Dominican orders in the early thirteenth century has been called 'the most distinctively and uniquely urban contribution made by the church in the long history of Christianity' (Dobson 1984, 110). But because of the almost total destruction of their written records, we know little of the social setting of the British friaries. Only ten per cent of the sites of English friaries can now be identified by fragments above the ground, and very few are as extensive as a typical monastic ruin kept in guardianship. Friaries are especially noteworthy for three reasons: the information they may provide about previous land-use beneath their precincts, the nature of the buildings of a peculiarly urban religious order, and their increasing role as foci of patronage and the arts.

The normal (but by no means universal) extramural siting of friaries, when there must have been plenty of cheap land within the comparable security of the town defences, is demonstrated by the Welsh towns which were additionally in a troubled frontier zone. At Cardiff, the Blackfriars and Greyfriars both lay outside the town, but near the castle (see Fig 2.1 on pp. 26–7, the sites marked F); in other Welsh towns friaries lay at the water's edge (Haverfordwest), across rivers (Brecon), at the limits of settlement or off suburban roads (Carmarthen, Denbigh, Newport (Gwent)); that at Rhuddlan, in existence adjacent to the Norman defences by the 1260s, was left in the countryside when Edward I had the new borough laid out on the far side of the castle in 1281–92 (Fig 2.3 on pp. 30–1; Soulsby 1983, 226–30).

Figure 6.11 The chapel is raised on a concrete raft and moved across the building site during construction works by developers Speyhawk (Museum of London Archaeology Service)

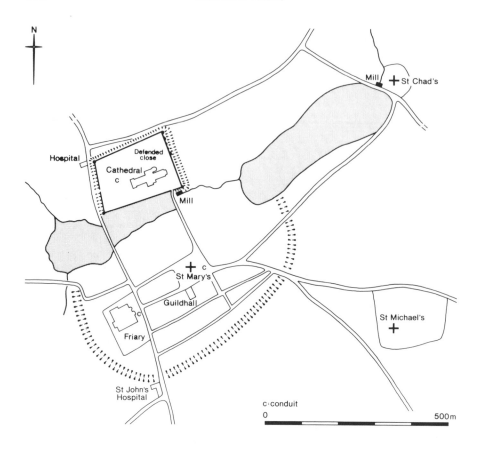

Figure 6.12 Lichfield at the end of the Middle Ages, showing the sites of both the cathedral in its defended precinct and the friary, near the market-place and next to the town conduit (Gould 1976)

The fact that friaries often settled on marshy land (which may have been used as a rubbish-tip by the adjacent town) should produce archaeological dividends, for in these waterlogged conditions the survival of organic materials, as well as seeds, insects and parasites should be high. In the case of the Austin Friars at Leicester (to be examined below), an ecological history of the site before, during and after the occupation by the friars can be sketched out.

Some friaries, however, were occasionally also sited within towns, and near market-places: at Maldon, or Lichfield (Fig 6.12), for instance. The great church of the Greyfriars in London was also next to the Shambles or meat-market in the middle of Newgate Street, and in Canterbury the Austin Friars had a gate into the nearby High Street; here, all three friaries were within the walls (Fig 2.3). In several French towns it has been noted that friaries first settled outside the walls, but later moved inside; perhaps their particularly urban mission was calling them closer to the markets and places of public resort. Indeed, Pope Clement IV eventually had to issue a papal bull in 1268 commanding that there should be a distance of about 500 m. between the mendicant convents in any town (Le Goff 1980, 236–7). Change of site by friaries should therefore be looked out for in British towns.

The friars were determined to preach to the largest audiences possible, and this directed their choice of locality for their church (a populated town) and the development of their church architecture. But unlike some of the other orders, the friars did not build to a rigidly characteristic plan; it is difficult to isolate the 'typical' friary church. It may be that friary architecture, in contrast, drew ideas rather from other friaries in the region, as seems to be the case in Ireland.

Sometimes the cloistral plan would be arranged so that the church, the principal focus of the complex for townspeople, was near the principal approach road; the cloister and other friary buildings would be placed on the other, private side (as at Greyfriars and Austin Friars in London, where the cloister is thus on the north). The emphasis upon the secular nature of most of the church continued inside. Usually, by the fifteenth century, the church was a large aisled nave without appendages such as private chapels or large transepts (though large transepts do occur, for instance in the Greyfriars at Oxford). The nave was divided into two unequal parts by a solid screen or pulpitum; the choir was kept within the nave bays east of this screen, to allow the maximum space for movement around the church. Between the choir and nave, supported by two parallel walls or arches which crossed the church, was usually a steeple or belfry containing one large bell. The architectural emphasis of these walls and the adjacent pulpitum formed a natural break in the building for through-traffic and, later, partial demolition after the Dissolution.

The domestic buildings of friaries also had their own character. Often the cloister was moved slightly away from the body of the church, so that a lane or alley ran between. The position and size of the cloister is much more a commentary on the success of the friars in obtaining land to build on than upon any planning instructions they were working to (Butler 1984, 132). The walks of the cloister were often built over with rooms above: not only the dormitory and special rooms such as a library, but also sometimes the refectory. Archaeological excavation, concerned with foundations and below-ground evidence, may not detect these first-floor functions and is likely to be most fruitful when investigating the drains and trying to identify the kitchen. We should also keep an eye out for the industries or crafts which the friars may have practised to keep themselves; and several friaries built wharves into their adjacent rivers.

In distinction to the Benedictines or Cistercians, the friars were forbidden to own property, and were supposed to espouse poverty. This very ideal made the friaries attract much attention and benefactions. Especially in the larger towns such as London and York, kings, nobles and rich townspeople wished to be associated with the friars in life and especially in death. Some friaries grew lavish in their decoration, and this became a source of resentment: the author of the fourteenth-century poem *Pierce the Ploughman's Creed* walked round the London Blackfriars dryly noting wide windows wrought with numberless writings and knightly shields or merchants' marks, tombs railed with iron, knights and ladies in gilded alabaster images. The cloister was roofed in lead and had a pavement of painted tiles; the Chapter House was as large as another church, with a painted ceiling; even the domestic buildings such as the frater and dormitory had glass windows. This is perhaps the most extreme case, but the tension between avowed poverty and the friars' inability to stem the tide of secular patronage is a theme to pursue in the excavated remains of their buildings, their diet and their bodily health. Future work on friaries may thus illustrate the interlacing of secular and religious motives in monument-building.

Friaries in many towns were examined in the 1970s, notably at Guildford, Leicester and Oxford. The Guildford and Leicester friaries are instructive not only in their individual findings, but also in their contrasting and complementary results.

In 1974 excavations on the site of a brewery on the outskirts of medieval Guildford uncovered the cloister and ranges on its north and east sides, the choir and most of the nave of the church on the south side, and part of the churchyard to the south of the church of the Dominican friary (Fig 6.13; Poulton and Woods 1984). With the exception of a chantry chapel and an extension to the chancel, all these buildings were laid out in a single operation. The nave had a single additional aisle from the beginning, but apparently never needed to expand further (as was the case in some other friaries, e.g. at Beverley). The area beneath the choir stalls produced a large number of bronze objects – jettons, pins, strap ends, book studs and lace tags. The excavators suggested that these were the debris of bored friars, fiddling with anything to hand and often losing it.

Only the nave of the church and the cemetery to the south were investigated for burials. The 28 in the nave included wooden coffins, and one case of a lead coffin with the body of a young woman. A further brick vault had been robbed of its occupant, whose bones were apparently dumped to one side. Outside in the cemetery, coffins were less frequent.

Were different kinds of person buried in different parts of the friary? The few skeletons found in the cloister walks were male and almost certainly friars. In the graveyard south of the church a boundary wall may have divided a main cemetery for the friars, to the east, from lay burials (which included women). Female burials were also found in the nave, where burials were generally of richer patrons. Here, however, areas kept clear of burials included the altar and the area around the probable site of the pulpit.

The pattern of burials within friaries has not been widely studied, largely because only small parts of each complex are available during rescue excavation: but burials at the Dominican friary at Oxford seem to have divided into friars in the cloister walks, lay people (presumably dignitaries) in church, and a main cemetery north of the church (Lambrick and Woods 1976; Lambrick 1985). This is the pattern also at Guildford. In addition at Oxford, several children were buried at the west end of the chapter house. At the Franciscan friary at Hartlepool, more people were buried in the church than outside to the north, and there was more evidence of coffins inside the church than outside, a probable distinction of status (Daniels 1986, 271–2).

In contrast to Guildford, the development of a friary site over time is the

Figure 6.13 Aerial view from the east of the excavation of the Dominican friary at Guildford in 1974, showing the location of the extensive remains in relation to the medieval town which lay to the left, where the street marks the outer edge of the city defences (National Monuments Record, Crown Copyright)

main point of interest at Leicester. The site of the Austin Friars, immediately outside the west gate of the town (Fig 6.14), was well-preserved due to its being a garden in the eighteenth century and the site of a railway station in the nineteenth. The friary also lay on an island in the River Soar, which ensured the exceptional survival of material which illustrates the lifestyles and some aspects of the economy of the friars (Mellor and Pearce 1981).

The excavation site lay to the north of the friary church, and ten phases of activity charted the development through time and expansion across the site of its associated religious buildings (Fig 6.15). The friars arrived in Phase 2 (1254 on documentary grounds), dug a drainage ditch to limit the site and put up two buildings, one of timber. They made and repaired shoes; refuse in

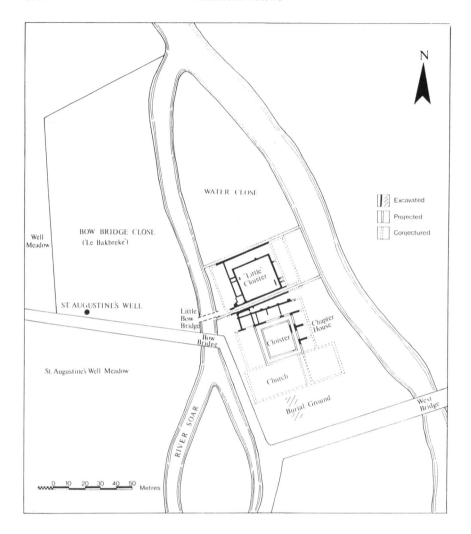

Figure 6.14 Overall plan of the Austin Friars, Leicester, on its island in the River Soar (Mellor and Pearce 1981)

the ditch included wooden table vessels and fragments of clothing. A high number of cereal pests in samples from the ditch sediment suggests grain stores nearby, and household pests appeared for the first time.

In the early fourteenth century the friary expanded over the ditch with regular cloistral buildings; and a second cloister followed in the middle of the century (Phases 3–4). The ditch was rebuilt into a major drain beneath a new range in the fifteenth century, along with other modifications (Phases 5–9), and the site destroyed after being surrendered in 1538 (Phase 10).

Finds and environmental material from the site contribute to a detailed impression of life in the friary. Much of the building materials had been removed, but in the destruction levels were many pieces of painted window

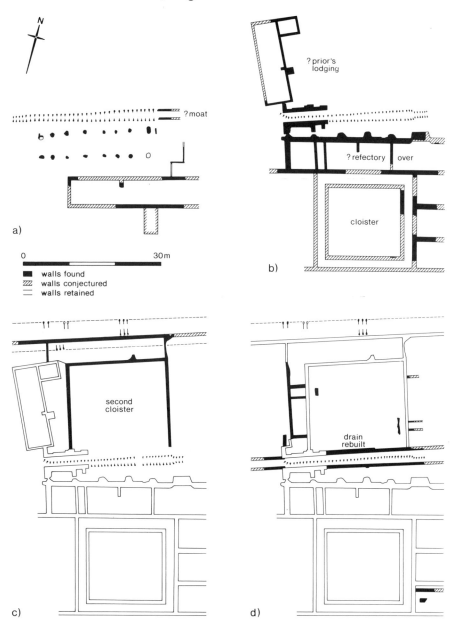

Figure 6.15 Successive period plans of the Austin Friars, Leicester (Mellor and Pearce 1981): (a) phase 2; (b) phase 3; (c) phases 4 and 5; (d) phases 6, 7 and 8. The building histories of friaries may be a more sensitive indicator of urban fortunes than those of the houses of other monastic orders

glass; the buildings were roofed in clay tiles and local Swithland stone slates, the ridges adorned with ornamented pottery crests. Floor-tiles were laid in the south cloister alley, shown by loose fragments and tile impressions left in the mortar. Three sources were identified by X-ray fluorescence of the clay: from Nottingham, north-east Warwickshire and Northampton. Pottery wasters suggest that the pre-friary land-use may have included kilns. The friars' meat diet was mainly cattle, sheep, pig, chicken, goose and duck; the pigs may have been slaughtered on the site, as bones from most parts of the animal's body were recovered. Fallow deer were similarly introduced in one piece; they were the only wild species showing butchery marks. Eleven species of fish were eaten, of which nine were marine; they may have come in salted form. The insect assemblages reflected building on the site (wood-boring beetles), nearby grazing animals (dung beetles) and, after a flood sediment of the early sixteenth century in the drain, a complete absence of food pests. At its dissolution in 1538, the friary had only four inmates.

Thus friaries, as the particularly urban form of religious community in Britain, have much to contribute not only about an important facet of medieval religious life, but also about many aspects of life in towns. A recent discussion paper (Gilchrist 1988) highlights at least three further topics which have only been touched on here. First, even when outside the walls, and especially when within, friaries were placed near major thoroughfares, and therefore routes of transportation may be glimpsed through their situations; like market buildings and gates, they may indicate the major axes of the town. Secondly, since friaries, unlike monastic orders, did not rely on a system of providing food from rural manors and granges in the possession of the house, but had to get their food where and when they could from the town itself, so friaries must have shared the town's sources of food supply. Thus excavated evidence of diet will have an urban character, and the comparatively well-isolated assemblages possible on friary sites may stand as reference material for the usually more jumbled evidence on house-sites in the town. And thirdly, the observed variety in friary architecture across the country may be related, in due course, to variables of time (early–late), situation (urban–rural) and houses of greater or lesser standing and wealth.

Besides its friaries, any reasonably vigorous town could expect to maintain three or four hospitals. Since the main enthusiasm for hospital foundation dates from the early twelfth century, study of the position of hospitals in the town can give clues as to the extent of built-up areas and lines of defences; though some hospitals were sited within towns, most were on the edges, and some, such as leper hospitals, were deliberately placed at some distance from the town. The majority of hospitals looked like the monastic infirmaries from which they were derived, with a wide, undivided hall; but some leper hospitals may have given their inmates individual cells in a single range. By the fifteenth century the courtyard plan is found in hospitals as it was then becoming usual in academic and secular colleges and almshouses (Butler 1987, 175–6).

Currently, a large research programme at the Museum of London concerns St Mary Spital, an Augustinian priory and hospital founded in 1197 outside Bishopsgate to the north-east of the city. Excavations of 1982–8 have revealed much of the hospital's plan and its development (Thomas et al.

1989; and in prep). The recorded remains date largely from after 1235, when the hospital was refounded and the original church was presumably demolished.

The main new building at first combined both church and hospital; the church had a choir but no nave, and a four-bay northern arm which served as the hospital. This may have continued to the south to give a T-shape to the building, as at St John's Hospital, Canterbury. Traces of a foundation probably for a rood screen (forming the entrance to the choir) were found between two of the pillars. The floors of the church were of mortar or clay, replaced many times during the lifetime of the building, and there was no sign of floor-tiles or their impressions (sometimes tile floors were lifted in the medieval period, leaving impressions in their clay bedding layers). An orderly cemetery was laid out between the church and Bishopsgate.

About 1280, however, a new infirmary block was built adjacent to the old infirmary wing, over its cemetery. This new building was five bays long and had an arcade down the middle; it was extended by half as much again to the west in the 1320s (Fig 6.16). The old north wing probably reverted to being part of the church, since burials were now made in it; a total of fifteen were recovered. To the north lay stables and a drain; a latrine block and a long hall which may have been the nuns' dormitory was added about 1350. North-east of the church lay the thirteenth-century canons' cloister (i.e. not the lay sisters who functioned as nurses) with further prestigious buildings on two sides, including the Prior's Lodging, the canons' dorter, frater and chapter-house. The last two had fine decorated tiled floors. In a garden west of the new infirmary, a sluice-pit contained a large group of pottery and wooden vessels, shoes and seed evidence possibly of patients' food. The cemetery now lay to the south-east of infirmary, away from Bishopsgate; 102 skeletons were analysed.

Thus there were three groups of skeletons: the first, of 1235–80; the second, of 1280–1538; and a third small high-status group buried within the church of the hospital, of 1280–1538 (some fragments of tombs survived, and their names are known from documentary records). In the first group, a significant portion of the 101 recorded invididuals were adolescents, evidence of the known specialism at this hospital with orphans. There were also more men than women – why in a hospital? One theory is that these were rootless migrants coming to London, but not surviving long. The remains of skeletons buried in the church had the highest level of dental disease and were older, as one might expect from well-fed prosperous citizens who wished for burial in chapels or near the altar in the church. They also had the highest level of diffuse idiopathic skeletal hyperostosis (DISH), a condition associated with a rich diet – about 20 per cent of the skeletons, as opposed to a frequency of about 2–3 per cent in modern populations. This well-off group of persons had also been less exposed to knocks and skeletal traumas in their working lives than the other two groups who were laid in the external cemeteries (Conheeny in prep). Thus the study of human bones from St Mary Spital is demonstrating how cemeteries in different parts of the complex show differences which can be explained in terms of the groups of people who patronised the hospital, both migrants (as it appears) and wealthy citizens.

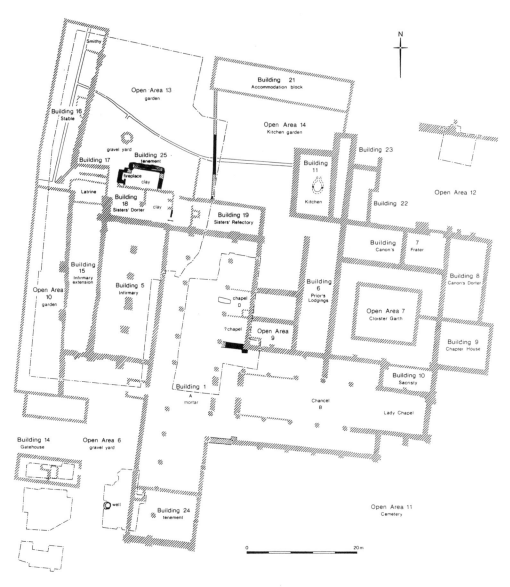

Figure 6.16 Plan of the hospital of St Mary Spital, London, from recent excavations: principal features of the period 1280–1320. The black walls are the new work; the diagonal hatching without lines indicates the previous period (Museum of London Archaeology Service)

Conclusions

When we look at the specialised character and functions of the church building, whether a parish church or the centre of a religious community, four topics are noteworthy: how churches grew; how the building and its spaces helped to make the liturgy or services work; what the fittings and decoration tell us about patronage and the way people used churches as a form of expression for themselves and their families; and how churches reflected the resources, aspirations and failures of their locality.

It is therefore important that once the outline of a church's development is known, its secular surroundings should be analysed; and the same, on a larger scale, goes for the buildings comprising a monastery, friary or hospital. Documents are remarkably uninformative about the disposition of monastic buildings in the majority of cases, and excavation must usually provide the plan and its internal details (Palliser 1993, 7). Only then can we approach larger questions such as whether churches or monastic houses competed with other functions, or with each other, for space, custom or prestige in towns; or to what extent a monastery or a large parish church was the dominant factor in town life. And in the larger towns, it may be that we can learn about the spending power and taste of the wealthy burgesses as much from their patronage of religious art and architecture (especially their tombs) as from the design and decoration of their own homes.

Further, behind their high walls, religious houses were little towns in microcosm. Each house had a church (often larger than the local parish church), a centre for official administration (the chapter house), and buildings for eating, sleeping, working and storage; many of them of stone, and with drains that worked. When civic leaders searched for models to improve the town, its standard of construction and perhaps the arrangement of its major buildings, they must have looked at the monasteries and friaries in their towns.

7 The environment of medieval towns

Environmental archaeology is a self-contained branch of archaeology which includes specialists in flora, fauna, microbiology, dendrochronology, and human bone studies (Shackley 1981). The urban archaeologist has many questions of these specialists: the appearance of the town site in its pre-urban phase (i.e. the pre-town landscape), the disruption to the environment caused by the initial settlement, the information on the town's phases of expansion which is provided by preserved organic remains, the function and social status of parts of the town at various periods, and specific aspects of use of individual buildings (Addyman 1982). Here we review four topics: (i) the influence on medieval town life of physical factors (climatic regimes, air and water pollution); (ii) man's interaction with the environment (plants, insects, and wild animals; woodland management); (iii) biological factors affecting townspeople (dietary changes, infestations, viruses and disease); and (iv) environmental consequences of social practices (overcrowding and other effects of urban living).

Physical factors

The high concentration of human activity and density of population in towns has an affect on their climate and atmosphere (Brimblecombe 1982). The climate of the medieval period in Britain can be reconstructed to some extent from documents (the earliest weather diary describes the weather in Oxford in 1269–70), movement of glaciers, tree rings and pollen assemblages. From this emerges a picture of general warming to around 1000 and then cooling throughout the medieval and post-medieval period. Around 1200, however, winters became noticeably milder than before (ibid., Figs 3 and 4). During the thirteenth century there was a period of little rainfall, but the fifteenth and sixteenth centuries were up to twice as wet, and there were periods of excessive storminess at the end of each century. This increased rainfall seems to have been one cause of a change in rural house construction, from structures laid on the ground-surface to those surrounded by deep eaves gullies, drains on the inside of walls and construction of some houses on platforms (Steane 1985, 175). A recent discussion of the role of climate in English medieval history concludes that *long-term* climatic changes had a limited effect on the standards of living of the inhabitants of lowland England, though settlements and arable land were given up in uplands due to increased rainfall and the gradual drop in temperature (Dyer 1989, 258–60). The country lost thousands of acres of land, but because of a drop in population, it was no longer needed. In contrast, *short-term* fluctuations in weather had profound effects: poor harvests meant widespread starvation, surges in grain prices, and the danger of urban unrest. The archaeological contribution to this debate is hesitant and self-critical, as archaeologists are 'merely noting environmental and economic coincidences, and we need to develop our enquiry to see if they are related' (Astill and Grant 1988, 232–3).

Further topics of interest are differences between town and countryside in temperature, wind velocity and visibility, and air and water pollution. We know that present-day Manhattan, or the City of London, generate their own micro-climate, largely because of the intense generation of heat (now central heating, but formerly thousands of fires and ovens). 'Heat islands' of this kind in late medieval Britain might have reached as much as four degrees Centigrade above their surroundings. On the other hand, life in towns may have been less comfortable when it rained. Since stone and brick buildings, and gravelled streets, are more waterproof than rural landscapes, precipitation will run off quicker, and thus towns which had not developed wide storm drains would be flooded in storms. This flooding would contaminate drinking water, as we know from documentary references.

There are differences between town and countryside today in the ferocity of winds and visibility in the atmosphere; it is difficult to suggest how research on such differences might take us back into the pre-modern period. There are, however, some potential lines of enquiry concerning air pollution. Concern was expressed about the possible damage to health of coal smoke as soon as coal became widely used in the thirteenth century. The smoke concentration over the City of London in the medieval period, for instance, must have been far higher than rural levels. During the post-medieval period of industrialisation there was evident concern about the effect of fogs and smoke in aggravating respiratory conditions, diminishing sunlight, damaging plants, buildings and clothing, but study of these factors has yet to be extended back into the medieval period. Brimblecombe (1982, 22–4) suggests that worthwhile examinations might take place of corroded metal and stonework, and dust deposits, to give information on the nature of urban air pollution in the past.

A study by Boyd (1981) of sediments on two sites at the junction of the Fleet river with the Thames, along the west side of the medieval City of London, suggested correlations between events in the sedimentary record and pollution and climatic 'events' recorded in medieval documents. Beneath six metres of man-made deposits, up to four metres of prehistoric and historic (pre-fifteenth century) sediments of the Fleet were sampled. From medieval sediments came many species of diatoms (microscopic unicellular algae), small molluscs, sponges, foraminifera and ostracods (a type of crustacean). The 140 species of aquatic organisms were a mixture of freshwater, brackish (salty) water and marine species. Two successive layers of sediment, both of fourteenth-century date, produced significantly different assemblages, suggesting something happened in between. The upper layer contained a higher proportion of a diatom associated with polluted water; at the same time molluscs, ostracods and mussels which prefer fresh water, and which were abundant in the lower stratum, suddenly disappeared from the upper. This evidence suggests increasing pollution of the Fleet river, at the time when Edward III was repeatedly demanding that the mayor of London clean up the area. This study further claims that some of the brackish water microfossil organisms may have been deposited by tidal surges during periods of reduced freshwater flow, which are also mentioned in documents.

Molluscs can indicate the ancient environment, particularly on virgin sites where the influence of settlement is still to be felt. At Oxford, the Blackfriars covered the ground surface with a dump of clay, perhaps to raise their intended friary buildings above the adjacent river level. The thirteenth-century surface they buried contained aquatic molluscs, suggesting seasonally flooded grassland (Robinson 1976, 227–31). Parallel exercises have studied the environmental impact of new towns in the Roman period, for instance the first century of development of Roman London (Maloney and DeMoulins 1990).

There is therefore the potential within medieval urban archaeology, as with the archaeology of other urban periods, to study both the history of pollution and the effects of urban growth upon the landscape.

People and their environment: flora, insects and wild vertebrate fauna

Botanical evidence, assemblages of insects and of wild vertebrate fauna in towns (specifically small animals like voles and mice) are grouped for consideration here because they reflect both the influence of the natural world on human habitats and alterations by people to their natural surroundings. Are such assemblages indications of natural habitats, or of human presence? The problem is, they could be either. Excavated seeds or pollen may indicate what was growing nearby or they may suggest cultivation or industrial uses. Similarly, insect assemblages may suggest natural happenings or the decomposition of human rubbish, sometimes of a particular character which indicates it is trade or industrial waste. Bones of small rodents and other wild animals and birds may indicate, by their presence, the character of the immediate surroundings of the deposits.

The rich botanical results from waterlogged sites in Winchester and Southampton, for instance, have illustrated this fundamental problem (Green 1982). These deposits preserve a wide range of seeds, but in many cases they could be from either human or natural sources, and could reflect long periods of residuality; seeds can lie in the ground for hundreds of years without alteration, and can even germinate again after such long periods. In addition, peculiar circumstances ensure the survival of certain restricted kinds of seed: carbonised (burnt) material is often mainly cereals, chaff or associated seeds which have been exposed to fires, and mineralised material is also found in human faeces, reflecting those plants which have been eaten. Over 5000 samples from Winchester of the tenth to fifteenth centuries were examined, but the pessimistic conclusion was that detailed and reliable statistical analysis on pits of a particular century (i.e. to chart change) could not yet be undertaken (Green 1982, 46). Current work in London suggests that there were no real changes in plant use during the medieval period, but considerable changes between the medieval and the Roman or Saxon periods.

Study of plants may continue to be bedevilled by such uncertainties of analysis, and sometimes only local or anecdotal information will be obtained. For instance, samples from the ditch of Oxford castle, dating to the fourteenth to mid-fifteenth centuries, produced 'the usual diverse range of species from many different habitats which tends to be found in urban waterlogged deposits' (Robinson and Wilson 1987, 63). They included weeds which tend to grow around places of human habitation, edible fruits (grape and fig, probably imported) and cultivated plants, including clippings from box hedges which must have adorned the castle garden. It seems at present that cesspits contain more variety of seeds than dump layers: in medieval Constance (Switzerland), for instance, over three times as many varieties from layers of the same early fourteenth-century date (Küster 1993).

One local but extremely useful area of plant studies is that of food plants which passed through the human body and ended up in cesspits (Fig 7.1). The interpretation of some layers in these pits as human faeces is often supported by the occurence of human parasite ova (see below), though it is also clear that cesspits were used as general dustbins for the waste of food preparation in the kitchen (a topic of equal interest). To take only one example from a recent excavation, that of a cesspit attached to a fifteenth-century hall in the precinct of the minster at Beverley, on the Lurk Lane site, here much was deduced from samples from three layers (McKenna 1991, 215). The most abundant food residue was cereal bran, from wheat and/or rye, which had been ground into flour to make bread. Those who used the site also ate figs, strawberries, hazelnuts, apples, raspberries, sloes, bullace (another member of the *prunus* family), wild cherries and elderberries. Grape pips came from raisins, which we know were imported into Hull in the fourteenth century, though grapes were growing in monastic gardens. The food or drink was flavoured with fennel, coriander, poppy and possibly dill. All three contexts produced fragments of corncockle – a widespread weed in the medieval period – but not many, indicating that the bread consumed was made from good-quality grain. Corncockle makes bread unpalatable and produces mild intoxication, and its ingestion has been associated with susceptibility to leprosy.

To make more general statements, plants can be grouped by habitat or association, so that observed variations are between groups rather than individual species. Following standard works such as *Flora of the British Isles* (Clapham et al. 1987), nine different broad habitat and usage categories are recognised and have been used in analysis in London, for instance on 106 samples from 60 tenth- to thirteenth-century features (pits, occupation layers, and hearths or ovens) on sites around Cheapside in the City (Jones et al. 1991). Many plants fall into more than one category, and evaluation according to the quantity of seeds and the archaeological context is also necessary. Five of the categories deal with the localities in which wild plants are found; three categories with their potential uses; and the ninth is cultivated plants.

Weeds of cultivated land are usually brought into towns with the cultivated plants with which they were grown. In this group of pits and other features, as in other towns, they included corncockle and fool's parsley. *Plants of waste places and disturbed ground* are probably the most numerous on urban sites since they reproduce quickly; such species include

Figure 7.1 Thirteenth-century cesspit, Milk Street, London. Environmental analysis
of the deposit in this pit produced a great number of fruit seeds (Museum of London
Archaeology Service)

goosefoot, nettle, thistle and dandelion. *Plants of woods, scrub and hedgerows* were not well represented in the London pits, except as edible fruit and nuts which are better discussed as a separate group. Inedible plants in this category, such as stitchworts and chickweeds, may have been imported casually by animals or people. *Grassland plants* may also have been brought in accidentally. Some, such as sedges, were probably imported for flooring or thatching material, and seeds of the grass family (along with other species) may have been from hay. *Plants of damp or marshy land* included rushes and other plants growing on the banks of ditches or streams; they were also used for roofing or flooring. *Edible wild plants* included blackberry or raspberry. Edible woodland plants included wild strawberry, sloe and hazlenut; apples may have come from hedgrows or managed orchards, along with pears. *Medicinal plants* included opium poppy, which contains strong alkaloids, and henbane, which is a sedative; many other wild plants had some kind of medicinal property, if herbals and folklore are to be believed. *Wild plants with other economic uses* included elderberries, which could be used in tanning, and weld, which produces a yellow dye but is also a common weed. At present, it seems that seeds of wild plants with uses in medicine, as food, and in industry rarely occur in large enough concentrations to justify interpretation as anything but weeds. Finally, *cultivated plants* included peas, beans, carbonised cereals, cherries, fennel, grape and fig. In the London case there were few instances where the botanical evidence pointed clearly to specialised uses or high-status food consumption, but this method holds some hope for future results.

A further but less significant problem concerns imports. The earliest appearance of new foodplants or exotic fruits in documents can be compared with their earliest appearance in the archaeological record; this is one of the current approaches (Greig 1988, 125–7; Jones et al. 1991, 353). Imports from other countries in Europe are likely to have been a significant part of the diet and therefore of the archaeological debris. By the end of the medieval period, the level of imports in the larger centres was high. To take the most extreme case, import duties in 1480–1 in London were levied on ships coming from the Low Countries and northern Spain, carrying almonds, aloes, aniseed, apples, barley, bay-tree (laurel) berries, cinnamon, cloves, figs, flour, garlic, ginger, hemp, hops, mistletoe, mustard seed, nutmeg, nuts, oats, olives, onion seed, oranges, peas, pine-cone kernels, pomegranates, prunes, raisins, saffron, teazles and wheat (Cobb 1990). All these commodities would have spread through the capital to smaller towns and, to a lesser extent, they were imported through many other ports. It is ultimately more important to know how people on an excavated site were using spices, cereals and fruit, rather than to know whether the produce was native or foreign.

The problems of 'background noise' associated with plants in general also attend study of pollen in urban archaeological deposits. Two main types of pollen spectra can be distinguished. The first is rich in pollen of grasses and *compositae* (e.g. daisies, dandelions, marigolds), probably the result of natural transport and deposition. The second type is rich in pollen of cereals and sometimes of *Ericales* (heather, ling, heaths), and the deposits producing it are often well-fills or buried soils; thus it is probably a sign of human activity.

There are a number of caveats which have to be made. Some plants produce far more pollen than others, and clearly wind-pollinated plants such as dock, sorrel and nettle will produce higher numbers of far-travelling pollen when compared with insect-pollinated plants such as bedstraw or the herb avens. The pollen in any town deposit will be a mixture of 'regional pollen' from outside the town, a 'local pollen' component from features such as moats and ditches, and a third human component (Fig 7.2).

Greig (1982, 50–64) based conclusions on 34 sampled sites, of which 20 were urban, and six of these were medieval; all were in England. Certain types of feature seem to have distinctive pollen spectra. Ponds, wells and ditches have spectra with abundant evidence of grass and other plants which together derived from local sources. A second distinctive spectrum is characterised by a preponderance of cereal pollen, and one possibility is that this represents straw or chaff. This was the character of samples from a ditch at Bolebridge Street, Tamworth, a ditch at Nantwich, and a pond or dump in York. A third type has a large amount of *Gramineae* (grasses) pollen, together with signs that the pollen was dispersed by humans, and probably represents hay somewhere nearby (as from a sample from a barrel-latrine in Worcester). Fourthly, pollen of heather and ling is occasionally found in urban samples, and presumably reflects the introduction of cartloads of such plants for roofing or flooring, as indicated by seed remains in urban deposits.

The plant most used in the medieval town was, of course, wood; especially for buildings and constructions of all kinds, artefacts, and for firewood (for a general survey of the crafts using wood in the medieval period, see Munby 1991). By the thirteenth century, in England, woodlands were a managed resource (Rackham 1976, 69–95). Man expected to live off renewable resources, and woods were managed on this basis. Felling at set intervals, and programmes of coppicing (which as a practice is known by 1068), ensured vigorous regrowth.

Oak was the most widespread timber used in buildings and other wooden constructions such as waterfront revetments (Fig 7.3); it was used for structural timbers, laths and boards. Oak for royal contracts, such as the roof of Westminster Hall, came from royal woods in Hampshire, Berkshire, Surrey and Hertfordshire; the leaders of the church could also rely on royal or noble assistance for large structural timbers. Religious houses could use wood sent as part of the *firmae* (rents) of their manors.

Elm was used for piles in waterfront structure, but was also supplied in the form of boards. It was used for doors and window shutters, privies, floors and for benches, dressers and shelving. Even in London, the sources of elm were local: the Bridge Account Rolls for the brief period 1381–97 mention eighteen specified places in Essex, Kent, Middlesex and Surrey as sources. Ash was used for handles of tools, the uprights in wattling and as planks in certain situations, especially pastry boards (the long table attached to the wall in many kitchens). Beech was used for laths, occasionally for shelving, and sometimes used for scaffolding or other forms of poles, as was alder, fir and willow. Wicker (horizontal and vertical rods woven together) was used chiefly for fences, weirs and other external situations. During the tenth to twelfth centuries wicker was also used to line rubbish pits (Fig 7.4).

Demand for timber from towns had a number of consequences. First, areas

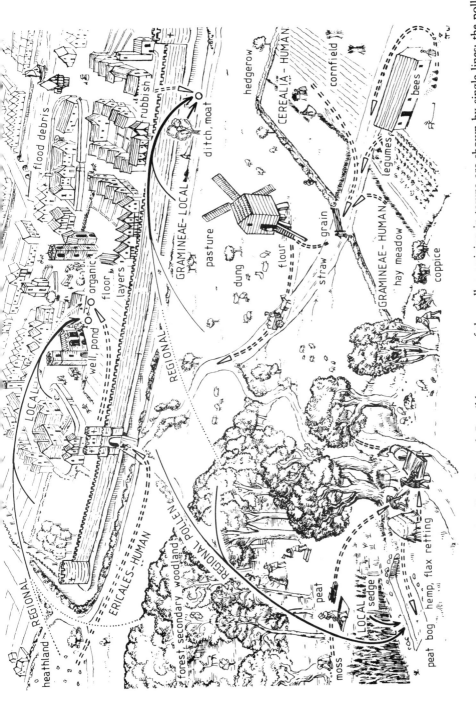

Figure 7.2 A model of urban and rural pollen dispersal. Possible sources of the pollen arriving in towns are shown by single lines; the pollen dispersal through human action, by double dashed lines (Greig 1982)

Figure 7.3   Well-preserved oak timbers comprising a waterfront revetment of *c.* 1220 at Billingsgate, London (Museum of London Archaeology Service)

around at least the major towns were denuded of a large part of their tree cover. As we have seen, most of the major species could be used either in construction or as fuel. This continuous and, in some cities, increasing need for timber led to the import of some species from mainland Europe early in the medieval period. By the thirteenth century, in London, it was as cheap to import oak and fir (deal) from the Baltic as it was to bring it from anywhere outside the home counties; this was presumably a function of the extraordinary demand in the city as well as difficulties with overland transport. Secondly, it is probably the case (though more work is needed on this to fill out the picture) that the possibility of finding larger trees for construction work became rarer as the period progressed, and therefore that the timbers provided for building work in towns gradually became smaller. This seems to be the case in London, where building contracts specify the sizes of many of the principal timbers. A range of documents suggest a general diminution in timber sizes between the middle of the fourteenth century and the latest, in 1602.

Study of insects in the medieval period does not seem to have advanced as much as that for the Roman and Saxon or Viking periods (e.g. O'Connor et al. 1984, 171). In York, where much work has been undertaken, it is suggested that changes occur in typical beetle faunas through the medieval period, with domestic species like furniture beetle, spider beetles and species which graze moulds becoming gradually more numerous than those found in

Figure 7.4 A medieval rubbish pit lined with wicker, Milk Street, London (Museum of London Archaeology Service)

rotting matter, and grain pests, common in the Roman period, appearing again in the late medieval centuries (ibid.). Study of insect and small mammal assemblages is very site-specific, but can, on occasion, make suggestions as to the ebb and flow of the boundaries of settlement. The onset of urbanisation on the west fringe of medieval Oxford, for instance, was revealed by insect assemblages (Robinson 1980, 199–206). Samples from mid to late twelfth century ditches at the Hamel contained insect faunas characteristic of damp grassland. Ditches and pits of the next two human generations contained urban faunas: the proportion of outdoor insect species fell. The 'urban' insects had habitats such as rotten thatch, damp corners of buildings or decaying straw and animal remains. One pit contained many puparia of a bloodsucking sheep parasite, suggesting the washing of sheep or carding of wool on the site.

A detailed understanding of the appearance of some urban areas, especially open spaces, can be obtained by studying small mammals, such as mice, rats and voles. Armitage (1985) applies principles developed from the study of animals on islands to medieval urban ecosystems, proposing that large gardens, churchyards and waste ground can be seen as 'habitat islands' or refuges for small mammals, separated by areas of dense human occupation without much greenery. A greater range of species might be expected in open spaces near the edges of town than in the centre, but this has still to be tested. Certainly analysis of a late fifteenth-century well at

Greyfriars, London, and fourteenth- to fifteenth-century pits in the collegiate grounds at Beverley (Lurk Lane), both peripheral sites in their towns (though within the walls), showed a variety of species: on both sites, rats, mice, fieldmice, field (short-tailed) voles, bank voles, pygmy shrews, water shrews, and weasels; in addition, at London, yellow-necked mice and hedgehogs, and at Beverley, moles. These habitat islands might therefore furnish much useful information on the history of small faunal species and their frequency in towns. But further, from their preferred micro-habitats, we can reconstruct the immediate surroundings of the deposits in which their bones were found. Armitage and West (1985) suggested, from the range of small animals which had been trapped or had fallen into the disused well of the London Greyfriars, that the garden contained thick grass, scrub, water-filled ditches (for some additional frogs in the well), possibly hedges and orchard; but all contributing to an impression of 'an overgrown and bankrupt garden'.

It is currently thought that the more dramatic aspects of small animals, and in particular their role in the transmission of disease, would be difficult to recognise in archaeological bone assemblages (Rackham 1982, 92). Mice and rats form a significant pest of Roman settlements and are clearly transported by man. Although the black rat was introduced in the Roman period, extensive sieving at York of Anglian and later levels suggests that the species was not present again in this town until late in the Anglo-Scandinavian period; that is, it was re-introduced, perhaps reflecting trade with Europe or the Mediterranean. Since these small mammals are only hosts of the vector of many diseases, while their presence is esssential for some diseases such as the Black Death (in epidemic proportions), their actual presence is not in itself an indicator of disease, although it may reflect hygiene levels.

All kinds of site may produce evidence of seeds, use of timber, insects, and small animals. But to advance, the discipline needs groups or assemblages which are tightly dated, low in residuality, exceptionally well-preserved, large in sample size, and not too far removed from their original point of use or deposition. In other words, the 'more secondary' the deposits become, through being churned about or physically transported, the less reliable will be our conclusions.

Work in London and other medieval ports shows that waterfront sites often have all the required merits (though there has to be an assumption that the waterfront dumps were 'fresh' and therefore not removed too far from their primary state). Many deposits on each large site are dated accurately by dendrochronology of timber structures; if there are stone river walls, naturally, the tightness of dating is far less exact. Large samples from well-defined deposits should be bulk sieved for bone, shell, pottery and other finds on a mesh of 2–4 mm.; the resulting domestic animal and fish bone assemblages need to be sufficiently large for statistical comparisons (Fig 7.5). If several waterfront sites are excavated, we can document the chronology of introductions of imported foodstuffs as well as new types of pottery or other artefacts, though new species rarely appear in the archaeological record until some time after their first documented appearance, and it is more likely that the archaeological specimens are from the period when the species' use becomes more common. Further, both finds and environmental analysis in

Figure 7.5 Environmental archaeologists at work, with tower sieves, London. A: Siraf-style flotation tank, B: wet-sieve facility, C: cement mixer for difficult clay-rich samples, D: settling tanks (Museum of London Archaeology Service)

London have demonstrated that the dumps used to reclaim land reveal differences between sites which may reflect either nearby rubbish heaps from different social groups (royal households, poorer ones) or variations in local activities (including trade waste). The dumps may have incorporated rubbish from the tenement which was itself being extended, thus forming a reservoir of information to match the structural remains. Even better evidence comes when a building, often of timber, survives exceptionally well in the riverside deposits, and environmental analysis can make a contribution to study of its function and appearance.

A third focus of waterfront investigation concerns the foreshore which accumulates against each revetment. The amount of silting may indicate the lifespan of the revetment, though floods and scouring action may have also had their effect. Foreshore deposits can document changes in river level, salinity and pollution. Again, to make sound inferences about these things, several sites should be sampled, on both sides of the town's waterway.

Biological factors: diet

As the previous discussion has shown, the influences at work on the provision of foodstuffs in towns are several and intertwined. When towns are relatively small and depend for their food supplies on the adjacent land, the diet of townspeople and rural food-producers are very similar. Urbanisation,

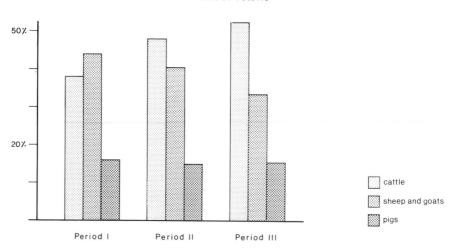

Figure 7.6 Main domestic species of meat-bearing animals in King's Lynn (Noddle 1977)

however, moves towards abolishing the seasons, for town authorities try to store grain and other basic foodstuffs to offset seasonal variations in the availability of food. The meat diet of townspeople will perhaps be different from that of rural folk, since farmers will sell excess stock to town butchers, and the town itself may demand certain kinds of meat. Alternatively, the town may be fed with what the countryside around is producing for other purposes, as in the case of sheep reared predominantly for wool.

Further, the increasing urban population puts a huge load on the surrounding countryside. Agriculture becomes more intense, since farmers can make money by supplying the towns, and rural estates thus begin to mirror prosperity in towns which they have helped to support. This section will deal with the provision of meat, which has to be transported, butchered and marketed. The food industry has many by-products; urban manufacturing crafts use the waste from animal slaughter, especially tanners (who supplied the leather industry) and bone-workers.

Discussion of animal bones must start with those of the main domesticated animals: cattle, sheep or goat (which are often discussed together, partly because of the difficulty of telling the bones apart), and pig. Our first example shows how sites in a town demonstrate the exploitation of these species over time. At King's Lynn, ten thousand animal bones were identified by Noddle (1977); they represent, however, probably less than 0.025 per cent of the bone deposited since the eleventh century. Here, three periods covering the whole town were used: I, *c.* 1050–1250; II, *c.* 1250–1350; III, *c.* 1350–1500. The percentages of fragments of the three main domesticated species are shown in Figure 7.6. By weight, this indicates that beef was the main meat consumed; the number of bone fragments was similar in Period I, but a dressed carcase of beef probably gave 36kg or more of beef or veal, as against 3kg for one of mutton or lamb (the problems of arguing from bones to carcases, and from the sample to the animal population, are addressed in studies which put forward the various different methods of analysing bones:

Chaplin 1971; Maltby 1979, 5–8; Scott 1991). The increasing availability of beef in King's Lynn over the medieval period is marked. This diet was varied with a wide selection of domestic and wild fowl and varieties of fish, all sea species, increased from three in Period I (cod, haddock and plaice) to nine in Period II (the new species being ling, conger, hake, halibut, ray and flatfish). It is suggested that of these, plaice, ray and possibly conger may have been raised in local fisheries. Cod was evidently the most important for food, followed by ling, haddock and plaice.

A different pattern of meat consumption over time was found at Lurk Lane, Beverley, in a study of buildings forming part of the precinct of the medieval minster from the eleventh to the fifteenth centuries (Scott 1991). Cattle, sheep and pig were the most common mammals, but when measured both by number of fragments and by minimum number of individuals (MNI) methods, the percentage of cow bones present fell during the twelfth and thirteenth centuries, to pick up again in the fourteenth. At the same time, the percentage of sheep bones rose, to fall back as the proportion of cattle rose again. Throughout, the proportion of pig bones stayed roughly the same.

The significance of the proportions of the three species was underlined by study of the age at death of the animals (i.e. when they were brought to market for butchery). Most of the cows were aged 3.5 years or older; they had presumably been used for milk production or, in the case of the old ones, as draught animals. Similarly, two-thirds of the sheep were aged three years or more, up to two years later than would be necessary to obtain the maximum meat from the body. Pigs, on the other hand, were reared primarily for meat and were slaughtered as soon as a worthwhile body weight was attained.

Pigs were probably also raised in the backyards of the town, and were not subject to economic forces influencing the availability of cattle and sheep driven in from the countryside (i.e. their usefulness for other purposes). At Beverley, the relative increase in the sheep numbers in the twelfth and thirteenth centuries probably reflects the importance of the area for providing wool for the expanding textile industry. Similarly at Lincoln and York, although beef was also the main meat, the consumption of mutton increased at the expense of beef in the medieval period (O'Connor 1989). Since wool was an important export, it is seen to be a consequence that sheep became predominant in the urban diet (i.e. economic factors pertaining to an agricultural product, not a consequence of urban desires). In Oxford, near the Cotswolds, analysis from large samples on the St Ebbe's sites suggests that the townspeople ate meat from sheep which were surplus to requirements in a wool-producing area (i.e. the young males and older females, which had presumably outlived their usefulness (Wilson 1989, 264)). Similarly, most of the beef came from cows, not oxen, which probably had longer working lives as draught animals on the farms. In the fourteenth and fifteenth centuries there was an increased availability of veal (i.e. unwanted male calves), which has been noted in Exeter, Northampton and Oxford (Wilson 1989, 261–2).

Rabbit appears to have been introduced during the eleventh and twelfth centuries (Grant 1988, 166); it became a common food. Wild mammals such as deer are generally occasionally to be found in early medieval deposits, but rare in later towns. The role of wild mammals and birds in urban economies in Wessex is discussed by Coy (1982), who concludes that the nutritional significance of wild vertebrates may be greater than their meat values imply. Study of wild species may provide information on the relationship between hunting practices and the town, domestication of wild species, and control of the landscape. At Lurk Lane, Beverley, for instance, hunting must have been responsible for a profusion of deer, hare, wild boar and wild birds: 28 species of birds were identified, three-quarters of which were edible (the others being scavengers), and half the species present came from wetland environments which surrounded the town (Scott 1991, 222–3).

Fish was an important element in the medieval diet, since the Church forbade eating of four-legged animals for up to three days each week and during Lent. Freshwater fish for institutions and households of status came from private fishponds. This seems to have given some species of fish a status which might seem unjustified on grounds of palatability (Grant 1988, 170, quoting C. Dyer). Towns on rivers could expect a variety of freshwater species in their diets: ten species were identified in a sieved deposit from Abingdon. But strata generally contain more evidence of marine species, even on inland sites. At ports and coastal towns, as one might expect, the variety of available fish was larger. At Great Yarmouth, where fishing was a staple industry, deposits of the eleventh and twelfth centuries produced nineteen species of mainly marine fish (Rogerson 1976, 208–23), incidentally proving the value of sieving; a previously excavated site at Baker's Lane in King's Lynn had produced eight marine species from normal retrieval (hand-picking of bones), and these tended to be the large specimens with heavy bones. The Yarmouth fish included species inhabiting both inshore and deep water, and those which live near the surface and in depths of over 100 m. A variety of fishing techniques, with trawls, seine nets, and hooks (several of which were found on the excavation), is indicated.

To revert to the major mammals, a problem is how to distinguish food debris from deposits left by butchery or industrial processes concerned with animal products, for example tanning or horn-working. Serjeantson and Waldron (1989, 3) suggest four criteria: the context is a residential building; the bones are exclusively or mainly of food animals; there is evidence of butchery; and the parts of the skeleton which have the most meat predominate. At Exeter, despite the variability in the groups, it seems likely that all parts of animal carcases were dumped on these domestic sites. This could be because either householders did their own butchery, or that they bought all parts of the carcase, even those without much meat, from the market. By contrast, in early medieval Southampton, the bones derived from twelfth-century pits behind stone houses on the High Street were derived from large joints or carcases, suggesting butchery on the site; but in the thirteenth century, as butchery became a specialised trade, with markets of its own in the town, the size of the joints was reduced and the choice of meats on this comparatively well-off site widened (Platt 1976, 68–9).

A model of the exploitation of meat-bearing animals in Lincoln over the period 850–1500 has been provided by O'Connor (1982, 46–50), using material from the Flaxengate site. He assumes that the studied bones came from both domestic consumption and butchers' or slaughterhouse debris, and the relative absence of luxury animals indicates that the site was of middling status. Hunting and wildfowling were incidental providers of food; venison was rare. Figure 7.7 shows how butchery practices for sheep changed in the mid-eleventh century, when also younger pigs appear noticeable in the diet; the rabbit makes an appearance shortly before 1300.

The degree to which animal bones produce information on craft-working has already been examined (pp. 109–11). Further analyses can tell us about the way animal carcases were prepared for the table, at least in major institutions such as religious houses. For example, Levitan (1989) analysed bones from nine areas of St Katherine's priory, Exeter. The study is also a warning, for each of the nine locations gave a different view of the relative numbers of species over time; in other words, small-scale excavation, say of one or two areas, would have given an over-selective picture. The priory was apparently buying in carcases whole or halved, and much secondary butchery took place on site. The main results were that outside the kitchens, large bones were dumped as carcases were deboned and meals were prepared. Smaller bones, which represent table waste, were found in deposits closer to the eating and living areas, and were perhaps disposed of in a more haphazard fashion. Monastic sites hold out the possibility of progress in this area because they are, to some extent, closed sites with limited functions (as opposed to the burgage plot, subject to many forces), but they generally seem to produce a small amount of animal bones; perhaps the excavators are too keen on chasing walls (for a review, see O'Connor 1993).

Can we detect differences in social standing between ordinary households from their diet? One would expect so, if we can assume that most bones on a site are food debris and not industrial waste. Sometimes, not surprisingly, there are no differences: a study of two adjacent properties in medieval Hull produced no clear differences and considerable similarity (Berg 1987). On the other hand, an instructive case comes from seventeenth- and eighteenth-century Amsterdam, where Ijzereef (1989) was able to suggest, from bones in cesspits, which households were Jewish and which were not (5 per cent or more pig bones indicates a non-Jewish household), and although pottery and glass did not indicate much social differentiation, he proposed a range of rich–poor households based on 'rich' and 'poor' bone assemblages. Rich meant the better cuts of beef, high proportion of chicken, turkey and goose, freshwater fish and oysters; poor meant cattle skulls and metapodials, with bones often smashed open for the marrow, and fish skulls. If such distinctions could be found in British assemblages, and correlated with similar indices of social status in the artefacts (or possibly documentary records, if present), it would be a significant step forward. Differences in social status might also be indicated by differences in seed remains, for instance if there was a higher proportion or variety of imported plants or foodstuffs (grapes, figs, oranges) on one property than on another.

Further, modern anthropological studies show that socially defined custom is a major determinant of what we eat (e.g. Fieldhouse 1986). In previous centuries, as today, food is a vehicle for social cohesion. It was, and is, used in rituals or on ceremonial occasions (the wedding feast, the wake); there have always been prestige foods which were only found at rich tables, such as venison, wild birds and the rarer fish (Grant 1988, 178–82, where a high

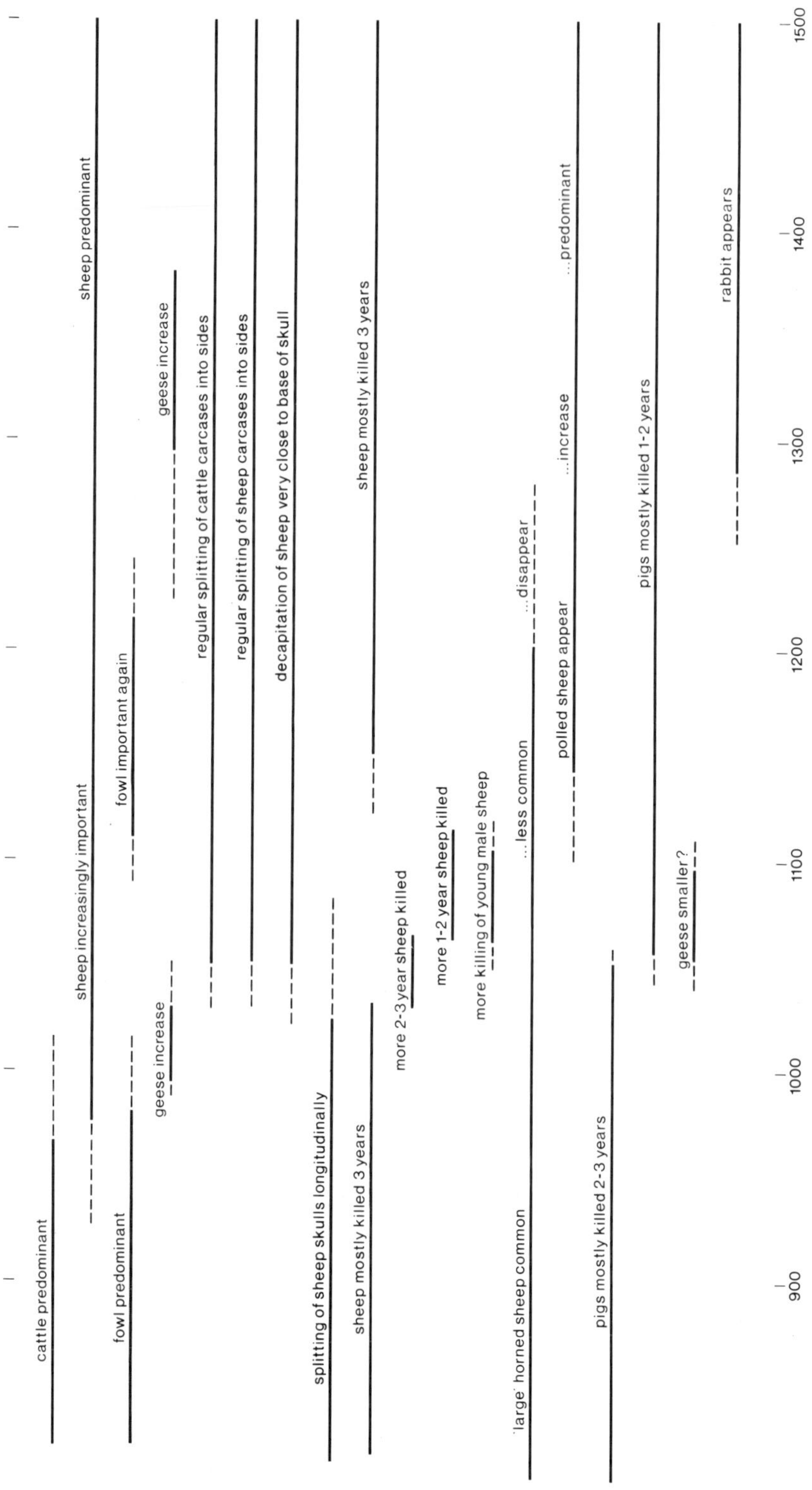

cattle predominant

fowl predominant

sheep increasingly important

fowl important again

geese increase

geese increase

regular splitting of cattle carcases into sides

regular splitting of sheep carcases into sides

decapitation of sheep very close to base of skull

sheep predominant

splitting of sheep skulls longitudinally

sheep mostly killed 3 years

more 2-3 year sheep killed

more 1-2 year sheep killed

more killing of young male sheep

sheep mostly killed 3 years

'large' horned sheep common

...less common

...disappear

polled sheep appear

...increase

...predominant

pigs mostly killed 2-3 years

pigs mostly killed 1-2 years

geese smaller?

rabbit appears

900　　1000　　1100　　1200　　1300　　1400　　1500

Figure 7.7 Chronology of some of the variables noted in animal bone assemblages, tenth to fifteenth centuries, at Lincoln (O'Connor 1982)

proportion of pig bones is also thought to be a mark of status). In medieval towns, the waste of food preparation and what was left on the table were regularly tipped into cesspits to join the human waste. A wide range of animal, bird and fish bones in such deposits might indicate a degree of wealth and feasting, as is suggested by documentary records such as accounts of foodstuffs for specific meals. The Carpenters' Company in London, for instance, had feasts when the Mayor was presented to the king at Westminster (November), on St Laurence's Day, and on a special Feast Day. Records of what was purchased for these meals each year survive for much of the period 1491–1521. The Feast Day meal in 1491, for instance, included a whole sheep, veal, beef, necks of mutton, two swans, 17 geese, 22 conies, seven dozen pigeons, nine pikes, as well as ingredients for sweet dishes. On other occasions variety was provided by lamb, kid, marrow-bones, and pork. Other poultry and game included the occasional buck, chickens, peacocks, plovers, rabbits, sparrows and other small birds; and the fish included bloaters, bream, cod, crab, cray-fish, dace, four kinds of eel, flounders, haddock, herring, lamprey, ling, minnows, mullet, oysters, roach, salmon, salt-fish, shrimps, smelt, sole, sturgeon and turbot (Marsh 1914). This was not a royal or a noble household, but a prosperous guild in London; in general, there was a high proportion of animals and birds that had not previously served a useful purpose on the farm. One way forward may be to characterise such luxurious meal assemblages from documentary records and then look for similar groups in the archaeological record, starting with high-status sites.

Studying the physical and environmental background to towns is interesting and necessary, but in urban archaeology the economic factors will be the most significant in terms of results. The best archaeological evidence for the management of sheep flocks in the countryside probably comes from towns (Grant 1988, 153). We have already noted that an increasing proportion of sheep bones at Beverley may indicate an emphasis on sheep-farming in the area. From a large sample such as the 28,000 bones now studied from medieval sites in the St Ebbe's district of Oxford, Wilson (1989, 265–6) has outlined the contribution of animal bone studies to the study of the local economy and the organisation of the town. The high proportion of bones from cows rather than oxen suggests that dairying husbandry supplied most of the cattle killed in Oxford, in turn implying that arable farming was less prevalent in the area. The subsistence economy of the town may have been geared to this farming style. The post-medieval organisation of butchery, in which cattle were brought long distances and fattened in meadows near the town, may have started in the medieval period; along with breeding and husbandry improvements, this was to result in larger animals. Within the town itself, pigs and calves were slaughtered on the tenements; they may have been kept there. The tenements would have had a superficial scatter of bone debris about them, but most of the animal debris was safely buried in pits, and exposed bones would be scavenged by dogs, cats, foxes and birds. The investigation could not demonstrate that fowl were reared on the site, since the bones could be from birds bought in the market. The small size of the bones of domesticated animals during the medieval period points to poor feeding and housing conditions, especially meanness in provision of fodder.

How good was the standard of living in medieval towns? Townspeople generally probably had a better diet than their neighbours in the countryside. If they had money, they could buy several kinds of bread, ale, wine, meat and fish. Fruit and vegetables came from town and suburban gardens. Over the period, there is some evidence that town-dwellers ate more meat, and less cereals or fish; after 1350, such a desire was part of the strengthened bargaining powers of the workers (Dyer 1989, 201–2).

Biological characteristics of urban people: disease

Urbanisation was perhaps the greatest social transition suffered by man since remotest antiquity, and some changes in man's health may well have followed from it. There might be alterations in nutrition, changes in the pattern and ferocity of diseases, differences in height, age at death, or changes due to the nature of urban living and work. This discussion follows the outline of Waldron (1989).

We are constrained to examination of the human skeleton for evidence, and only a portion of conditions and diseases are manifest on human bones. Of vitamin deficiency diseases, only scurvy and rickets are detectable in skeletons. Scurvy (lack of vitamin C) is indicative of a restricted diet, and was epidemic in medieval Europe in winter months when fresh fruit and vegetables were unavailable. Rickets (lack of vitamin D) is a disease of children, enlarging epiphyses (the ends) of growing bones; common among medieval skeletons, it was endemic in areas of low incident sunlight, and perhaps therefore it might be more prevalent in crowded parts of towns. White (1988, 41) suggests that there are no recorded archaeological examples in the early medieval period in England, indicating that people were sufficiently exposed to the high degree of sunshine then prevalent.

Infectious diseases which might have been particularly rife in towns include leprosy, tuberculosis and syphilis. The first two in particular were common in the medieval period, though it has also been suggested that the spread of pulmonary tuberculosis led to the decline of leprosy in the post-medieval period, since the tubercle bacillus seems to have given some immunity from the bacterium which causes leprosy. So far few sites in Britain have produced examples of leprous bones, though the disease was common enough for there to be about 200 leper hospitals in thirteenth-century England (Steane 1985, 96–7). Five cases of tuberculosis and some possible cases of syphilis were noted at St Helen's in York (Dawes and Magilton 1980, 58). The suggestion that tuberculosis and syphilis were particularly urban diseases should be tested. Other diseases known to have been virulent in medieval Europe included amoebic dysentery and smallpox (Cipolla 1981, 50–7).

Not enough is yet known about people's height in the medieval period to distinguish between rural and urban populations (Fig 7.8), but it is notable that an observable decline in height among British youths in the nineteenth century could be related to industrialisation and urbanisation. We also do not have enough samples yet to form conclusions about differences in age at

| Site | Date | Heights | | Sample |
		male	female	size
Bidford-on-Avon	Saxon	5'7½" (171.45)	5'1½" (156.21)	large
North Elmham, Norfolk	"	5'7¾" (172.09)	5'2" (157.62)	20
Porchester Castle	"	5'9¼" (175.90)	5'5" (165.10)	15
St Helen, Aldwark, York	10th–16th	5'6½" (169.30)	5'2" (157.50)	large
Durham Cathedral	12th	5'7½ (171.45)	— —	20
Pontefract Priory	12th–14th	5'7½" (171.45)	— —	34
Wharram Percy DMV	medieval	5'6" (168.00)	— —	large
Greyfriars, Chester	"	5'6½" (168.82)	5'3" (160.98)	20
Austin Friars, Leicester	"	5'10" (177.80)	5'2" (157.50)	13
Bordesley Abbey	"	5'8" (172.80)	— —	19
Rothwell Charnell House	"	5'5" (165.10)	5'2" (157.60)	large
Dominican Priory, Chelmsford	"	5'7" (170.18)	5'1½" (156.20)	25
Guildford Friary, Surrey	"	5'8" (175.00)	5'3" (157.50)	56
St Mary's Priory, Thetford	12th–13th	5'9¾" (177.17)	— —	5
South Acre, Norfolk	12th–14th	5'6" (167.64)	5'1½" (156.21)	5
St Leonard's, Hythe, Kent	14th–15th	5'7" (170.20)	5'2" (157.40)	large
St Nicholas Shambles, London	11th–12th	5'8" (172.75)	5'2" (157.50)	94

Figure 7.8 Mean stature heights, in inches and centimetres, for Anglo-Saxon and English medieval populations (White 1988)

death; certainly people lived shorter lives in the past, but the only comparisons which can be made are between then and now, rather than between communities of the same historical period. More pessimism attends hope of distinguishing work-related conditions in the medieval period, since the actual occupations are never known; though in a case of an eleventh-century (presumably late Saxon) group recovered from beneath the levels of the bailey at Norwich Castle in 1979, widespread occurrence of deficiency in vitamin D (resulting in rickets) and a number of pathologies associated with lifting and labouring strains among the male skeletons suggested occupations where hard physical work was undertaken away from sunlight. This could cover many medieval trades, but in this case mining was suggested (Stirland 1985). More success may be achieved by studies of post-medieval cemeteries, where documentary evidence, particularly name-plates on coffins and parish registers, may give details of occupations of the deceased. Then comparisons could be made with similar pathological cases from medieval contexts.

Let us take a recently studied medieval urban population as an example of what is found. The cemetery of the small parish church of St Nicholas Shambles in London was excavated in 1975–7 and 234 articulated skeletons of eleventh- to twelfth-century date recovered (White 1988). A large proportion of adults could only be said to be 'over 17', and thus the finding that only 6.4 per cent of the others reached 45 is probably unreliable (many older persons were probably in the 'over 17' group). Similarly, few infants were found, a common feature of cemetery excavations where the small bones have probably been greatly disturbed. The skeletons of those identifiably under about 13 years old could not be assigned a sex (Fig 7.9).

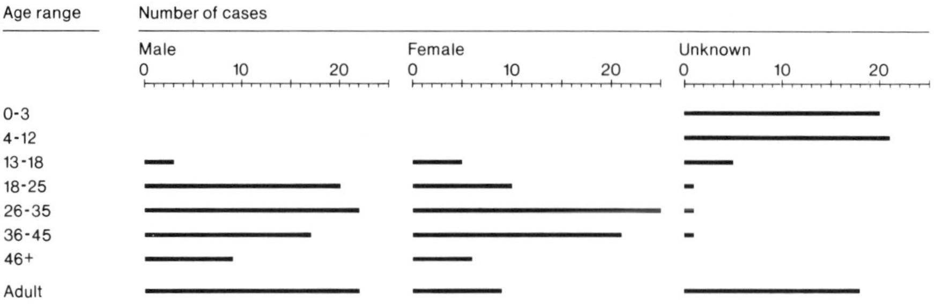

Age range	Number of cases		
	Male	Female	Unknown
	0 10 20	0 10 20	0 10 20
0-3			
4-12			
13-18			
18-25			
26-35			
36-45			
46+			
Adult			

Figure 7.9 Age at death and apparent mortality rate at the St Nicholas Shambles cemetery, London (White 1988)

This group of townspeople was comparatively healthy, with few pathological conditions evident on their bones. Only 12 per cent of the adult jaws were free from some kind of dental defect, mainly either a high degree of calculus deposit, indicating a lack of cleaning of the teeth, or caries (Fig 7.10). On average, people lost 7.6 per cent of their teeth during life. Nutritional disease was evident in 17 per cent of the skulls in a mild form of pitting of the inside of the eye cavity called *cribra orbitalia*. Osteoarthritis, especially of the vertebrae, was found in many skeletons – at least 40 per cent of the adults were affected, men and women equally. Deformities of the toes might be a result of wearing tight shoes. Individual cases of note included a girl with a missing left leg who had survived to be a teenager, and another, tall and probably overweight, who was left with a prominent limp probably through a congenital disorder of the hip joint called *coxa vara* (Fig 7.11). One girl died in childbirth (Fig 7.12). A much larger group of 1041 skeletons has been published from the cemetery of St Helen on the Walls, York (Dawes and Magilton 1980), but the date range of this population stretches from the tenth to the sixteenth century, and conclusions can therefore only be of a general character. The low expectation of life, with 27 per cent of the sample dying as children and only 9 per cent living beyond the age of 60, confirms documentary evidence for high mortality rates all over medieval England. Unexpectedly, men seemed to outnumber women at all ages over 35, whereas in modern societies women usually have a higher expectation of life then men. It may be that females suffered poorer nourishment than males in medieval (and here, Tudor) towns, as well as the special hazards of child-bearing. More tightly dated groups of skeletons are required; and groups from different parts of the same town, to study local variations.

When archaeological survival is exceptional, a detailed medical and anthropological programme of research can produce far-reaching results. One such programme, for instance, is that being conducted on the human remains from two sites in Svendborg, Denmark (Jansen 1987), as part of a multi-disciplinary study of the medieval town. About 200 individuals were excavated. Child mortality was high. The average age at death was 33 for men and 28 for women, several of whom died in childbirth. The average height was 175 cm. for men and 163 cm. for women; at St Nicholas in

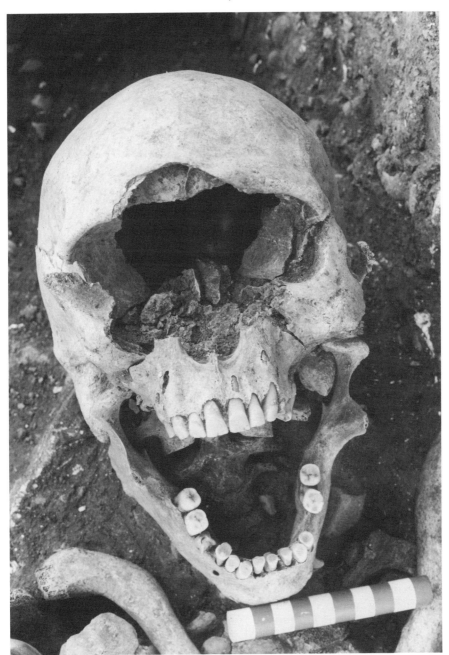

Figure 7.10 A good set of teeth on a skeleton from St Nicholas Shambles. A man aged 32–35, he had lost six teeth during life (White 1988)

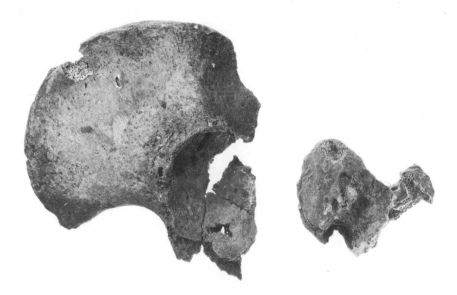

Figure 7.11 Detail of the congenital orthopaedic disorder of the hip, *coxa vara*, on a skeleton from St Nicholas Shambles. This woman lived to be 25–28, but her femur had been disposed to slipping in the joint through adolescence; this led to it growing distortedly, and some discomfort (White 1988)

London it was 173 cm. and 157.5 cm. The medieval Danes were also larger than nineteenth-century Danes; in 1850 when National Service was introduced, the average height of the first intake was 162 cm. Osteoarthritis was widespread, reflecting the hard physical labour and lack of labour-saving devices of the time. A notable feature of the Svendborg group is that 57 of the skeletons still had their brains, due to the anaerobic alkaline soil conditions. Scanning electron microscopy clearly shows the brain structures.

The level of hygiene on urban properties can be ascertained by study of human coprolites (faeces) and evidence of parasites such as tapeworms, which are found in both cesspits and floor layers. At High Street/ Blackfriargate, Hull, for instance, samples from cesspits of thirteenth- and fourteenth-century date produced ova of intestinal parasites; floors produced parasite ova probably from rat and mice droppings. Human parasites included whipworm (*Trichuris* sp.) and maw-worm (*Ascaris* sp.), which have also been found in medieval faecal deposits in York and Beverley (McKenna 1987, 255–7; 1991, 214). Absence of the ova can also aid interpretation. At Beverley, for instance, a twelfth-century pit attached to an aisled hall in the minster precinct served as a dump for food waste, including fish bones and fruitstones, but the very low concentration of intestinal parasite ova ruled out the possibility that this was a cesspit – more likely the pit was dug simply for rubbish disposal, possibly during the demolition of the associated building (McKenna 1991, 214).

Towns were often ravaged by disease. The Black Death of 1348–9 cut the

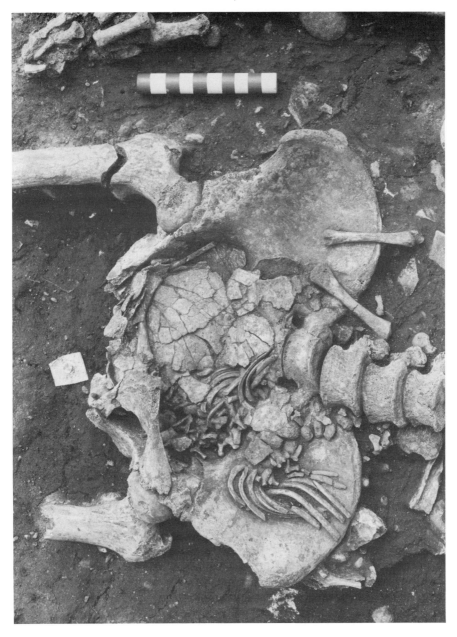

Figure 7.12 Detail of a young woman who died in childbirth – the foetus was never born (White 1988). The bones of small children are often dispersed by later digging in a cemetery, and thus their number is probably underestimated

population of England by between 20 and 40 per cent (Postan 1975, 33–4, 41–4; Ziegler 1971; for comments on black rats in medieval towns: Armitage, Locker and Straker 1987, 278). It is estimated that in Europe, over a three- or four-year period, 25 to 50 million people died, a quarter to a third of the entire population. The plague was especially disastrous in certain towns, for instance Lübeck, where nine out of ten people perished. It may have been especially lethal because it struck at a population already weakened by chronic undernourishment after a generation of agrarian disasters and famine. Plagues occurred between 1328 and 1377, perhaps resulting in an overall fall in population of over 50 per cent; the population did not really resume an upward trend until about 1470.

By the early fifteenth century, it seems that plague had become a particularly urban disease: by the 1420s the habit of fleeing to the country to avoid contagion was already well established. Between 1400 and 1485 only five plagues affected the whole country, whereas seven hit the capital. But did these plagues always result in a reduction in the population? Perhaps not, since a significant increase in the birth rate often follows a high death rate. Significant rises in the replacement rate may have helped restore population levels as the frequency of plagues lessened.

Were townspeople different genetically from those in rural areas? At any period, a proportion of town-dwellers will be migrants from the countryside. Modern research suggests that migrants sometimes select themselves, in that they are taller (Tanner and Everleth 1976, 146). Whether it is a result of their genetic make-up or the urban environment, however, several modern studies around the world suggest that urban children grow up taller and heavier than rural children (ibid., 147–59) and urban girls reach puberty earlier than rural girls (ibid., 159–60) – a feature observed in 1610 by a writer called Quarinonius. In one modern study, village children erupted their permanent teeth, on average, later than urban children. It seems probable that most, if not all, these differences are due to the economic differences between town- and country-dwellers, resulting in the better feeding of the well-off. Such differences might be apparent in medieval populations.

Conclusions

This chapter has considered the ecology of the medieval town: the degree to which urban settlement affected its rural surroundings, the environment in towns, and the degree to which nature's products – the weather, animal and plant foodstuffs, and man's own biology – affected life in towns. It is evident that environmental archaeology has a great potential. From soil samples the archaeologist can extract detailed description of how and under what conditions deposits formed. Pollen gives information on vegetation and land-use, diatoms on salinity and levels of water pollution, seeds and charred plant remains on vegetation, diet, materials used in buildings, technology and fuel. Though useful, however, this is at present largely anecdotal evidence. Some broad changes can be seen, for instance in the consumption of varieties of meat, but we cannot yet say much about how, or whether, environmental factors actually contributed to change. It does appear to be the case that the environment of towns had an effect on people's state of health and perhaps exposed them to a wider range of conditions and possibly fatal diseases than living in the countryside.

At least two other approaches could be taken to the one adopted here. The environmental archaeology of a particular town might be arranged as a study in the progression from the rural (pre-urban) to the modern urban environment: colonisation of the countryside, early food supply, commercialisation of that food supply, development of secondary animal product industries. Within the town we would then pursue local variations in craft activities, development of craft control, and, in general, the late medieval migration to larger towns which produce density of urban population and its concomitant urban diseases. At all times we should explore, if we can, the extent to which the bundle of variables studied as environmental archaeology will demonstrate that life in towns was different from that in the countryside.

Medieval urban archaeology uses concepts derived from economic history deduced from documents, and perhaps this should be resisted. There is, secondly, a potential within environmental archaeology to add a further dimension to the study of towns and their surrounding areas. The current emphasis on proportions of animal bones, meat weight, wheat varieties, and food storage and processing might be matched with studies into the natural history of the medieval farmyard and field or the ecological consequences of drainage or woodland clearance. What were the ecological effects on a village which was economically dominated by the self-interest of a nearby town? Instead of seeing the space around us, and around our archaeological sites, as a natural resource, emphasising modes of production and systems of redistribution of wealth, we could see it as context for living and stress the finiteness of the resource and our responsibilities to the ecosystem (Austin 1990). This is a challenging new way of looking at the past.

8 Unfinished business and further questions

The discoveries and speculations surveyed in this book are the work of many archaeologists in medieval towns in Britain, especially in the last thirty years. Medieval urban archaeologists have argued and shown that towns can claim to be more representative of the nature of society of which they formed part than any other type of site. In towns, as the previous chapters have demonstrated, we are most likely to find archaeological evidence of both long-distance and local trade, of exploitation of natural resources, of specialisation and of technological evidence in manufacturing, of social differentiation, of the means of political control, and of the religious aspirations of the population. This is our continuing agenda, and much remains to be done.

The archaeological investigation and study of medieval towns should go through four stages. These stages are: (i) data gathering; (ii) the construction of chronologies and typologies; (iii) study of archaeological evidence of specific activities; and (iv) study of the archaeology of groups which functioned within towns, including their contacts with the region around the town and other towns. At the wider regional and national levels we also need consistent data collection, the construction of typologies of artefacts, and the comparison of similar functional groups, for instance artisans engaged in manufacture, working within several towns in a region or up and down the land. Finally, we can suggest how archaeology, by working to its own agenda, can make a contribution to answering some of the many historical questions concerning towns in the Middle Ages.

Data gathering

If nothing or little is known about the archaeology of a town, then data must be gathered. This was the phase which many medieval (and pre-medieval) towns went through in the 1970s and 1980s as their centres were drastically altered. At this first stage, many would argue that there is really no appropriate archaeological strategy or question except Philip Barker's 'What is there?' Others would say, in contrast, that while it is important to produce consistent data over many investigations, it is also possible to apply research questions to the archaeology of a town, even where little is so far known. Rescue archaeologists who work every day on the archaeology of towns reply that research questions are by their very nature selective and exclusive. An emphasis on the Roman period will inhibit data gathering in the post-medieval period, as was traditional in British archaeology until the 1960s. By constantly unearthing the unexpected and yet significant, urban archaeology tends to point out the blinkered perspective of over-rigid research designs.

Excavation sites will continue to be dictated very largely by development pressures, and they will be all over the town. This should be used to provide a wide range of samples from different types of deposit – streets, backlands, churches, defences and waterfronts. The strategy must be to bring about, within the context of redevelopment, a comprehensive series of excavations sampling all the periods of the town in a wide variety of stratigraphic situations; for examples of this as a proposed strategy, see Biddle and Hudson (1973) on London and Carver (1980) on Worcester.

In the choice of sites, or as is often the case, assigning priorities of effort and time between sites which come up for redevelopment at roughly the same time within towns, archaeologists are guided by the nature of deposits. We need to map the survival of deposits within towns, to chart the archaeological resource which is still available to be managed (either by preservation or by interrogation before destruction in building works). This resource will be greatest in certain parts of town, for instance along the waterfront, in churchyards, and in zones not yet touched by comprehensive redevelopment. If we chronicle the earth-moving episodes in a town's history, as has been done for a handful of British towns (London, Worcester, Stafford, York), we not only have the menu of research possibilities (and an important tool in the necessary dialogue with urban planners), but the earth-moving operations themselves show us something about the town at those periods. The building of castle mounds or clearance of whole streets for public or religious complexes demonstrates power at work in the town; the expanding waterfront zone presumably reflects pressure on urban space, as a result of booming business, or rising population, or both.

At the same time as we gain a satellite view of the town's depositional history, we must use the close-up lens. The essence of town archaeology is the *sequence* of layers which form its stratification. From the sequence we can deduce change over time in building layout and design, in pottery and all other kinds of artefacts, and in the interaction of people with their natural environment. But layers in towns suffer from two kinds of interference. The first is the sheer weight of the actions of people over time, continually digging new holes and constructing new roads or buildings. In towns of the greatest age such as the ex-Roman centres, the medieval strata are often damaged, at least in part. Their buildings and yards, in any one period, are never complete. The second problem is residuality: an unknown proportion of the finds or inclusions (building material, bones, seeds or insect remains) within any stratum may have survived from a significantly earlier period and thus form a kind of misleading contamination. Bones, pottery and the hardier seeds or fruit-pips could be redeposited centuries after they were initially discarded. A 'background noise' is created, through which the true signals of each new period have to be heard.

To address both these problems, the archaeologist needs single-period sites, both individual building-types (an intact church or medieval house) and whole short-lived towns (i.e. a medieval town-site which is now deserted) for comparison with the often more fragmentary remains excavated in the centres of living towns. The abandoned sites, often in the countryside, will tell us what our fragmentary buildings looked like in their full plan. But what these rural sites gain in extent of plan, they will lose in not having long histories and useful sequences of layers. Often, therefore, dating frameworks will be urban in origin, whether pottery or artefact types, carpentry joints dated by dendrochronology (tree-ring dating), or moulded stones in buildings dated by documents. The key is the urban stratigraphy, hence the emphasis among urban archaeologists on the diagram of relationships between layers called the Harris matrix (Harris 1979) as the key to explanation and the starting point for interrogation of the archive, whether the site report or the multitude of finds.

Nor is the background noise of residuality necessarily a bad thing; in long-lived towns we have to work with it. Significant information can be gained particularly about artefacts from study of layers later than the period in question. Three-quarters of all the Romano-British objects of gold, silver and copper alloy recovered from the Winchester excavations of 1961–71 were found in post-Roman or residual contexts (Biddle 1990, 31). A similar situation probably pertains in London, where within the city walls late Roman levels have been comprehensively damaged by later activity and especially nineteenth-century cellars, so that future work on the third- and fourth-century city may have to concentrate on the extensive list of Roman coins found in dark earth and other Saxon deposits. Recognised and tackled correctly, residuality need not be a problem. We must, by preference, distinguish the types of deposit which are low in residuality, and here again waterfront dumps, being composed of largely contemporary and often fresh rubbish, are good candidates. It may be that waterfront dumps are better reservoirs of low-residuality than other secondary contexts such as pits on inland sites; the latter lay open for periods, whereas the process of dumping behind revetments was presumably quicker, being intended to function as reclaimed ground on which traffic and buildings could promote business.

At this first level of data recovery, there are some specific areas which require development. Three can be mentioned: how to deal with the sheer weight and variety of information from medieval towns (as for their other periods); how to deal with small towns; and the special case of standing buildings.

Today, archaeological information is usually stored in computer files, and we can use the question of their structure and design to explore both the strengths and weaknesses of our information. Archaeologists in medieval towns, as on sites elsewhere, need four basic groups of files: those dealing with context (stratum) information, bulk finds, smallfinds, and pottery types. In the context file, we need to suggest an interpretation for the layer – construction, demolition, abandon, occupation – and a higher grouping such as a building, a road, or a streambed. Finds are conventionally divided into two kinds for practical purposes: those treated in *bulk* (large amounts of any material, for instance rooftiles or iron) and *smallfinds*, sometimes called registered or accessioned finds (they are individually accessioned into a museum collection), such as knives, barrels, pieces of furniture or hones. The file records the context number of the object, its material, what we think it is, and other practical information such as its state of conservation.

There are four sub-kinds of pottery files: provisional dating of the pottery (often called 'spot-dating') to help interpretation of the strata, sometimes a fabric type-series for the town (samples of wares analysed according to the geological composition of their clay), a form type-series, and files concerned with quantification. In this way the basic questions about pottery can be answered: (i) what date is it?; (ii) where was it made?; and (iii) what was it used for? (Orton et al. 1993). As a large number of stratified groups of pottery is collected from the town and its region, students can study types and functions, chronology, methods of manufacture and marketing.

To emphasise the value of deep stratification and major centres is not to abandon the archaeology of small towns, which have their own considerations. Size, by itself, does not make a town. What differentiates a town from a village is a preponderance of activity concerned with manufacture, food processing and trade, both wholesale and retail. Borough status and other privileges, and the buildings to illustrate this local independence, will follow. Townish villages and small towns are in some ways more difficult to study than larger towns – the stratigraphy in them is thin, and therefore extremely fragile and susceptible to damage from the lightest of foundations. It is one of the challenges facing archaeologists in rural areas today that small-town medieval society is less well understood, by documentary historians, than that of the manor and village (Hilton 1990, 73). We need an expansion of theory to deal with small towns; perhaps they should be dealt with as rural landscapes rather than as dense urban settlements.

Thirdly, a strategy is also required for standing buildings in towns, which might be used for elucidating the development of social needs such as that for privacy. Buildings, far more than excavation sites, are three-dimensional banks of information. Archaeologists should be involved far more than at present in the recording of changes to old buildings during refurbishment. Many opportunities have been lost. Indeed, a dedicated research strategy is required for the present urban environment as a historical and archaeological resource.

Construction of chronologies and typologies

This is the stage which archaeologists in many medieval British towns have now reached. A body of data has been gathered, and questions are being put to it. These questions concern both topography ('How did the town develop into its present shape?') and artefacts ('What equipment did the people use? What did the inside of their houses look like?').

Archaeologists should start with the topographical subjects where they can be most original and confident: street-plans, building types and the distribution of debris (Carver 1987, 20). The debris will include evidence of manufacturing and trade, and the objects will represent a whole level of popular material culture which is representative of the life of the majority of people who do not appear in documents (and which have not figured in traditional museum collections). Spatial studies will be informed by dating of the layers which is provided by artefacts, coins and dendrochronology, and, by careful use of the stratigraphic and dating evidence, typologies of individual forms of pottery or artefact – which type came first, and which later – can be constructed. These typologies, of which a pottery type-series is the most important for the town, can then be used to date artefacts in less

Ceramic phase	Date-range	New pottery types
1	850–1020	Late Saxon shelly ware
2	1000–1020	Early medieval sandy ware
3	1020–1050	Early medieval sand and shell ware
4	1050–1100	Andenne ware, Early medieval chalky ware, Early Surrey ware
5	1100–1150	London-type ware (and Coarse variant)
6	1150–1180	Shelly sandy ware
7	1180–1240	Rouen and northern French imitations in London-type ware
8	1240–1270	Kingston-type ware
9	1270–1350	Mill Green ware
10	1330–1380	Coarse Border ware in quantity
11	1360–1400	Cheam ware
12	1400–1480	Coarse border ware bifid rims
13	1480–1520	Raeren stoneware

Figure 8.1 Ceramic Phases constructed for the late Saxon and medieval periods in the City of London, from excavated waterfront assemblages of 1972–83 and earlier collections in the Museum of London (after Vince 1985). Can we apply these ceramic phases to the whole city, and apply them to other artefacts such as metalwork or building-types?

well dated contexts, which are perforce the majority in both urban and rural excavations.

The framework of pottery dates developed for London in recent years, for instance, can date most groups of pottery in the capital from the twelfth to the fifteenth century to 30-year bands (Fig 8.1; Vince 1985). This is soundly based on a framework of dendrochronological and coin dates. Such series of assemblages dated by dendrochronology should be sought in other towns. The potential of waterlogged places such as streams, and especially the waterfront zones of riverine or coastal ports, is such that even though many have been excavated in recent decades, they will continue to be very cost-effective producers of archaeological data. The rich finds from the waterfront zone are an index of all aspects of life in the medieval town. Further, if our analysis can be developed, it may be that the waterfront area will prove to be a comprehensive sample of the archaeological data of the town's region and hinterland.

Some of these chronologies of individual artefact-types (including buildings) will be informed by dates in documentary records, and medieval towns have, to varying degrees, the additional benefit of more records per square mile than rural places, or than towns in previous centuries. This is not the place for an extended discussion of the relative merits of archaeo-logical and documentary research. The two sources are complementary. Archaeology gives more depth on individual sites, while documentary study is wider and is effective at the level of larger units such as street or town. Each group of investigators scrutinises a different set of sources, and there is no overlap. Further, there is scope for much interesting comparison of results, even if (or perhaps, especially because) we do not yet know how the two sets of information will integrate in the short or long term.

Study of archaeological evidence of specific activities

It is at this third level of enquiry that analysis of research questions beyond those concerned with typologies and chronologies can truly start. The data have been gathered in a consistent manner and are in a repository where they can be studied for all time. The story told by the stratigraphic sequence of layers can be compared with that of the artefacts, so that the knotty evidence of intense occupation is teased out where justified and stretched on a framework of suggested dates. But there is also a law of diminishing returns; there is a danger of reduplication of data if we do not know when to start being selective in data gathering. For this reason it is vital that the urban archive is constantly, and repeatedly, worked over to produce the answers to the changing list of archaeological and historical questions. The answers should feed into future research priorities so that new excavation not only adds to knowledge, but also refines it.

A certain kind of study forms the bulk of archaeological reports today: excavations of the defences of town X, the cathedral at Y, the bridge of Z. Less common are studies of single facets of town life which bring together the evidence of several sites within the place. This is partly a consequence of a potentially over-rigorous division of archaeological reports, and of archaeological organisations, into site- and finds-specialists. There should now be a swing towards integration of structural and artefactual evidence, so that we can understand an activity – defence, or religious experience, or making cloth – in its entirety. When the structures associated with an activity, the heavy plant, changed, did the mobile equipment also change? We do not seem to be asking such questions.

In theory, it should be possible to add functional keywords to descriptions of strata in the computer, at least at the 'stratigraphic group' level. These functions, often based on study of the finds, will tend to be 'domestic', 'industrial' and such broader terms than the more specific 'religious' or 'military', but such justifiable associations cannot be ruled out. In the preceding chapters we have looked at a variety of activities in the medieval town – military, domestic, industrial, commercial, and religious – and often the function of a place at a certain time will be suggested by documentary study, since we know the site was a castle or a church (though the date-range of this function may not be certain). We have also, however, pointed to several pitfalls in attributing such functional associations, on archaeological or other grounds, to individual strata or stratigraphic events.

More immediate success is likely with the simpler connections we can establish between the town and its hinterland, and between the town and other towns, both in Britain and abroad. Imports in certain materials are easily perceptible, especially in pottery and glass, or exotic (non-native) materials such as ivory, gems or articles of wood species not grown in Britain. The imports may be from the hinterland or within Britain (such as building stones or bricks, identified according to their own ceramic fabric type-series), or from abroad. Here the computer model is at its most helpful, for the files will say how many objects, whether pottery or individual items, originated in a certain place (the north, or the Rhineland). They will not say how the objects got in the town, or by what route, but we may speculate and compare relative volumes of regional or foreign material.

A presently unanswered question concerns the role of towns in developing or promoting technological advancement. Were towns the crucible of innovation? For some scholars, such as Sjoberg (1960), the main influence on the development of society from prehistoric to industrial times was technology. That is, distinctive types of social structures were associated with varying levels of technology, by which term Sjoberg meant sources of energy, tools and know-how. According to this argument, the shift from copper or bronze implements to those of iron opened the way for proliferations of cities throughout the Old World. With iron, better wheeled vehicles became a reality, shipping goods and food to markets in towns. Improved tools built better and more permanent houses, and money made an appearance.

During the entire period 500–1500 the Near East was superior to the West; technologically the West had little to bring to the East, and techno-logical movement was in the other direction. Discoveries which came by this route included the tidal mill, water clock, segmental arches in buildings, reservoirs and dams, gunpowder and cannons, the magnetic compass, alcohol, sulphuric and hydrochloric acids, asphalt, soap, tin, glazed and lustre-painted pottery, the spinning wheel, paper, (including the airmail variety, which was developed so it could be carried by pigeons), many secrets of the tanning industry via Cordova in Spain, sugar, and coffee (al-Hassan and Hill 1986). The network of this movement was composed of European cities and ports, and its energy was supplied by trade. Towns as agents of technology transfer are as important as towns as seats of innovation itself. Medieval towns were accelerators of change, whether or not they were the source of it. Other historians emphasise what western Europe did to these ideas, having absorbed them, particularly the mechanisation of processes (Cipolla 1981).

Literacy was the key to Islamic advancement, which was at least partly based on technological innovation and achievement. Islam was, moreover, primarily an urban civilisation. In this case urban prosperity, local and international trade, literacy, and a flourishing culture of science were all linked together; and further, the Islamic empire, which stretched from Delhi to Marrakesh, made Arabic a common language of scientists and allowed interchange of ideas in that language over an immense geographical area. Transferring this to our own area, it may be that constructing an archaeology of literacy would be profitable, and we will probably find that towns were, as some contemporaries thought, crucibles of literacy. This skill aided technological as well as other advances.

Study of archaeology of groups in towns

Between 1150 and 1340 a new urban society came into being in European towns. Many towns were autonomous or fought to be so, but these apparently united communities contained disparate groups and classes. Friction between these component groups often resulted in violence. Even with the caveats of the previous section, archaeology has an important role to play here in describing the extent and character of the material lifestyle of the various groups.

Some can be perceived relatively easily, such as the nobles who occupied distinctive and large town houses, or the churchmen and women in their walled-off convents. The ordinary people who made up the majority of citizens were dispersed and arranged through the town according to factors which are revealed by a combination of archaeological and documentary study, which can be called urban socio-topography. Especially within larger towns, taxation records show that some areas were in general richer than others. This may be because people in one zone were generally richer, or because the richer area had in it one or two very rich tax-payers. Archaeological study of sites in both rich and poor areas may help clarify the fiscal data. Alternatively, street-name evidence often implies quarters for individual trades; but in Britain, as in France and Germany, such quarters seem to have been more prevalent in the twelfth and thirteenth centuries and, significantly, not later, when, after the plague, these local boundaries appear to have broken down. Again, archaeology could make a contribution to this matter when a sufficient number of sites in a town have been excavated.

Archaeology should not be solely a matter of fine workmanship and high-status sites. We should investigate the mass market, where the majority of people operated; one recent study has shown the popularity of shoddy, mass-produced items in base metals (Egan and Pritchard 1991). We must establish the baseline of the archaeology of the ordinary. To reset the balance further, there is a need for more study of the marginal groups and outcasts of medieval urban society. First, the poor, because they formed an important and numerous part of the urban population. Other specifically outcast groups include lepers, Jews, and, in a more subtle way, partially acceptable foreigners (Lombards). Study of these groups will complement and correct the bias of currently published work.

Secondly, women in towns. This may seem harsh following the excluded people of the previous paragraph, but it is a fact that the medieval urban milieu was first and foremost a masculine milieu. Medieval towns were important in the struggle for emancipation of women (Power 1975). Medieval women in towns could be active in trade, ran schools, and held property. In many ways they were privately, though not publicly, on a par with men. For many urban trades, women were part of the labour market; in some towns their involvement in the crafts was curbed, because, as today, they could be used to undercut the cost of male labour. Several industries were largely in the hands of women, especially the making of silk and brewing of ale. Can we construct an archaeology of women's affairs in the medieval town? Papers arguing explicitly for gender studies in archaeology appeared in the early 1980s (Conkey and Spector 1984), but although attempts have been made to develop the subject in prehistory (e.g. Gero and Conkey 1991), scholars have generally fought shy of developing gender studies in historic periods (see now Gilchrist 1994).

Figure 8.2 Lincoln: reconstruction of the West Gate of the Upper City about 1180, by D.R. Vale (City of Lincoln Archaeological Unit). At this period the city was dominated by its two largest medieval topographical features, the Norman cathedral and the Norman castle

Wider chronological questions

Finally, the archaeologist can study large themes: towns in the medieval economy, or how towns functioned in their regions; how the history of towns, elucidated or illuminated by archaeology, mirrored the history of the country as a whole. The medieval period in most of Britain, as we saw at the beginning of this book, falls into two parts: the apogee of towns in 1100–1350, and crises and consolidations in 1350–1500 (or to some scholars, 1530).

Of these two parts, the first is easier to study, as is its equivalent in the first two centuries of Roman occupation of Britain. Urban consumption, urban markets, new standards in housing, waves of religious orders are all clearly perceptible in the archaeological record. The archaeology of medieval towns can be dealt with as a study of definable monuments and sites, since the larger topographical features were often clear and stark (e.g. Fig 8.2). There should be more work in Wales, Scotland, and Ireland; many themes could be listed for treatment. But at least we roughly know what evidence survives, and how to record it.

The second part of the Middle Ages, from 1350 to about 1500, is, by comparison, poorly understood, in towns as in the countryside, and this is partly because we do not yet know effective ways to study it (for

Figure 8.3 Lincoln: reconstruction of the Newland Gate and the Lucy Tower about 1500, by D.R. Vale (City of Lincoln Archaeological Unit)

commentary and some notable archaeological attempts, see p. 21 above). In large and small centres, the strata of this later period are thin; the waterfront zones are increasingly unhelpful, as stone walls take over from timber revetments and the dated groups of artefacts become far less frequent. It seems the case that after the Black Death, because there were considerably fewer people in towns, several processes took place. Shops disappeared from central streets, some houses became larger, while the unwanted margins of settlement crumbled, decayed and were covered with their own version of dark earth, the deposit normally associated with the Saxon centuries. Some of these processes, for instance the amalgamation of properties into larger units, can be seen in other European cities and towns (e.g. Zürich: Schneider 1993, 242–3). Within towns, we can expect that the poor and disadvantaged areas suffered disproportionately from the main urban plagues. From England to Italy, the Black Death was, without doubt, a proletarian epidemic; the rich escaped when they could, or lived in parts of town where the quality of life, and sanitation, gave them some protection. Thus, the marginal areas will show more radical evidence of change to the archaeologist. At the same time, long-established towns tried to keep up their defences and large religious buildings (Figs 8.3 and 8.4).

During the fifteenth century some towns recovered. They tended to be the larger centres (and above all, London), or those which could depend upon a rich hinterland for their industrial wealth (e.g. cloth towns in Yorkshire and the West Country). Others, like Winchester, went into a gentle decline. At

Figure 8.4 Excavation of the thirteenth-century Lucy Tower, Lincoln, in 1972–3
(City of Lincoln Archaeological Unit)

first, there were fewer people around, and therefore less need for towns. But
during the fifteenth century, and into the sixteenth, new centres of political,
commercial and cultural influence and power attracted immigrants, both rich
and poor. After a period of stagnation and desolation, sixteenth-century
towns looked for their future prosperity to a new network of connections,
beyond Britain and Europe, to Asia and the New World.

While remaining critical about the nature of the evidence from the ground
or in standing structures, the archaeologist can produce an archaeological
account of the stages in the life of a medieval town. The emphasis in this
book on words like *sequence* and *chronology* shows the archaeological
strength of urban deposits. Archaeological investigation excels in the
recording of times of change and crisis. Strata and the activities they indicate,
such as construction and demolition, above all indicate *change*, whether for
good or ill. One building or waterfront or industrial process or circuit of
defences is replacing another. Archaeological work in towns should, by
preference, therefore investigate evidence of change, and seek to suggest the
reasons for change which have rarely been written down. Were these changes
caused by social conflicts, or by new technologies, or by environmental
factors such as a worsening climate and river silting? By concentrating on
these crucial phases or turning-points in our urban history, archaeology will
provide independent and unique explanation of the past.

Bibliography

Addyman, P.V.A. (1982), 'The archaeologist's desiderata', in Hall and Kenward, 1–5.

Addyman, P.V.A. and Black, V. (eds) (1984), *Archaeological Papers from York Presented to M.W. Barley*, York Archaeological Trust, York.

Aldsworth, F. and Freke, D. (1976), *Historic Towns in Sussex: an archaeological survey*, Institute of Archaeology, London.

Alexander, J. and Binski, P. (eds) (1987), *Age of Chivalry: art in Plantagenet England 1200–1400*, Royal Academy of Arts, London.

al-Hassan, A.Y. and Hill, D.R. (1986), *Islamic Technology: an illustrated history*, Cambridge University Press, Cambridge.

Andrews, G. (1984), 'Archaeology in York: an assessment', in Addyman and Black (eds), 173–208.

Armitage, P.L. (1982), 'A system for ageing and sexing the horn cores of cattle from British post-medieval sites (17th to early 18th century) with special reference to unimproved British longhorn cattle', in B. Wilson, C. Grigson, and S. Payne (eds) *Ageing and Sexing Animal Bones from Archaeological Sites*, Brit. Archaeol. Report 109, 37–53.

Armitage, P.L. (1985), 'Small mammal faunas in later medieval towns', *Biologist* 32(2), 65–71.

Armitage, P.L. (1989), 'The use of animal bones as a building material in post-medieval Britain', in D. Sergeantson and T. Waldron (eds) *Diet and Crafts in Towns*, Brit. Archaeol. Report 199, 147–60.

Armitage, P.L. and West, B. (1985), 'Faunal evidence from a late medieval garden well of the Greyfriars, London', *Trans. London and Middlesex Archaeol. Soc.* 36, 107–36.

Armitage, P.L., Locker, A. and Straker, V. (1987), 'Environmental archaeology in London', in H. Keeley (ed.) *Environmental Archaeology: a regional review, II*, Historic Buildings and Monuments Commission Occ. Paper 1, 252–331.

Armstrong, P. and Ayers, B. (1987), 'Excavations in High Street and Blackfriargate', Hull Old Town Report Series 5, *East Riding Archaeologist* 8.

Armstrong, P., Tomlinson, D. and Evans, D.H. (1991), *Excavations at Lurk Lane Beverley 1979–82*, Sheffield Excavation Reports 1, University of Sheffield/ Humberside Archaeological Unit.

Astill, G.G. (1978), *Historic Towns in Berkshire: an archaeological appraisal*, Berks. Archaeol. Committee Pubn 2.

Astill, G.G. (1985), 'Archaeology and the smaller medieval town', *Urban History Yearbook 1985*, 46–53.

Astill, G.G. and Grant, A. (1988), *The Countryside of Medieval England*, Blackwell, Oxford.

Aston, M. and Leech, R. (1977), *Historic Towns in Somerset*, Committee for Rescue Archaeology in Avon, Gloucestershire and Somerset.

Atkin, M. (1985), 'Excavations on Alms Lane', in M. Atkin, A. Carter and D.H. Evans, 'Excavations in Norwich 1971–78, Part II', *East Anglian Archaeol.* 26, 144–260.

Austin, D. (1990), 'The "proper study" of medieval archaeology' in D. Austin and L. Alcock (eds), *From the Baltic to the Black Sea*, 9–42.

Ayers, B. (1981), 'Hull', in Milne and Hobley (eds), 126–9.

Ayers, B. (1985), 'Excavations within the North-east Bailey of Norwich Castle, 1979', *East Anglian Archaeol.* 28.

Ayers, B. (1988), 'Excavations at St Martin-at-Palace Plain, Norwich, 1981', *East Anglian Archaeol.* 37.

Ayers, B.S. (1991), 'From cloth to creel – riverside industries in Norwich', in Good et al., 1–8.

Ayers, B. (1992), 'The influence of minor streams on urban development: Norwich, a case study', conference pre-printed paper, *Medieval Europe 1992: pre-printed papers 1, Urbanism*, York.

Ayers, B. and Murphy, P. (1983), 'A waterfront excavation at Whitefriars Street car park, Norwich, 1979', *East Anglian Archaeol.* 17, 1–60.

Baart, J.M. (1977), *Opgravingen in Amsterdam*, Haarlem.

Baker, D., Baker, E., Hassall, J. and Simco, A. (1979), 'Excavations in Bedford 1967–1977', *Bedfordshire Archaeol. Journal* 13.

Barley, M.W. (ed.) (1977), *European Towns: their archaeology and early history*, Academic Press, London.

Barley, M.W. (1986), *Houses and History*, Faber and Faber, London.

Barron, C.M. (1974), *The Medieval Guildhall of London*, London.

Barry, T. (1987), *The Archaeology of Medieval Ireland*.

Bassett, S.R. (1982a), 'Medieval Lichfield: a topographical review', *Trans. S. Staffordshire Archaeol. Hist. Soc.* 22, 93–121.

Bassett, S.R. (1982b), *Saffron Walden: excavations and research 1972–90*, Council for British Archaeol. Research Report 45.

Baudry, M.-T. (ed.) (1982), *Archéologie urbaine: actes du colloque international, Tours, 17–20 Novembre 1980*, Association pour les fouilles archéologiques nationales, Paris.

Beresford, M.W. (1988), *New Towns of the Middle Ages* (2nd edn), Alan Sutton, Gloucester.

Beresford, M.W. and St Joseph, J.K.S. (1979), *Medieval England: an aerial survey* (2nd edn), Cambridge University Press, Cambridge.

Berg, D.S. (1987), 'The faunal remains' in Armstrong and Ayers, 245–52.

Biddle, M. (1967), 'Excavations at Winchester, 1967, sixth interim report', *Antiq. Journal* 48, 250–85.

Biddle, M. (1974), 'The future of the urban past', in P.A. Rahtz (ed.) *Rescue Archaeology*, Penguin, Harmondsworth, 95–112.

Biddle, M. (1990), *Object and Economy in Medieval Winchester*, Winchester Studies 7.ii, Oxford University Press, Oxford.

Biddle, M. and Hudson, D. (1973), *The Future of London's Past*, Worcester.

Biddle, M. and Keene, D.J. (1976), 'Winchester in the eleventh and twelfth centuries' in M. Biddle (ed.) *Winchester in the Early Middle Ages* (Winchester Studies 1), Oxford University Press, Oxford, 241–448.

Binski, P. (1987), 'Monumental brasses', in Alexander and Binski (eds), 171–3.

Blair, C. and Blair, J. (1991), 'Copper alloys', in Blair and Ramsay (eds), 81–106.

Blair, J. and Ramsay, N. (eds) (1991), *English Medieval Industries*, Hambledon Press, London.

Bogdan, N.Q. and Wordsworth, J.W. (1978), *The Medieval Excavation at the High Street, Perth, 1975–76: an interim report*, Perth High Street Archaeological Committee.

Bolton, J.L. (1980), *The Medieval English Economy 1150–1500*, Dent, London.

Bond, C.J. (1987), 'Anglo-Saxon and medieval defences', in Schofield and Leech, 92–116.

Boockmann, H. (1987), *Die Stadt im späten Mittelalter*, C.H. Beck, Munich.

Boyd, P.D.A. (1981), 'Medieval estuarine sediments in London', in J. Neale and J. Brasier (eds) *Microfossils From Recent and Fossil Shelf Seas*, Ellis Horwood, Chichester.

Brachmann, H. and Herrmann, J. (eds) (1991), *Frühgeschichte der europäischen Stadt*, Akademie Verlag, Berlin.

Bradley, J. (ed.) (1984), *Viking Dublin Exposed: the Wood Quay saga*, O'Brien Press, Dublin.

Brimblecombe, P. (1982), 'Early urban climate and atmosphere', in Hall and Kenward, 10–25.

Britnell, R.H. (1981), 'The proliferation of markets and fairs in England before 1349', *Economic History Review* 2nd ser. 34, 209–21.

Brown, A.N., Grenville, J. and Turner, R.C. (1987), *Watergate Street: third interim report of The Rows Research Project*, Chester City Council and Cheshire County Council.

Bruce-Mitford, R. (ed.) (1956), *Recent Archaeological Excavations in Britain*, Routledge and Kegan Paul, London.

Butler, L. (1975), 'The evolution of towns: planned towns after 1066', in M.W. Barley (ed.) *The Plans and Topography of Medieval Towns in England and Wales*, Council for British Archaeol. Research Report 14, 32–47.

Butler, L. (1984), 'The houses of the mendicant orders in Britain: recent archaeological work', in Addyman and Black, 123–36.

Butler, L. (1987), 'Medieval urban religious houses', in Schofield and Leech, 167–76.

Campbell, M. (1987), 'Metalwork in England, *c.* 1200–1400', in Alexander and Binski, 162–8.

Campbell, M. (1990), 'Gold, silver and precious stones', in Blair and Ramsay, 107–66.

Campbell, R.M.S. (1990), 'People and land in the Middle Ages, 1066–1500', in R.A. Dodgshon and R.A. Butlin (eds), *An Historical Geography of England and Wales* (2nd edn), Academic Press, London, 69–122.

Caple, C. (1991), 'The detection and definition of an industry: the English medieval and post-medieval pin industry', *Archaeol. Journal* 148, 241–55.

Carter, H. (1981), *The Study of Urban Geography* (3rd edn), Edward Arnold, London.

Carver, M.O.H. (1978), 'Early Shrewsbury: an archaeological definition in 1975', *Trans. Shropshire Archaeol. Soc.* 59, 225–63.

Carver, M.O.H. (1979), 'Three Saxo-Norman tenements in Durham City', *Medieval Archaeol.* 23, 1–80.

Carver, M.O.H. (ed.) (1980), 'Medieval Worcester: an archaeological framework', *Trans. Worcestershire Archaeol. Soc.* 7.

Carver, M.O.H. (ed.) (1983), 'Two town houses in medieval Shrewsbury', *Trans. Shropshire Archaeol. Soc.* 61.

Carver, M.O.H. (1987), 'The nature of urban deposits', in Schofield and Leech, 9–26.

Chaplin, R. (1971), *The Study of Animal Bones from Archaeological Sites*, Academic Press, London.

Charleston, R.J. (1991), 'Vessel glass', in Blair and Ramsay, 237–64.

Cherry, J. (1991), 'Leather', in Blair and Ramsay, 295–318.

Chew, H.M. and Kellaway, W. (1973), 'London Assize of Nuisance 1301–1431', *London Record Soc.* 10.

Chitwood, P.J. (1988), 'St Mark's Yard East', in *Archaeology in Lincolnshire 1987–8: Fourth Annual Report of the Trust for Lincolnshire Archaeology*, 24–6.

Ciolek-Torrello, R. (1984), 'An alternative model of room function from Grasshopper Pueblo, Arizona', in H. Hietala (ed.), *Intrasite Spatial Analysis in Archaeology*, Cambridge University Press, Cambridge, 127–53.

Cipolla, C.M. (1981), *Before the Industrial Revolution: European society and economy 1000–1700* (2nd edn), Methuen, London.

Cipolla, C.M. (ed.) (1981), *The Middle Ages*, Fontana Economic History of Europe **1**, London.

Clapham, A.R., Tutin, T.G. and Warburg, E.F. (1987, 3rd edn), *Flora of the British Isles*, Cambridge University Press, Cambridge.

Clark, P. (1984), *The English Alehouse: a social history 1200–1830*, Longman, London.

Clarke, D. (1968), *Analytical Archaeology*, Methuen, London.

Clarke, H. (1973), 'King's Lynn and east coast trade in the Middle Ages', in D.J. Blackman (ed.) *Marine Archaeology, Proceedings of the 23rd Symposium of Colston Research Society, Bristol*, 277–91.

Clarke, H. (1981), 'King's Lynn', in Milne and Hobley, 132–6.

Clarke, H. (1984), *The Archaeology of Medieval England*, British Museum Publications, London.

Clarke, H. and Carter, A. (1977), *Excavations in King's Lynn 1963–1970*, Soc. for Medieval Archaeol. Monograph 7.

Clarke, H.B. and Simms, A. (eds) (1985), *The Comparative History of Urban Origins in Non-Roman Europe*, Brit. Archaeol. Report S255.

Clevis, H. (1989), 'Nijmegen: investigations into the historical topography and development of the lower town between 1300 and 1500', *Berichten van de Rijksdienst voor het Oudheidkundig Bodemonderzoek* 37, 275–390.

Cobb, H.S. (1990), *The Overseas Trade of London: Exchequer Accounts 1480–1*, London Record Soc. 27.

Conheeney, J. (in prep), 'The human bone', in Thomas et al.

Conkey, M.W. and Spector, J.D. (1984), 'Archaeology and the study of gender', in M.B. Schiffer (ed.), *Advances in Archaeological Method and Theory*, 7, New York, 1–38.

Coppack, G. (1986), 'The excavation of an Outer Court building, perhaps the Woolhouse, at Fountains Abbey, North Yorkshire', *Medieval Archaeol.* 30, 46–87.

Coppack, G. (1990), *Abbeys and Priories*, Batsford, London.

Council for British Archaeology (1987), *Recording Worked Stones: a practical guide*, Practical Handbooks in Archaeology **1**, London.

Cowgill, J., de Neergaard, N. and Griffiths, N. (1987), *Knives and Scabbards*, Medieval Finds from Excavations in London 1, HMSO, London.

Coy, J. (1982), 'The role of wild vertebrate fauna in urban economies in Wessex', in Hall and Kenward, 107–16.

Crossley, D.W. (ed.) (1981), *Medieval Industry*, CBA Research Report 40.

Crowfoot, E., Pritchard, F. and Staniland, K. (1992), *Textiles and Clothing c. 1150–c. 1450*, Medieval Finds from Excavations in London 4, HMSO, London.

Crummy, P. (1981), *Aspects of Anglo-Saxon and Norman Colchester*, Council for British Archaeol. Research Report 39.

Curnow, P.E. and Thompson, M.W. (1969), 'Excavations at Richard's Castle, Herefordshire, 1962–4', *Journal Brit. Archaeol. Ass.* 3rd ser. 32, 105–27.

Daniels, R. (1986), 'The excavation of the church of the Franciscans, Hartlepool', *Archaeol. Journal* 143, 260–304.

Daniels, R. (1990), 'The development of medieval Hartlepool: excavations at Church Close, 1984-5', *Archaeol. Journal* 147, 337–410.

Davey, P. and Hodges, R. (eds) (1983), *Ceramics and Trade: the production and distribution of later medieval pottery in north-west Europe*, University of Sheffield.

Davies, R.R. (1991), *The Age of Conquest: Wales 1063–1415*, Oxford University Press, Oxford.

Dawes, J.D. and Magilton, J.R. (1980), *The Cemetery of St Helen-on-the-Walls, Aldwark*, The Archaeology of York **12/1**, York.

Dawson, D.P., Jackson, R.G. and Ponsford, M.W. (1972), 'Medieval Kiln Wasters from St Peter's Church, Bristol', *Trans. of the Bristol and Gloucestershire Archaeol. Soc.* **91**, 1–9.

Dejevsky, N.J. (1977), 'Novgorod: the origins of a Russian town', in Barley (ed.), 391–404.

Dickinson, R.E. (1961), *The West European City: a geographical interpretation* (2nd edn), Routledge and Kegan Paul, London.

Dobson, B. (1977), 'Urban decline in late medieval England', *Trans. Royal Hist. Soc.* **27**, 1–22.

Dobson, B. (1984), 'Mendicant ideal and practice in late medieval York', in Addyman and Black, 109–22.

Dodgshon, R.A. (1987), *The European Past: social evolution and spatial order*, Macmillan, London.

Dolley, M. (1975), 'The coins and jettons', in Platt and Coleman-Smith, ii, 315–31.

Drage, C. (1987), 'Urban castles', in Schofield and Leech, 117–32.

Draper, P. (1987), 'Architecture and liturgy', in Alexander and Binski, 83–91.

Dunning, G.C. (1959), Anglo-Saxon Pottery – A Symposium, *Medieval Archaeol.* **3**, 31–78.

Dunning, G.C. (1977), 'Mortars' in H. Clarke and A. Carter (eds), *Exavations in King's Lynn 1963–1970*, Soc. Medieval Archaeol. Monograph 7, 320–47.

Durham, B. (1977), 'Archaeological investigations in St Aldates, Oxford, *Oxoniensia* **42**, 83–203.

Durham, B., Halpin, C. and Palmer, N. (1983), 'Oxford's northern defences: archaeological studies 1971–1982', *Oxoniensia* **48**, 13–40.

Dyer, C. (1986), 'English peasant buildings in the later Middle Ages', *Medieval Archaeol.* **30**, 19–45.

Dyer, C. (1989), *Standards of Living in the Later Middle Ages*, Cambridge University Press, Cambridge.

Dyson, T. (1989), *The Medieval London Waterfront*, Annual Archaeology Lecture for 1987, Museum of London.

Eames, E. (1980), *Catalogue of Medieval Lead-glazed Earthenware Tiles in the Department of Medieval and Later Antiquities, British Museum* (2 vols), British Museum.

Ebner, H. (1991), 'Die Frühgeschichte Wiens', in Brachmann and Herrmann, 60–7.

Eddy, M.R. and Petchey, M.R. (1983), *Historic Towns in Essex*, Essex County Council.

Egan, G. (1985–6), 'Finds recovery on riverside sites in the City of London', *Popular Archaeol.*, December 1985/January 1986, 42–50.

Egan, G. (1991), 'Industry and economics on the medieval and later London waterfront', in Good et al., 9–18.

Egan, G. (in prep), *The Medieval Household: daily living c. 1150–c. 1450*, Medieval Finds from Excavations in London 6, HMSO, London.

Egan, G. and Pritchard, F. (1991), *Dress Accessories*, Medieval Finds from Excavations in London 3, HMSO, London.

Ekwall, E. (1960), *The Concise Oxford Dictionary of English Place-names* (4th edn), Oxford.

Ersgård, L., Holmstrom, M. and Lamm, K. (eds) (1992) *Rescue and Research: reflections of society in Sweden 700–1700 AD*, Riksantikvarieambetet, Stockholm.

Evans, D.H. and Carter, A. (1985), 'Excavations on 31–51 Pottergate', in M. Atkin, A. Carter and D.H. Evans, 'Excavations in Norwich 1971–78 Part II', *East Anglian Archaeol.* **26**, 9–86.

Evans, D.H. and Tomlinson, D.G. (1992), *Excavations at 33–35 Eastgate, Beverley, 1983–86*, Sheffield Excavation Reports 3, Sheffield.

Evans, J. (1949), *English Art 1307–1461*, Oxford University Press, Oxford.

Everitt, A. (1976), 'The market towns', in P. Clark (ed.) *The Early Modern Town: a reader*, Longman, London, 168–204.

Ewan, E. (1990), *Townlife in Fourteenth-Century Scotland*, Edinburgh University Press, Edinburgh.

Fehring, G.P. (1991), 'Lübeck und die hochmittelalterliche Gründungsstadt im einst slawischen Siedlungsraum: Vorraussetzungen, Entwicklungen und Strukturen', in Brachmann and Herrmann, 281–93.

Fieldhouse, P. (1986), *Food and Nutrition: customs and culture*, London.

Flüeller, M. and Flüeller, N. (eds) (1993), *Stadtluft, Hirsebrei und Bettelmönch: Die Stadt um 1300*, Stuttgart.

Foard, G. (1991), 'The medieval pottery industry of Rockingham Forest, Northamptonshire', *Medieval Ceramics* 15, 13–20.

Frere, S.S., Stow, S. and Bennett, P. (1982), *Excavations on the Roman and Medieval Defences of Canterbury*, Archaeology of Canterbury II, Canterbury Archaeological Trust, Canterbury.

Gardam, C.M.L. (1990), 'Restorations of the Temple Church, London', in Grant, 101–27.

Gardner, A. (1935), *A Handbook of English Medieval Sculpture*, Cambridge University Press, Cambridge.

Gero, J.M. and Conkey, M.W. (eds) (1991), *Engendering Archaeology: women and prehistory*, Blackwell, Oxford.

Gilchrist, R. (1988), 'Friaries', Monument Protection Programme, Class Description Paper, English Heritage.

Gilchrist, R. (1994), *Gender and Material Culture: the archaeology of religious women*, Routledge and Kegan Paul, London.

Gilchrist, R. and Mytum, H. (1993), *Advances in Monastic Archaeology*, Brit. Archaeol. Report 227.

Gilmour, B.J.J. and Stocker, D.A. (1986), *St Mark's Church and Cemetery*, The Archaeology of Lincoln XIII–1, Lincoln.

Goldthwaite, R. (1980), *The Building of Renaissance Florence*, London.

Good, G.L., Jones, R.H. and Ponsford, M.W. (eds) (1991), *Waterfront Archaeology: Proceedings of the Third International Conference, Bristol, 1988*, Council for British Archaeol. Research Report 74.

Goudge, C.E. (1983), 'The leather from 38–44 Eastgate Street', in C.M. Heighway (ed.) *The East and North Gates of Gloucester*, Western Archaeological Trust Monograph 4, Bristol, 173–85.

Gould, J. (1976), *Lichfield: archaeology and development*, West Midlands Rescue Archaeology Committee, Birmingham.

Grant, A. (1988), 'Animal resources', in Astill and Grant, 149–87.

Grant, L. (ed.) (1990), *Medieval Art, Architecture and Archaeology in London*, British Archaeol. Assoc. Conference Transactions for 1984.

Green, F.J. (1982), 'Problems of interpreting differentially preserved plant remains from excavations of medieval urban sites', in Hall and Kenward, 40–6.

Greene, J.P. (1992), *Medieval Monasteries*, Leicester University Press, London.

Grenville, J. (in prep), *Medieval Housing*, Leicester University Press, London.

Greig, J. (1982), 'The interpretation of pollen spectra from urban archaeological deposits', in Hall and Kenward, 47–65.

Greig, J. (1988), 'Plant resources', in Astill and Grant, 108–27.

Grew, F. and de Neergaard, M. (1988), *Shoes and Pattens*, Medieval Finds from Excavations in London 2, HMSO, London.

Grimes, W.F. (1968), *The Excavation of Roman and Medieval London*, Routledge and Kegan Paul, London.

Guy, C.J. (1986), 'Excavations at Back Lane, Winchcombe, 1985' *Trans. of the Bristol and Gloucestershire Archaeol. Soc.* 104, 214–20.

Habovstiak, A. (1991), 'Bratislava – Die Anfange der heutigen Hauptstadt der Slowakei', in Brachmann and Herrmann, 159–65.

Hall, A.R. and Kenward, H.K. (eds) (1982), *Environmental Archaeology in the Urban Context*, Council for British Archaeol. Research Report 43.

Hall, A.R., Tomlinson, P.R., Taylor G.W. and Walton, P. (1984), 'Dyeplants from Viking York', *Antiquity* 58, 58–60.

Hanawalt, B. (1986), *The Ties that Bound: peasant families in medieval England*, Oxford University Press, Oxford.

Harbottle, B. and Clack, P. (1976), 'Newcastle-upon-Tyne: archaeology and development', in P. Clack and P.F. Gosling (eds) *Archaeology in the North*, 111–31.

Harden, G. (1978), *Medieval Boston and its Archaeological Implications*.

Harris, C.J. (1985), 'An Outline of Ropemaking in Bergen', in Herteig, 144–50.

Harris, E. (1979), *Principles of Archaeological Stratigraphy*, Academic Press, London.

Harrison, G.A. and Gibson, J.B. (eds) (1976), *Man in Urban Environments*, Oxford University Press, Oxford.

Harvey, P.D.A. (1969), 'Banbury', in M.D. Lobel (ed.) *Historic Towns [Atlas]* 1, Oxford.

Hassall, J. (1979) 'The pottery' in Baker et al., 147–240.

Hassall, T.G. (1976), 'Excavations at Oxford Castle, 1965–73', *Oxoniensia* 41, 232–308.

Hassall, T., Halpin, C.E. and Mellor, M. (1989), 'Excavations in St Ebbe's, Oxford, 1967–1976: Part I, late Saxon and medieval domestic occupation and tenements, and the medieval Greyfriars', *Oxoniensia* 54, 71–278.

Hawthorne, J.G. and Smith, C.S. (eds) (1979), *Theophilus. On Divers Arts: The Foremost Medieval Treatise on Painting, Glassmaking and Metalwork*, Dover, New York.

Heighway, C.M. (1972), *The Erosion of History*, Council for British Archaeology, London.

Heighway, C.M. (1974), *Archaeology in Gloucester*, Gloucester City Museum, Gloucester.

Heighway, C.M. (1983), 'Tanner's Hall, Gloucester' *Trans. of the Bristol and Gloucestershire Archaeol. Soc.* CI, 83–109.

Henderson, C.G. (1985), 'Archaeological investigations at Alphington Street, St Thomas', in C.G. Henderson (ed.) *Archaeology in Exeter 1984/5*, Exeter City Council, Exeter, 1–14.

Herrmann, J. (1991), 'Siedlunggeschichliche Grundlagen und geschichtliche Voraussetzungen für die Entwicklung Berlins', in Brachmann and Herrman (eds), 7–18.

Herteig, A.E. (ed.) (1985), *Conference on Waterfront Archaeology in North European Towns No. 2, Bergen 1983*, Bergen.

Herteig, A.E. (1991), *The Buildings at Bryggen: their topographical and chronological development*, Bryggen Papers Main Series 3, pt 1 and 2, Bergen.

Hewett, C. (1969), *The Development of Carpentry 1200–1700: an Essex study*, David and Charles, Newton Abbott.

Hewett, C. (1980), *English Historic Carpentry*, Phillimore, Chichester.

Higham, M.C. (1989), 'Some evidence for twelfth- and thirteenth-century linen and woollen textile processing', *Medieval Archaeol.* 33, 38–52.

Hill, D. (1981), *An Atlas of Anglo-Saxon England*, Blackwell, Oxford.

Hill, J.W.F. (1948), *Medieval Lincoln*, repr. 1990, Paul Watkins, Stamford.

Hilton, R.H. (1982), 'Towns in English medieval society', in D. Reeder (ed.) *Urban History Yearbook: 1982*; repr. in R. Holt and G. Rosser (eds), 19–28.

Hilton, R.H. (1984, reprinted in 1990), 'Small town society in England before the Black Death', in Holt and Rosser (eds), 71–96.

Hindle, B.P. (1982), 'Roads and tracks' in L. Cantor (ed.) *The English Medieval Landscape*, 193–218.

Hinton, D.A. (1990), *Archaeology, Economy and Society: England from the fifth to the fifteenth century*, Seaby, London.

Hodges, R. (1982), *Dark Age Economics: the origins of towns and trade AD 600–1000*, Academic Press, London.

Hohenberg, P.M. and Lees, L.H. (1985), *The Making of Urban Europe 1000–1950*, Harvard University Press, London.

Holdsworth, P. (ed.) (1987), *Excavations in the Medieval Burgh of Perth 1979–1981*, Soc. of Antiquaries of Scotland Monograph 5.

Holt, R. (1985), 'Gloucester in the century after the Black Death', *Trans. of the Bristol and Gloucestershire Archaeol. Soc.* 103, repr. in R. Holt and G. Rosser, 141–59.

Holt, R. and Rosser, G. (eds) (1990), *The Medieval Town: a reader in English urban history 1200–1540*, Longman, London.

Hooper, J., Wilmot, A. and Young, J. (1989), 'Pottery from St Marks East', *Archaeology in Lincolnshire 1987–1988: Fourth Annual Report of the Trust for Lincs. Archaeol.*, 29–32.

Horrox, R. (1978), *The Changing Plan of Hull 1290–1650*, Kingston upon Hull City Council, Kingston upon Hull.

Horsman, V., Milne, G. and Milne, C. (1988), *Aspects of Saxo-Norman London, I: building and street development*, London and Middlesex Archaeol. Soc. Special Paper 11.

Howarth, C.I. (1976), 'The psychology of urban life', in G.A. Harrison and J.B. Gibson (eds) *Man in Urban Environments*, Oxford University Press, Oxford.

Huggins, P.J. (1972), 'Monastic grange and outer close excavations, Waltham Abbey, Essex, 1970–72', *Essex Archaeol. and Hist.* 4, 30–127.

Huggins, P.J. and Bascombe, K.N. (1992), 'Excavations at Waltham Abbey, Essex, 1985–1991: three pre-Conquest churches and Norman evidence', *Archaeological Journal* 149, 282–343.

Izjereef, F.G. (1989), 'Social differentiation from animal bone studies', in Serjeantson and Waldron, 41–54.

Jansen, H.M. (1987), 'Svendborg in the Middle Ages: an interdisplinary investigation', *Journal of Danish Archaeol.* 6, 198–219.

Johnson, C. and Vince, A. (1992), 'The South Bail Gates of Lincoln', *Lincolnshire Hist. and Archaeol.* 27, 12–16.

Jones, B. (1984), *Past Imperfect: the story of rescue archaeology*, Heinemann, London.

Jones, G., Straker, V. and Davis, A. (1991), 'Early medieval plant use and ecology', in Vince, 347–85.

Keene, D. (1975), 'Suburban growth', in M.W. Barley (ed.) *The Plans and Topography of Medieval Towns in England and Wales*, Council for British Archaeol. Research Report 14, 71–82.

Keene, D. (1985a), *Cheapside Before the Great Fire*, Economic and Social Research Council, London.

Keene, D. (1985b), *Survey of Medieval Winchester*, Winchester Studies II, Oxford University Press, Oxford.

Keene, D. (1989), 'Medieval London and its region', *London Journal* 14, 99–111.

Keene, D. (1990a), 'Shops and shopping in medieval London', in Grant (ed.), 29–46.

Keene, D. (1990b), 'The character and development of the Cheapside area', in Schofield et al., 178–93.

Kellett, J.H. (1969), 'Glasgow', in M.D. Lobel (ed.) *Historic Towns [Atlas]* 1, Oxford.

Kenyon, J.R. (1990), *Medieval Fortifications*, Leicester University Press, London.

Knight, J. (1983) 'Montgomery: a castle of the Welsh March, 1223–1649', *Chateau Gaillard* **XI**, 169–82.

Küster, H. (1993), 'Pflanzliche Ernährung', in Flüeller and Flüeller, 289–92.

Lambrick, G. (1985), 'Further excavations on the second site of the Dominican priory, Oxford', *Oxoniensia* **50**, 131–208.

Lambrick, G. and Woods, H. (1976), 'Excavations on the second site of the Dominican priory, Oxford', *Oxoniensia* **41**, 168–231.

Lauret, A., Malebranche, R. and Seraphin, G. (1988), *Bastides: villes nouvelles du Moyen Age*, Editions Milan, Toulouse.

Leach, P. (ed.) (1984), *The Archaeology of Taunton*, Western Archaeological Trust Excavation Monograph 8, Gloucester.

Le Goff, J. (ed.) (1980), *La ville medievale*, Histoire de la France urbaine 2, Seuil, Paris.

Levitan, B. (1985), 'Early eighteenth-century horncores from Shooting Marsh Stile', in C.G. Henderson (ed.) *Archaeology in Exeter 1984/5*, Exeter City Council, 15–17.

Levitan, B. (1989), 'Bone analysis and urban economy: examples of selectivity and a case for comparison', in Serjeantson and Waldron, 161–88.

Lohrum, B. (1993), 'Fachwerkbau', in Flüeller and Flüeller, 248–66.

Lunde, O. (1985), 'Archaeology and the medieval towns of Norway', *Medieval Archaeol.* **29**, 120–35.

Lynch, M., Spearman, M. and Stell, G. (1988), *The Scottish Medieval Town*, London.

MacGregor, A. (1991), 'Antler, bone and horn', in Blair and Ramsay (eds), 355–78.

Mahany, C., Burchard, A. and Simpson, G. (1982), *Excavations in Stamford Lincolnshire 1963–1969*, Soc. of Medieval Archaeology Monograph 9.

Maloney, C.M. and DeMoulins, D. (1990), *The Upper Walbrook Valley in the Roman Period*, Council for British Archaeol. Research Report **69**.

Maltby, M. (1979), *Faunal Studies on Urban Sites: the animal bones from Exeter 1971–75*, Exeter Archaeological Report 2, University of Sheffield.

Marks, R. (1987), 'Stained glass *c.* 1200–1400', in Alexander and Binski, 137–47.

Marsh, B. (ed.) (1914), *Records of the Carpenters' Company, ii: Wardens' accounts 1438–1516*.

Martin, D. and Martin, B. (1987), *A Selection of Dated Houses in Eastern Sussex 1400–1750*, Rape of Hastings Architectural Survey: Historic buildings in Eastern Sussex 4.

McCarthy, M.R. and Brooks, C. (1988), *Medieval Pottery in Britain, AD 900–1600*, Leicester University Press, London.

McKenna, W.J.B. (1987), 'The environmental evidence' in Armstrong and Ayers, 255–62.

McKenna, W.J.B. (1991), 'The plant, molluscan, insect and parasite remains', in Armstrong et al., 209–15.

McNeil, R. (1983), 'Two twelfth-century Wich Houses in Nantwich, Cheshire', *Medieval Archaeol.* **27**, 40–88.

Mellor, J.E. and Pearce, T. (1981), *The Austin Friars, Leicester*, Council for British Archaeol. Research Report 35.

Michelmore, D.J.H. (1979), *A Current Bibliography of Vernacular Architecture 1970–76*, Vernacular Architecture Group.

Middleton, A. (1984–5), 'Examination of ash from the experimental firing group pottery bonfire held at Leicester in July 1984 and comparison with some archaeological ashes', *Bull. Experimental Firing Group* 3, 19–24.

Milne, G. (1987), 'Waterfront archaeology in British towns', in Schofield and Leech, 192–200.

Milne, G. (1992), *Timber Building Techniques in London c. 900–c. 1400*, London and Middlesex Archaeol Soc. Special Paper 15.

Milne, G. and Hobley, B. (eds) (1981), *Waterfront Archaeology in Britain and Northern Europe*, Council for British Archaeol. Research Report 41.

Milne, G. and Milne, C. (1982), *Medieval Waterfront Development at Trig Lane, London*, London and Middlesex Archaeol. Soc. Special Paper 5.

Moorhouse, S. (1983), 'The medieval pottery', in P. Mayes and L.A.S. Butler (eds) *Sandal Castle Excavations 1964–73*, Wakefield Historical Publications, Wakefield.

Morris, R. (1987), 'Parish churches', in Schofield and Leech, 177–91.

Morris, R. (1989), *Churches in the Landscape*, Dent, London.

Munby, J. (1975), '126 High Street: the archaeology and history of an Oxford house', *Oxoniensia* 40, 254–308.

Munby, J. (1978), 'J C Buckler, Tackley's Inn and three medieval houses in Oxford', *Oxoniensia* 43, 123–69.

Munby, J. (1987), 'Medieval domestic buildings', in Schofield and Leech, 156–66.

Munby, J. (1991), 'Wood', in Blair and Ramsay, 379–406.

Munby, J. (1992), 'Zacharias's: a medieval Oxford inn at 26–8 Cornmarket', *Oxoniensia* 57, 245–309.

Noddle, B. (1977), 'Mammal bone', in Clarke and Carter, 378–98.

O'Brien, C. (1991), 'Newcastle upon Tyne and its North Sea trade', in Good et al., 36–42.

O'Connell, M.G. (1977), *Historic Towns in Surrey*, Surrey Archaeol. Soc. Research Vol. 5.

O'Connor, T.P. (1982), *Animal Bones from Flaxengate, Lincoln, c. 870–1500*, The Archaeology of Lincoln XVIII–1, Lincoln.

O'Connor, T.P. (1983), 'Feeding Lincoln in the 11th century – a speculation', in M. Jones (ed.) *Integrating the Subsistence Economy*, Brit. Archaeol. Report S181, 327–30.

O'Connor, T.P. (1991), *Bones from 46–54 Fishergate*, The Archaeology of York.

O'Connor, T. (1989), 'Deciding priorities with urban bones: York as a case study', in Serjeantson and Waldron, 189–200.

O'Connor, T.P. (1993), 'Bone assemblages from monastic sites: many questions but few data', in Gilchrist and Mytum, 107–12.

O'Connor, T., Hall, A.R., Jones, A.K.J. and Kenward, H.K. (1984), 'Ten years of environmental archaeology at York', in Addyman and Black, 166–72.

Orton, C., Tyers, P. and Vince, A. (1993), *Pottery in Archaeology*, Cambridge University Press, Cambridge.

Palliser, D.M. (1987), 'The medieval period', in Schofield and Leech, 54–68.

Palliser, D.M. (1993), 'The topography of monastic houses in Yorkshire towns', in Gilchrist and Mytum, 19–28.

Palmer, N. (1980), 'A Beaker burial and medieval tenements in the Hamel, Oxford', *Oxoniensia* 45, 124–225.

Pantin, W.A. (1947), 'The development of domestic architecture in Oxford', *Antiq. Journal* 27, 120–50.

Pantin, W.A. (1962–3), 'Medieval English town-house plans', *Medieval Archaeol.* 6–7, 202–39.

Park, D. (1987), 'Wallpainting', in Alexander and Binski, 125–30.

Parker, V. (1971), *The Making of King's Lynn*, Phillimore, Chichester.

Parsons, D. (ed.) (1990), *Stone: quarrying and building in England AD 43–1525*, Phillimore, Chichester.

Parsons, D. (1991), 'Stone', in Blair and Ramsay, 1–28.

Pattison, I.R., Pattison, D.S. and Alcock, N.W. (1992), *A Bibliography of Vernacular Architecture: III, 1977–89*, Vernacular Architecture Group.

Pearce, J.E. and Vince, A.G. (1988), *A Dated Type-series of London Medieval Pottery: Part 4, Surrey Whitewares*, London Middlesex Archaeol. Soc. Special Paper **10**.

Pearce, J.E., Vince, A.G. and Jenner, M.A. (1985), *A Dated Type-series of London Medieval Pottery: Part 2, London-type ware*, London and Middlesex Archaeol. Soc. Special Paper **6**.

Penn, K.J. (1980), *Historic Towns in Dorset*, Dorset Natural Hist. and Archaeol. Soc. Monograph **1**.

Perring, D. (1981), *Early Medieval Occupation at Flaxengate Lincoln*, The Archaeology of Lincoln **IX–1**, Lincoln.

Platt, C. (1976), *The English Medieval Town*, Secker and Warburg, London.

Platt, C. (1978), *Medieval England: a social history and archaeology from the Conquest to 1600*, Routledge and Kegan Paul, London.

Platt, C. and Coleman-Smith, R. (1975), *Excavations in Medieval Southampton, 1953–69 Vol. 1, The Excavation Reports; Vol. 2, The Finds*, Leicester University Press, Leicester.

Ponting, K.G. (1957), *A History of the West of England Cloth Industry*, Adams and Dark, Bath.

Portman, D. (1966), *Exeter Houses 1400–1700*, Phillimore, Chichester.

Postan, M. (1975), *The Medieval Economy and Society*, Penguin, Harmondsworth.

Poulton, R. and Woods, H. (1984), *Excavations on the Site of the Dominican Friary at Guildford in 1974 and 1978*, Surrey Archaeol. Soc. Research Vol. **9**, Guildford.

Pounds, N.J.G. (1990), 'Buildings, building stones and building accounts in south-west England', in Parsons, 228–37.

Power, E. (1975), *Medieval Women*, Cambridge University Press, Cambridge.

Priddy, D. (1983), 'Excavations in Essex 1982', *Essex Archaeology and History* **15**, 163–72.

Pritchard, F.A. (1984), 'Late Saxon textiles from the City of London', *Medieval Archaeol.* **28**, 46–76.

Pritchard, F.A. (1991), 'Small finds', in Vince, 120–278.

Rackham, J. (1982), 'The smaller mammals in the urban environment: their recovery and interpretation from archaeological deposits', in Hall and Kenward, 86–93.

Rackham, O. (1976), *Trees and Woodland in the British Landscape*, Dent, London.

Rapoport, A. (1990), 'Systems of activities and systems of settings', in S. Kent (ed.), *Domestic Architecture and the Use of Space*, Cambridge University Press, Cambridge, 9–20.

Reaney, P.H. (1967), *The Origin of English Surnames*, Routledge and Kegan Paul, London.

Redman, C.L. (1986), *Qsar es-Seghir: an archaeological view of medieval life*, Academic Press, London.

Reynolds, S. (1977), *An Introduction to the History of English Medieval Towns*, Clarendon Press, Oxford.

Robertson, J.C. (1989), 'Counting London's horn cores: sampling what?', *Post-Medieval Archaeol.* **23**, 1–10.

Robinson, M. (1976), 'The natural alluvium and dumped clay', in Lambrick and Woods, 227.

Robinson, M. (1980), 'Waterlogged plant and invertebrate evidence', in Palmer, 199–206.

Robinson, M. and Wilson, B. (1987), 'Survey of the environmental archaeology in the South Midlands', in H.C.M. Keeley (ed.) *Environmental Archaeology: A Regional Review Vol. 2*, English Heritage Occasional Paper **1**, 16–100.

Rodwell, K. (ed.) (1975), *Historic Towns in Oxfordshire: a survey of the new county*, Oxford.

Rodwell, W.J. (1976), 'The archaeological investigation of Hadstock church, Essex: an interim report', *Antiq. Journal 56*, 55–71.

Rodwell, W.J. (1981), *The Archaeology of the English Church*, Batsford, London.

Rodwell, W. (1987), *Wells Cathedral: excavations and discoveries*, Friends of Wells Cathedral, Wells.

Rogers, K.H. (1969), 'Salisbury', in M.D. Lobel (ed.) *Historic Towns [Atlas] 1*, Oxford.

Rogerson, A. (1976), 'Excavations on Fuller's Hill, Great Yarmouth', *East Anglian Archaeol. 2*, 131–246.

Rothschild, N. (1990), *New York City Neighborhoods: the eighteenth century*, Academic Press, London.

Royal Commission on Historical Monuments (England) (1977), *The Town of Stamford*, HMSO, London.

Royal Commission on Historical Monuments (England) (1980), *City of Salisbury: i*, HMSO, London.

Royal Commission on Historical Monuments (England) (1987), *Houses of the North York Moors*, HMSO, London.

Royal Commission on Historical Monuments (England) (1993), *Salisbury: the Houses in the Close*, HMSO, London.

Royal Commission on Historical Monuments (Wales) (1960), *Caernarvonshire* (2 vols), HMSO, London.

Salter, H.E. (1926), *Oxford City Properties*, Oxford Historical Soc. 83, Oxford.

Salzman, L.F. (1923), *Medieval English Industries*, Clarendon Press, Oxford.

Salzman, L.F. (1952), *Building in England Down to 1540* (2nd edn, 1965), Oxford University Press, Oxford.

Salzman, L.F. (1964), *English Trade in the Middle Ages*, Fordes, London.

Samuel, M.W. (1989), 'The fifteenth-century garner at Leadenhall, London', *Antiq. Journal 59*, 119–53.

Sarfatij, H. (1973), 'Digging in Dutch towns: 25 years of research by the ROB in medieval town centres', *Berichten ROB 23*, 367–420.

Saunders, A.D. (1980), 'Lydford Castle, Devon,' *Medieval Archaeol. 24*, 123–86.

Schneider, J.E. (1993), 'Der mitelalteriche Steinbar in Zürich', in Flüeller and Flüeller, 239–47.

Schofield, J. (1975–6), 'Excavations south of Edinburgh High Street, 1973–4', *Proceedings of the Soc. of Antiq. of Scotland 107*, 155–241.

Schofield, J. (1977), 'New Fresh Wharf, 3: the medieval buildings', *London Archaeol. 4*, 66–73.

Schofield, J. (1981), 'Medieval waterfront buildings in the City of London', in Milne and Hobley, 24–31.

Schofield, J. (1984), *The Building of London from the Conquest to the Great Fire*, British Museum Publications, London.

Schofield, J. (1987), *The London Surveys of Ralph Treswell*, London Topographical Soc. 135, London.

Schofield, J. (1990), 'Medieval and Tudor domestic buildings in London', in Grant, 16–28.

Schofield, J. (1994), *Medieval London Houses*, Yale University Press, London.

Schofield, J. (in prep), *Medieval London Parish Churches*.

Schofield, J. and Palliser, D., with Harding, C. (1981), *Recent Archaeological Research in English Towns*, Council for British Archaeol., London.

Schofield, J. and Leech, R. (eds) (1987), *Urban Archaeology in Britain*, Council for British Archaeol. Research Report 61.

Schofield, J., Allen, P. and Taylor, C. (1990), 'Medieval buildings and property development in the area of Cheapside', *Trans. London and Middlesex Archaeol. Soc.* **41**, 39–238.

Schofield, J. and Lea, R. (in prep), *Holy Trinity Priory, Aldgate.*

Scott, S. (1991), 'The animal bones', in Armstrong et al., 216–33.

Serjeantson, D. and Waldron, T. (eds) (1989), *Diet and Crafts in Towns: the evidence of animal remains from the Roman to the post-medieval periods*, Brit. Archaeol. Report **199**.

Seyer, H. (1991), 'Die Entstehung von Berlin und Cöln im Spiegel archaeologischer Ausgrabungen', in Brachmann and Herrmann, 19–24.

Shackley, M. (1981), *Environmental Archaeology.*

Sharpe, R.R. (1889–90), *Calendar of Wills Proved and Enrolled in the Court of Husting, London*, 2 vols, Corporation of London, London.

Shead, N.F. (1988), 'Glasgow: an ecclesiastical burgh', in Lynch et al., 116–32.

Short, P. (1980), 'The fourteenth-century rows of York', *Archaeol. Journal* **137**, 86–137.

Simpson, G.G. (ed.) (1972), *Scotland's Medieval Burghs: an archaeological heritage in danger.*

Sjoberg, G. (1960), *The Preindustrial City*, London.

Slade, C.F. (1969), 'Reading', in M.D. Lobel (ed.) *Historic Towns [Atlas]* **1**, Oxford.

Slater, T. (1980), *The Analysis of Burgages in Medieval Towns*, University of Birmingham, Department of Geography, Working Paper, **4**, Birmingham.

Slater, T.R. and Wilson, C. (1977), *Archaeology and Development in Stratford-upon-Avon*, University of Birmingham.

Smith, T. (1985), *The Medieval Brickmaking Industry in England 1400–1450*, Brit. Archaeol. Report **138**.

Spearman, M. (1988), 'The medieval townscape of Perth', in Lynch et al., 42–59.

Spencer, B. (1990), *Pilgrim Souvenirs and Secular Badges*, Salisbury and South Wilts. Museum Medieval Catalogue, Part 2.

Soulsby, I. (1983), *The Towns of Medieval Wales*, Phillimore, Chichester.

Steane, J.M. (1985), *The Archaeology of Medieval England and Wales*, Croom Helm, London.

Steedman, K., Dyson, T. and Schofield, J. (1992), *Aspects of Anglo-Norman London, 3: Billingsgate and the bridgehead to 1200*, London and Middlesex Archaeol. Soc. Special Paper **14**.

Stephenson, D. (1984–5), 'Colchester: a smaller medieval English Jewry,' *Essex Archaeology and History* **16**, 48–52.

Stevenson, A. (1988), 'Trade with the South', in Lynch et al., 180–206.

Stirland, A. (1985) 'The human bones', in Ayers, 49–58.

Stocker, D.A. (1990), 'Rubbish recycled: a study of the re-use of stone in Lincolnshire', in Parsons, 83–101.

Stocker, D.A. (1991), *St Mary's Guildhall, Lincoln*, The Archaeology of Lincoln **12/1**, Lincoln.

Stocker, D.A. (1993), 'Recording worked stone', in R. Gilchrist and H. Mytum (eds) *Advances in Monastic Archaeology*, Brit. Archaeol. Report **227**, 19–28.

Tanner, J.M. and Everleth, P.B. (1976), 'Urbanization and growth', in Harrison and Gibson, 144–66.

Tatton-Brown, T. (1978), 'Canterbury', *Current Archaeol.* **62**, 78–82.

Tatton-Brown, T. (1990), 'Building stone in Canterbury, *c.* 1070–1525', in Parsons, 70–82.

Thomas, C., Phillpotts, C., Sloane, B. and Evans, G. (1989), 'Excavation of the priory and hospital of St Mary Spital', *London Archaeol.* **6**, 87–93.

Thomas, C., Sloane, B. and Phillpotts, C. (in prep) *Excavations at the Priory and Hospital of St Mary Spital.*

Thrupp, S. (1948), *The Merchant Class of Medieval London*, University of Michigan Press, Ann Arbor.

Tolley, T. (1991), 'Eleanor of Castile and the "Spanish" style in England', in M. Ormrod (ed.) *England in the Thirteenth Century*, Harlaxton Medieval Studies I, 167–92.

Tracy, C. (1987), 'Woodwork', in Alexander and Binski, 118–21.

Tracy, C. (1988), *English Medieval Furniture and Woodwork*, Victoria and Albert Museum, London.

Urry, W. (1967), *Canterbury under the Angevin Kings*, Athlone Press, London.

Van Regteren Altena, H.H., (1970), 'The origin and development of Dutch towns', *World Archaeol.* 2, 128–40.

Velay, P. (1991), 'Die Entstehung und die frühe Entwicklung der Stadt Paris', in Brachmann and Herrmann, 85–91.

Verhaeghe, F. (1991), 'Frühmittelalterliche Städte in Belgen: ein voläufiger Uberblick', in Brachmann and Herrmann, 97–115.

Verlinden, O. (1963), 'Markets and fairs' in M.M. Postan, E.E. Rich and E. Miller (eds) *The Cambridge Economic History of Europe, Vol. 3: Economic organization and policies in the Middle Ages*, Cambridge University Press, Cambridge, 119–56.

Vince, A.G. (1977), 'The medieval and post-medieval ceramic industry of the Malvern region; the study of a ware and its distribution', in D.P.S. Peacock (ed.) *Pottery and Early Commerce*, Academic Press, London, 257–305.

Vince, A.G. (1984), 'The use of petrology in the study of medieval ceramics: case studies from Southern England', *Medieval Ceramics* 8, 31–46.

Vince, A.G. (1985), 'Saxon and medieval pottery in London: a review', *Medieval Archaeol.* 29, 25–93.

Vince, A.G. (ed.) (1991), *Aspects of Saxo-Norman London: Vol. 2, Finds and Environmental Evidence*, London and Middlesex Archaeol. Soc. Special Paper 12.

Vince, A. (1993), 'People and places: integrating documents and archaeology in Lincoln', in M.J. Jones (ed.) *Lincoln Archaeology 1992–1993*, Annual Report of City of Lincoln Archaeology Unit 5, Lincoln, 4–5.

Waldron, T. (1989), 'The effect of humanisation on health: the evidence from skeletal remains', in Serjeantson and Waldron, 55–76.

Wallace, P.F. (1981), 'Dublin's waterfront at Wood quay: 900–1317', in Milne and Hobley, 109–18.

Walton, P. (1991), 'Textiles', in Blair and Ramsay, 319–54.

Walton, P. (1992), 'The dyes', in Crowfoot et al., 199–201.

Waters, W.B. (1912), *Church Bells of England*, London.

Webster, L. and Cherry, J. (1973), 'Medieval Britain in 1973', *Medieval Archaeol.* 17, 138–88.

West, S.E. (1963), *Excavations at Cox Lane (1958) and at the Town Defences, Shire Hall Yard, Ipswich (1959)*, Proc. Suffolk Institute of Archaeology, 29.

White, L. (Jr) (1981), 'The expansion of technology 500–1500', in Cipolla, 143–74.

White, W. (1988), *Skeletal Remains from the Cemetery of St Nicholas Shambles*, London and Middlesex Archaeol. Soc. Special Paper 9.

Williams, F. (1977), *Excavations at Pleshey Castle*, Brit. Archaeol. Report 42.

Williams, J.H. (1979), *St Peter's Street Northampton, Excavations 1973–76*, Northampton.

Wilson, R. (1989), 'The animal bones', in Hassall et al., 259–68.

Wilthew, P. (1987), 'Metallographic examination of medieval knives and shears', in Cowgill et al., 62–74.

Woods, A. (1989), 'Report on Silver Street shelly wares', in P. Miles, J. Young and J. Wacher (eds) *A Late Saxon Kiln-site at Silver Street, Lincoln*, The Archaeology of Lincoln 17/3.

Yentsch, A. (1991), 'The symbolic divisions of pottery: sex-related attributes of England and Anglo-American household pots', in R.H. McGuire and R. Paynter (eds), *The Archaeology of Inequality*, Blackwell, Oxford, 192–230.

Ziegler, P. (1971), *The Black Death*, Collins, London.

Index